W9-BKN-062

Sichuan and Tibetan China 137
Getting Your Bearings ✦ In Two Weeks
Don't Miss ✦ The Highest Railway in the World ✦ Lhasa
✦ Leshan and Emeishan ✦ Jiuzhaigou
At Your Leisure ✦ 6 more places to explore
Where to... ✦ Stay ✦ Eat and Drink ✦ Shop ✦ Be Entertained

The Silk Road 157
Getting Your Bearings ✦ In Two Weeks
Don't Miss ✦ Xi'an ✦ Dunhuang ✦ Kashgar
At Your Leisure ✦ 4 more places to explore
Where to... ✦ Stay ✦ Eat and Drink ✦ Shop ✦ Be Entertained

Walks 173
✦ Beijing's Hutong
✦ Shanghai's French Concession
✦ Sheung Wan to Central, Hong Kong

Practicalities 183
✦ Before You Go
✦ When To Go
✦ When You Are There
✦ Useful Words and Phrases

Atlas 191
Index 211

Written by Graham Bond

Verified by George McDonald

Project editor Karen Kemp
Designer Nucleus Design
Cartographic editor Anna Thompson
Managing editor Clare Garcia

American editor Tracy Larson

Edited, designed and produced by AA Publishing
© Automobile Association Developments Limited 2008
Maps © Automobile Association Developments Limited 2008

Published in the United States by AAA Publishing,
1000 AAA Drive, Heathrow, Florida 32746-5063
Published in the United Kingdom by AA Publishing

ISBN-13: 978-1-59508-234-3

Cover design and binding style by permission of AA Publishing
Color separation by Keenes, Andover
Printed and bound in Thailand by Sirivatana

10 9 8 7 6 5 4 3 2 1

A03008
Maps in this title produced from mapping © MAIRDUMONT/
Falk Verlag 2007
with additional data from Mountain High Maps ®
Copyright © 1993 Digital Wisdom, Inc

AAA SPIRAL GUIDES

Travel With Someone You Trust®

CHINA

Contents

the magazine 5
✦ Economy of Scales ✦ Mother of Invention
✦ China goes Boutique ✦ Sic Fan La! ("Let's Eat" in Cantonese)
✦ Lights, Cameras, Crowds ✦ Different Strokes for Different
Folks ✦ The Opium Wars ✦ From Barbarians to Babes
✦ Disappearing China? ✦ China Opens its Arms to the World
✦ The Essential China Experiences

Finding Your Feet 31
✦ First Two Hours
✦ Getting Around
✦ Accommodation
✦ Food and Drink
✦ Shopping
✦ Entertainment

Beijing and the Northeast 43
Getting Your Bearings ✦ **In Five Days** ✦
Don't Miss ✦ The Forbidden City ✦ Tiananmen Square
✦ Beijing's Hutong ✦ Temple of Heaven
✦ The Summer Palace ✦ The Great Wall
At Your Leisure ✦ 6 more places to explore
Where to... ✦ Stay ✦ Eat and Drink ✦ Shop ✦ Be Entertained

Shanghai and the East 65
Getting Your Bearings ✦ **In Five Days**
Don't Miss ✦ The French Concession ✦ People's Square
✦ The Huangpu River ✦ Yuyuan and the Old City
✦ The Water Towns of Jiangnan ✦ Hangzhou
At Your Leisure ✦ 8 more places to explore
Where to... ✦ Stay ✦ Eat and Drink ✦ Shop ✦ Be Entertained

Hong Kong and the South 91
Getting Your Bearings ✦ **In Seven Days**
Don't Miss ✦ Hong Kong Island ✦ Kowloon
✦ Lantau Island ✦ Macau
At Your Leisure ✦ 6 more places to explore
Where to... ✦ Stay ✦ Eat and Drink ✦ Shop ✦ Be Entertained

The Southwest 115
Getting Your Bearings ✦ **In Two Weeks**
Don't Miss ✦ Guilin and Yangshuo ✦ Wulingyuan
✦ The Three Gorges ✦ Lijiang
At Your Leisure ✦ 8 more places to explore
Where to... ✦ Stay ✦ Eat and Drink ✦ Shop ✦ Be Entertained

the magazine

辽大中渔11047

ECONOMY
of Scales

"Let China sleep, for when she wakes, she will shake the world," said Napoleon Bonaparte. That comment, made two centuries ago, couldn't seem any more pertinent than it does today. China's meteoric rise from impoverished has-been to resurgent superpower has created ripples that have been felt across every continent. Its ability to sprout high-rises as quickly as green vegetables earns it regular headlines, while the country's size, energy and sheer "otherness" both amaze and daunt in equal measure.

Nothing quite captures China's scale and dynamism like a few choice statistics. Indeed, China probably wouldn't have it any other way. This is a country that revels in ranks, scales and percentages. Ask any Chinese citizen to name you the four "famous" classic novels, the five "famous" Taoist mountains, or the precise number of gold, silver and bronze medals accrued at the last Olympics and you'll have a well-rehearsed answer. Everything and everyone has its place and its value. Perhaps a country so big, old and complex needs numbers and figures to make sense of itself.

One of China's most repeated boasts is its 5,000 years of history (although only about 3,500 years have been verified by archaeological finds). Its population is 1.3 billion, which can be divided between 56 distinct ethnic groups and spread over 22 provinces, five "Autonomous Regions" (including Tibet), four "Municipalities" (including Beijing and Shanghai) and the two "Special Administrative Regions" of Hong Kong and Macau. China may or may not be the third largest country in the world, a position the USA also claims. China's border squabbles with India mean the truth rather depends on your politics.

China's brazen transformation from Communist bastion to Capitalist crusader has lifted more than 400 million people out of poverty, making some of them very wealthy indeed (Versace will be opening nine new stores in China during 2007). In 2006 the economy grew by 10.5 per cent and is expected to become the world's largest within 20 years. However, there are still an estimated 700 million people living on less than two US dollars a day – approximately the same as European cows consume daily in farm subsidies.

The tallest mountain in the world, like so much else today, has Chinese roots. The phrase "Mount Everest" means nothing in China. The 8,848m (29,030-foot) leviathan that soars skyward at the Chinese-Nepalese border is known only as Zhumulangma Feng (or Qomolangma in Tibetan). Some 2,000km (1,240 miles) to the north is Turpan, a town that lies 154m (505 feet) below sea level. It was here that China's highest temperature, 49.6°C (121.3°F), was recorded. Zoom 3,500km (2,175 miles) northeast and you'll find yourself in Mohe, on China's border with Siberia, where the temperature once dipped to -52.3°C (-62.1°F) and where the Northern Lights are sometimes visible.

Revolutionary politics may be a thing of the past in China, but its landscape will always be filled with jarring extremes.

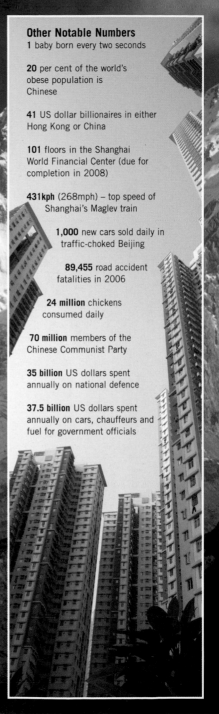

Other Notable Numbers

1 baby born every two seconds

20 per cent of the world's obese population is Chinese

41 US dollar billionaires in either Hong Kong or China

101 floors in the Shanghai World Financial Center (due for completion in 2008)

431kph (268mph) – top speed of Shanghai's Maglev train

1,000 new cars sold daily in traffic-choked Beijing

89,455 road accident fatalities in 2006

24 million chickens consumed daily

70 million members of the Chinese Communist Party

35 billion US dollars spent annually on national defence

37.5 billion US dollars spent annually on cars, chauffeurs and fuel for government officials

MOTHER *of Invention*

Maybe it's not so surprising that China appears slap bang in the middle of local world maps: every nation, it seems, has the sense that it resides at the centre of the universe. However, not every nation is so confident in the righteousness of this notion that it is prepared to stake its very name on it. China – or Zhong Guo – has no such quibbles. It is the self-proclaimed "Middle Kingdom", the land in which civilization began and from where everything worth anything was originally created and subsequently derived, borrowed or stolen.

Every schoolboy knows that paper and gunpowder originated in China. However, impressive as these inventions are, they represent the mere tip of the creative iceberg. In the latter half of the 20th century, British scholar Joseph Needham produced a comprehensive study of China's contributions to human progress. By the time he died in 1995, his *Science and Civilisation in China* had stretched to 16 volumes and remained a mere work-in-progress. The list is a long one.

Achievements Past

So where to begin? In terms of importance to the enlightenment of humanity, it's hard to beat the first printing press, which emerged in China during the 11th

The traditional pastime of kite-flying

century. The first printed book, a Buddhist text made using moveable type, was created earlier, in AD 868.

In engineering, China came up with the design for the suspension bridge and the segmented arch bridge – the first of which is still in use today in Zhaoxian, Hebei province. In industry, China can lay claim to the chain pump, the steam engine, the spinning wheel, gear cogs and the windmill, as well as the creation of cast iron and steel. The ultimate mechanization of bodies and machines that made Europe so rich during the Industrial Revolution could never have occurred without the mechanical clock, another Chinese invention of the late Tang dynasty (9th century AD).

In transport, China came up with the canal lock, rudders, the parachute and the compass (having first discovered magnetism, of course). In warfare, the Chinese invented the crossbow in the 4th century BC

and were still using it to fight the Japanese as late as 1895. They also invented the kite, playing cards, fishing reels and whisky.

Not neglecting the more refined arts, China created the first – and the finest – examples of porcelain and

Top: Decorative tiles in one of Beijing's metro stations

Above: The whole world celebrates with fireworks

silks. Wallpaper and wheel-barrows can be safely stashed in China's sizeable "miscellaneous" category of novelty inventions.

For much of the last 2,000 years, the Middle Kingdom has also been a leading exporter of wisdom. The thoughts of Confucius advocated ideal modes of behavior for both leaders and citizens and provided the basis for a social contract that sustained Chinese civilization for more than two millennia. His ideas influenced nearly every Eastern philosopher, and were brought to Europe by Italian Jesuit missionary Matteo Ricci in the 16th century. They've transfixed the Western world ever since. Taoism, a philosophy-cum-religion born out of the thoughts of Lao Zi and his book, the *Tao Te Ching*, is the basis for one of the world's best recognized symbols – the black-and-white symbol of yin-yang.

Any survey of China's contributions to humanity must include the 15th-century explorer and seafarer Zheng He, who travelled the oceans pioneering new trading routes throughout Asia and Africa. According to a recent book by British historian Gavin Menzies, Zheng actually circumnavigated the globe and discovered America 70 or so years before Columbus got there.

This isn't the only claim that has had traditionalists up in arms. A Chinese historian recently incurred the wrath of the small Scottish town of St Andrews after suggesting that golf was first played in the Middle Kingdom and exported to Europe by Mongol traders. The veracity of these boasts is perhaps not as important as their psychological impact.

It's clear that many people across the world are starting to sense that China can reclaim its former title of global trendsetter.

Achievements Present and Future

And there's evidence to suggest it's up to the task. In the last decade China has built the world's biggest dam (➤ 124), the highest railroad (➤ 142–143) and – with a little German help – the fastest train. It's currently building the world's longest trans-oceanic bridge (across Hangzhou Bay) and the world's tallest building (in Shanghai). In 2003, China joined the USA and Russia as the only countries to put a man in space and it plans to launch moon probes soon.

In the field of science and medicine, China already boasts a trailblazing pedigree thanks to ancient arts like acupuncture and reflexology. Now, they are complemented by Shanghai psychosurgeons who claim to cure drug addiction by burning holes in the brain and Shandong scientists who say they can plant microchips in pigeons' brains and control the birds by remote control.

As you travel around China, "deep" is an adjective you'll hear a lot in connection with the country's culture and history. There is an immense pride in what China achieved and what it is now showing signs of achieving again. Peruse the racks of pirated DVDs, shamelessly copied brand-name clothes and derivative pop CDs, and you'll be forgiven for thinking that China is master of only of one art – plagiarism. However, write the country off at your peril. China – the Middle Kingdom, no less – is back on the map.

Left: A painting of Confucius at the Confucian Temple in Suzhou

Below: The Maglev train uses electromagnetic force to propel it

CHINA
goes Boutique

Up until recently, shoppers in Shanghai might have faced something of a moral dilemma when it came to splurging in one of the city's emerging boutique stores. How could one justify lavishing hundreds, maybe thousands, of dollars on a new bag or pair of shoes when, just outside the door, millions of people were barely surviving on a few cents a day? Anyone who stops to ponder such questions these days is likely to find themselves left behind in the stampede. A people once famous for their frugality have become shopaholics *sans pareil.*

Conspicuous Consumption

China has gone from "communist conformity" to "glossy gorgeousness" in a generation. If you're very lucky, you might spot a classic faded-blue "Mao jacket" being worn on the streets of Shanghai, Beijing or Guangzhou. It's more likely that you'll find yourself making eyes at an outrageously ostentatious outfit being modelled by a hip-swinging waif. Rampant commerce has been both symptom and solution in China's economic miracle. Stressed-out city dwellers eagerly respond to the call of advertising TV screens cleverly engineered into bus stops, subway trains, taxi headrests and office-block elevators.

China recently became the world's third-largest market for luxury goods, and Shanghai, home to all of the world's biggest fashion brands (as well as a fair amount of home-grown talent), is where most of the cash is handed over. Those with big budgets and even bigger suitcases head for the Bund, an area now famous as much for its über-chic restaurants and designer stores as its elegant colonial architecture.

Luxury Hotels

China's new up-market tastes have filtered into the hotel industry. The past few years have seen a host of properties emerge that appear to fit the somewhat slippery "boutique" label. Singapore's Banyan Tree chain now has two luxurious retreats in the mountainous wilds of Yunnan province. The Commune by the Great Wall represents a veritable museum of modern Asian architecture located next to the most famous structure on the planet. The Fuchun

Resort, close to Hangzhou, offers golf and meditation with villa accommodation worthy of the emperors of old. Meanwhile, back in the urban arena, Shanghai's The Nine and Beijing's Red Capital Residence both offer super-expensive accommodation and novel perspectives on China's 20th-century history. The former is an art deco villa straight out of the hedonistic "Swinging '30s", the latter a courtyard guest house which revels in China's revolutionary history.

Mass Market

But the fun isn't only reserved for China's new wealthy elite. Stores offering facials, pedicures, manicures and massages have sprung up across the country. The price ranges – and corresponding quality controls – vary wildly, but they have made indulgence affordable for hundreds of millions, and signalled the return of a service culture that looked dead and buried just 30 years ago.

Above: Glass bathroom at the TMSK Café in Beijing

Left: The bar at Kathleen's 5 Rooftop Restaurant, Shanghai, offers terrific views across Renmin Park

SIC FAN LA!
("Let's Eat" in Cantonese)

Writing during a peasant rebellion in his native Hunan province, a young Mao Zedong famously described the inevitable traumas that would face China in its conversion to communism: "A revolution," he warned, "is not a dinner party."

canteen offerings of collectivization. Restaurant culture disappeared, farming was streamlined and one of the world's most diverse, cultured and spectacularly tasty cuisines stagnated. Not only did the art of cooking suffer – food itself disappeared. The most devastating famine the world has ever known occurred on Mao's watch. Thankfully, China's ancient culinary traditions survived and the dinner party is back in fashion.

It is difficult to overstate just how important

A Way of Life

In predicting the upheavals ahead, China's future leader touched upon a very sensitive subject. For far from being the bourgeois soirée of the West, the "dinner party" is China's most democratic leisure forum. There is nothing more natural or more common than settling down with friends for food. Under Chairman Mao's leadership, the dinner party was replaced with the meagre

Left: Dining out in Shanghai

Bottom left: A noodle stall in Xi'an

Right: Cooking kebabs and flat bread, near Turpan

food is to all tiers of Chinese society. It plays a crucial role, both as a social lubricant, a tool of business and a rhythm of life. It is medicinal, sacrificial and ceremonial. Fundamentally, it brings a lot of people a lot of pleasure.

Where in the West one might greet a friend with an enquiry after their health, in China the opening gambit is always about food. Expect to hear the phrase "*chi fan le mei you*?" ("have you eaten yet?") on a regular basis. Similarly, where Western friends might meet in a bar over a beer, in China the restaurant is the stage for the vast majority of all social interaction. The round tables so common to Chinese eateries are usually built for at least eight people and lunch breaks for schools and state-run businesses are usually three hours long. Slow dining is an almost holy principle. In China, you will never – ever – be encouraged to hurry along, no matter how late it is or how many people are waiting for a table.

Eating Out

In towns and cities, virtually every street corner boasts some form of food outlet, from hole-in-the-wall joints with black oil streaks decorating the walls, through opulent banquet halls all the way to super-expensive boutique restaurants. One of the most notable effects of China's economic reforms over the last 25 years has been the re-emergence of small, family-run restaurants. Surroundings are generally basic, but prices are fabulous and standards high.

The food you'll encounter in China will be different to what you might get from the local takeaway back home. The vast majority of Chinese restaurants and takeaways in the West have their roots in Hong Kong and Guangdong province, where Cantonese language, culture and cuisine reign supreme. Leaving aside the sizeable differences between "Western" Cantonese food and that which you'll find in Guangdong, Cantonese cuisine is only one of the four great "schools" of Chinese cooking and just a fraction of its rich and diverse culinary heritage. Move into other parts of the country and there's barely a chicken chow mein in sight.

The Four Cooking Schools

China's Northern School includes Beijing, Dongbei (Manchurian) and Shandong cuisine. As befits a land where growing options are limited by a frigid winter, northern food features lots of hearty meat dishes.

This area is also known as China's wheat bowl, and flour-wrapped dumplings (*jiaozi*) and steamed breads are hugely popular. Mongol influences can be sensed in the popularity of barbecued meats and hotpots. China's most famous dish, Beijing duck, is the region's most celebrated offering – crispy duck skin, separated from the soft flesh, all served on a wheat pancake with cucumber, spring onion and a dollop of plum sauce.

Crispy roast duck hanging in a window in Shanghai

The Western School is dominated by the hot and spicy cuisine of Sichuan province, where the food is famously flavoured with an exotic palette of spices, peppers and pastes.

The Eastern School, including Shanghai and surroundings, involves widespread use of dark vinegars, sugar and rice wine, and has a discernibly sweet flavour.

Cantonese food is remarkable for its diversity. The Cantonese are famously experimental and will eat virtually anything. In contrast to the heavy sauces and oils of the takeaway back home, the food is normally cooked with a light touch. The steam-basket *dim sum* breakfasts and lunches, so loved in the South, are a must for visitors – and much easier to enjoy than the snake or dog dishes you may come across.

What unites all forms of Chinese food is the wok. Stir-frying is far from the limit of the pan's capabilities: it is used for deep frying, stewing, steaming and smoking. To preserve freshness and fuel, Chinese food is normally cooked as briefly as possible and often arrives at the table with astonishing speed.

Eat Well, Live Well

The relationship between food and health is well understood by all Chinese and goes well beyond the "eat your greens" dictate so loved by Western matriarchs. Virtually every conceivable ailment or condition has a dietary prescription in China, with certain foods said to have very specific effects on particular parts of the body. "He that takes medicine and neglects diet wastes the physician's skills," runs one Chinese proverb. However, it's not only the doctor who knows best. Do so much as muffle a cough in the company of Chinese friends and expect an immediate diagnosis, shortly followed by a remedy served up fresh on the table.

Burgers and Coffee

Left: Barbecued sticks of meat for sale in Stalin Park in Harbin

Developing a sense of culinary adventure is key to getting the most out of a visit to China. However, if the sensory overload becomes too much, there is easy respite available. KFC, McDonalds and Starbucks are even more ubiquitous in Chinese cities than they are in the West.

Helpful hints for formal dining in China

Paying: To "invite" (*qing*) means to foot the bill. It does not, as is the case back home, mean simply "join me for dinner". Going Dutch is rare. When the bill arrives, feel free to have a gentle tug of war with your friend's arm as he reaches for his wallet. If he insists, cave in – but only after a few polite refusals.

Seating: The host (or the person doing the "inviting") will normally sit facing the door, with the most important people in the assembled company sitting either side. If you are being hosted, expect to be offered the place of honour. Refuse politely.

Toasting: Never drink alone. Always raise your glass to at least one person at the table. The most common Chinese toast, "*ganbei*", literally means "down in one", but is commonly used to mean, "cheers". Interpret as you see fit.

Singing: Regardless of ability, the Chinese love to sing and see the dinner table as a perfect venue for musical repartee. Expect to be asked to give a rendition of something from "your country".

Chopsticks: Try to use them, no matter how clumsy your pincer action might be. Avoid sticking chopsticks bolt upright into dishes (especially your rice bowl). It's considered bad luck.

Thanking: Try to resist the temptation to thank the waitstaff when something is brought to the table. It's likely to cause more confusion than comfort. For those who can't resist a show of gratitude, subtly tap the table with two fingers when tea is poured.

Leftovers: It's polite to leave a small amount of food in your bowl at the end of the meal. Failing to order enough food is considered a huge faux pas for any Chinese host and an empty bowl will be taken as a sign that you haven't had your fill, leading to either loss of face or several more dishes arriving at the table.

lI--HTS,
Cameras, Crowds

For many, China's hustle and bustle will be one of its great marvels. You haven't got to enjoy fighting for breath on the metro to appreciate the raw energy of Chinese street life. Walk out at night and your senses will be assailed: pungent smells from whirring extractor fans, loud music from shops that never seem to close, bright lights from overhanging street signs. Neon may have been discovered in France, but the Chinese have adopted it as if it were their own. Even trees, mountains and caves are decorated with it.

Come nightfall, locals often gather en masse in the large concrete plazas so beloved by China's town planners. Searchlights scan the skies and music plays from invisible PA systems. Within the mob there's little self-consciousness. Try not to stare too hard if you stumble across a frail septuagenarian pulling a pilates posture, twirling with a make-believe dancing partner or warbling loudly.

Singing doesn't only take place on the street. Like neon, karaoke may be a foreign import, but visiting aliens would surely conclude it was invented by the Chinese, for the Chinese, such is the extent to which it has been embraced in the Middle Kingdom. KTV parlours do a roaring trade and often provide sumptuous rooms, superb sound systems, waiter service and a smattering of English songs.

Above: Neon sign in Hong Kong

As the great travel writer Paul Theroux once observed, "The Chinese are comforted by crowds." To this may be added "noise". And "bright lights". And "cigarette smoke". This is important to remember for anyone who usually goes on holiday to get away from it all. In a nation of some 1.3 billion people, opportunities for moments of solitude and quiet contemplation will inevitably be few and far between.

Like the Japanese before them, the new wave of Chinese tourists who take whistle-stop tours of Europe have developed a reputation for group travelling, talking loudly and taking lots (and lots) of pictures. There's no reason to think domestic tourists are any different. The guides who lead the incessant flow of tour groups are famous for their fondness of battery-powered megaphones in their attempt to be heard above the noise.

A Little Peace

It's not impossible to escape the melee. Retreat into one of the country's ever-growing number of five-star hotels or exclusive social clubs and peace can be yours – at a price. Those seeking a more egalitarian solution are advised to head into the West. Eastern China may boast some of the world's most densely populated urban centres, but the desolate, windswept landscapes of Xinjiang, Inner Mongolia and Tibet tell a quite different story.

If relocating thousands of kilometres isn't feasible, note that most Chinese insist on observing "correct" mealtimes. Visit any of China's major tourist attractions around 8am, noon or 5pm and it's possible you might

Crowds of people outside Mao's Mausoleum in Tiananmen Square, Beijing

Whether you find yourself in the hushed rooms of a gallery or on a picturesque mountain peak, the babble rarely ceases. snatch some peace and quiet. Enjoy those moments. They probably won't last long.

DIFFERENT
Strokes for Different Folks

The rise of the Chinese language has mirrored the mother country's fortunes over the last three decades. The world's most spoken tongue is now taught in British and American schools, and Chinese script can be found on everything from cushion covers to T-shirts in Western homes. A word of warning, though: those same pretty "pictures" can lose their novelty when multiplied and printed on public signs and restaurant menus.

With a documented history of more than 3,200 years, Chinese is the world's oldest surviving written language. The earliest examples of Chinese were found on bone fragments used in divination rites during the Shang dynasty (*c*1500–1066 BC). Like ancient Egyptian, the Chinese of this era comprised a series of relatively simple picture signs, but evolved into today's more abstract and complex formations.

After 1949, China's Communist government set about simplifying many characters and creating a universal pronunciation system (known as *pinyin*) in the hope of boosting literacy and improving communication between its far-flung provinces and people. It was

a huge success. "Simplified Chinese" script (which still looks complicated to the uninitiated) is used across the mainland today and nearly everyone under the age of 70 can speak Mandarin, in addition to their own regional dialect. The word for Mandarin is *putonghua* – literally "normal speech".

There are pockets of resistance to Beijing's attempts to standardize the language. The former colonies of Macau and Hong Kong retain the dense "traditional" script and many residents speak only Cantonese – the mother tongue for most people in this part of China. Even less amenable to change are the "minority" regions of Tibet, Inner Mongolia and Xinjiang, where locals tend to resent the effect that Chinese has had on their traditional spoken and written languages. In these areas it's common to see trilingual signs, though sensitive Chinese authorities insist that Mandarin is the central, dominant mode.

Despite its own meddling, the government has frequently complained about the dilution of Chinese. Hundreds of new words are thought to enter the language each year, many of which mimic the sounds of their English equivalent. Even modern technology has come in for criticism. In a country where calligraphy is still considered one of the noblest art forms, some find it abhorrent that urban teens' only experience of creating Chinese script is in using mobile phones or computers. Without the practice required to remember the composition of Chinese characters, many worry the younger generation will simply forget how to write.

Those who never learned in the first place need not despair at the intimidating linguistic melange they'll experience in China. Thanks to increasing international attention, English signs are becoming common in the major cities. Moreover, learning English is now a passion for millions of Chinese, making for a large pool of wannabe translators only too delighted to have an opportunity to practise their English skills.

Left: A calligrapher at work
Right: Example of calligraphy at the Kong Residence, birthplace of Confucius

How Words are Made

The basic stock of 11,000 characters in use today is used to create tens of thousands of individual words. One word usually comprises between one and four characters, with each character representing a single syllable. Words composed of several characters often build on the individual meaning of its contingent parts, though there are seemingly arbitrary groupings, as the word *ma* (horse) proves.

马	*ma* horse
斑马	*ban* [striped] *ma* [horse] **zebra** (guessability: very easy)
马球	*ma* [horse] *qiu* [ball] **polo** (guessability: easy)
兵马	*bing* [soldier] *ma* [horse] **army** (guessability: moderate)
马上	*ma* [horse] *shang* [on] **immediately** (guessability: difficult)
马虎	*ma* [horse] *hu* [tiger] **careless** (guessability: very difficult)
马马虎虎	*ma* [horse] *ma* [horse] *hu* [tiger] *hu* [tiger] **so-so/passable** (guessability: impossible)

Chinese Place Names

北京	*Bei* [northern] *Jing* [capital] **Beijing**
上海	*Shang* [on] *Hai* [sea] **Shanghai**
广州	*Guang* [wide] *Zhou* [state/region] **Guangzhou**
香港	*Xiang* [fragrant] *Gang* [harbor] **Hong Kong**
长江	*Chang* [long] *Jiang* [river] **Yangtze River**
长城	*Chang* [long] *Cheng* [city wall] **The Great Wall**

THE *Opium Wars*

The two "Opium Wars" fought between China and Britain in the mid-19th century are crucial to understanding the country today. They explain the very existence of cities such as Shanghai and Hong Kong. More importantly, they mark the point when a once-mighty civilization finally realized it had fallen from its throne. Everything that has happened since can be seen as China's attempt to play catch-up, and never has this campaign been more obvious than today.

Opium for Tea

The 18th century saw international trade with China blossom, but there was a problem. The old-fashioned emperors of the Qing court failed to see the attractions of the goods that an increasingly industrialized West was offering. British merchants looking to supply huge demand for Chinese tea grew frustrated at a growing trade imbalance. They looked for a product the Chinese would find irresistible and found it in the colonial poppy fields of India.

Opium-smoking was banned in China in 1729, but British traders bribed local officials and began to ship large quantities of the drug from India to Guangzhou in the hope of creating a nation of addicts. It worked. Millions of Chinese found themselves in thrall to the brown resin and British merchants grew hugely wealthy off the profits.

Finally, in 1839, newly appointed imperial commissioner Lin Zexu decided to act. Within two months, a massive blitz had closed the

Above: The red opium poppy, cause of so much misery and Chinese humiliation

dens and destroyed thousands of chests of the drug. Queen Victoria herself found a letter on her table politely requesting a rethink of British policy.

Her response was to send in the troops. The military superiority of the British was overwhelming and soldiers seized control of China's strategic outposts with relative ease. Staring total defeat in the face, the Chinese court signed the infamous Treaty of Nanjing, which opened five cities to British trade – Shanghai included – and ceded Hong Kong to Her Majesty's authority.

In 1860, the British returned, this time with French allies. In their quest to secure the formal legalization of opium, the invading forces occupied Beijing and forced the Imperial court to retreat into the Northeast. China's humiliation was complete.

The End of Imperial Rule

These two humiliating defeats kick-started a protracted power struggle between reformers and traditionalists. As the European powers continued to expand ever more aggressively into China, the Imperial court disintegrated and finally fell apart in 1911, bringing to an end four millennia of dynastic rule.

In the years that followed, the country continued to suffer at the hands of outsiders – notably the Japanese in the 1930s and 1940s. The country's conversion to Communism in 1949 represented a radical strategy for ending the exploitation. Indeed, the Cold War alliance with the Soviet Union restored some measure of military strength. However, in 1979, when China decided to edge open its door to the world again, the country was economically crippled. Not anymore.

In the 21st century, every new dawn brings this proud nation a step closer to restoring its status as a global superpower and vanquishing the memories of arguably China's darkest age.

Diorama of the Flowery Smoking House, an opium den, in the Shanghai History Museum

FROM
Barbarians to Babes

毛主席语录
QUOTATIONS FROM
CHAIRMAN
MAO TSE-TUNG

Plaza 66
恒隆廣場

PATRIZIA PEP
FIRENZ

There was a time, not so long ago, when foreigners were known in China as "barbarians". The word was used in both casual conversation among Chinese people and in the official documentation of the Imperial Qing court, and testified to the unruliness of those unfortunates born outside the boundaries of the celestially favoured Middle Kingdom.

Foreigners visiting China these days are in no danger of suffering such scorn, but that isn't to say that Chinese views on the outside world have developed that deeply. The international isolation that preceded the 19th-century Opium Wars was repeated in the 20th century under Mao Zedong's Communist leadership. The result is that many Chinese still view the world as composed, essentially, of two parts: China and Foreign Places. Expect lots of curious stares and questions about what your *waiguo* (outside

China) food/money/houses/clothes/lifestyle are like. You may or may not be asked exactly which country it is you hail from.

One of the most interesting side-effects of this lack of subtlety is that anyone who looks remotely non-Chinese tends to become an instant celebrity, particularly outside the major cities. Many teachers of English as a foreign language have graduated from the classroom to take up starring roles in local TV programmes or illustrious modelling careers in advertising. China is the new "Wild East" – a land of opportunity where fame and fortune is just around the corner. Talent, or familiarity with your product, is not necessarily required.

One person who has thoroughly earned his extraordinary fame is a Canadian by the name of Mark Rowswell. Known to more

Far left: Signs and posters advertising Plaza 66 shopping mall, Shanghai

Inset: Mao's Little Red Book

Left: Enjoying a drink in Lan Kwai Fong, Shanghai

speaking – Rowswell is one of the most famous men on the planet.

In the same way that Chinese people can sometimes take a clichéd view on the outside world, many "foreigners" still view China as a mysterious kingdom where an idyllic way of life has been unmolested for millennia. Even now, there are some who return from China swearing they were the first foreign faces ever to have graced any given village, town or city. Unless you are planning on doing some serious trekking in the wilds of Tibet, it's extremely unlikely you'll be able to justify such a claim. The sight of a foreigner is no longer the traffic-stopper it once was. Indeed, in 2005, China became the fourth most visited country in the world.

than 1 billion Chinese as "Da Shan" (Big Mountain), Rowswell has been appearing on Chinese TV for nearly 20 years speaking flawless Mandarin on a variety of entertainment and language shows. He may be virtually unknown is his home country, but – statistically

Even the Middle Kingdom isn't immune to a rank-and-file tourist invasion.

Chinglish

China's curiosity about all things "foreign" manifests itself in the popularity of the English language. Nowhere is English studied and practised more enthusiastically. It doesn't mean it's always intelligible, though, as these (genuine) signs prove.

• **"Do not pi*s anywhere"** (Make proper use of the urinals), *Guangzhou Public Toilet*
• **"After first under on, do riding with civility"** (Let passengers disembark first), *Shanghai Metro Station*
• **"Cowboy Leg + Block Pepper Retchup"** (??? with Black Pepper Sauce), *Beijing restaurant*
• **"No fight and scrap. No rabble, no feudal fetish and sexy service"** (No fighting, freeloaders, perverts or prostitutes), *Ming Tombs, Beijing*

DISAPPEARING
China?

China's headlong rush into modernity is changing the landscape at a pace many find deeply unsettling. Critics complain the nation's heritage is being trampled under the march of so-called progress. Two examples are often cited as proof: the construction of the Three Gorges Dam and the demolition of Beijing's traditional *hutong* neighbourhoods.

Water, Water Everywhere

The Three Gorges Dam – the concrete colossus strung between the banks of the Yangtze River in Hubei province – has been the most controversial of Beijing's many grand schemes to propel the nation into the 21st century. The dam was built between 1993 and 2006 and created a 560km-long (350-mile) "reservoir" that forced 1.3 million people out of their ancestral homes.

While construction was taking place, the travelling rumour mill went into overdrive. The Three Gorges, one of China's most scenic locales, would be submerged. "Visit before it's

Doing Tai Chi exercises on the riverside promenade of the Bund, Shanghai

too late," went the rallying cry. Sure enough, in 2003 the dam was plugged and, in ten days, the watermark rose 65m (213 feet). By October 2006, the waters had risen a further 21m (69 feet), and will climb another 19m (62 feet) to reach a high watermark of 175m (575 feet) above sea level in 2008.

However, omitted from most reports was the fact that many of the mountains that created the Three Gorges were more than 1,000m (3,280 feet) high. Kneecapped they may well have been, but the Three Gorges were never in danger of disappearing. Indeed, tour boats still ply the route and do a roaring trade.

Demolition

The story of the *hutong* is similar. Much of the criticism surrounding the routine destruction of Beijing's historic neighbourhoods was legitimate. Hundreds of these attractive, low-rise housing compounds made way for bland apartment blocks and wide boulevards. The *hutong* may not have provided residents with mod cons, but they were the face of traditional Beijing charm, and many lamented their disappearance.

However, for the tourist, not a great deal has changed. Most of the *hutong* within the first ring road – the area most popular with visitors – are still intact and looking as lovely as ever. Moreover, as with the Three Gorges project, those forcibly relocated were not always unhappy at exchanging their rather cramped, run-down dwellings for modern apartments.

In with the New

Like its suffering environment, Chinese social mores are also in flux: ancient forms of exercise like Tai Chi – practised by the old – are shunned in favour of basketball by the young. The one-child policy has altered the nature of filial devotion. Where once children would go to extraordinary lengths to prove devotion to their elders, now a generation of spoiled "little emperors" has grown up more interested in serving themselves.

China is changing at an unprecedented rate and the government's management of this quiet revolution certainly isn't perfect. But given the 1.3 billion mouths to feed and the burden of thousands of years of history, perhaps it should be cut a little slack.

Below: Playing basketball in Zhaolin Park, Harbin

Bottom: View over the rooftops of one of Beijing's *hutong*

CHINA

Opens its Arms to the World

Big news for those who have spent the last few years in a cave: Beijing has won the rights to host the 2008 Olympics. While you've been away, China's capital has launched one of the most ambitious urban makeovers the world has ever known. Bold new business and residential districts are sprouting up, high-tech transportation networks are appearing magically and the city's many historic sites are undergoing painstaking renovation. When you went into hibernation, Beijing was all creaking bicycles, Communist-era tenement blocks and timeless imperial palaces. No more. "Old Beijing" has morphed into one of the world's biggest, brashest and most dynamic cities.

Main picture: The National Stadium in Beijing

Inset: Chinese athletes running towards the finishing line

The building effort for the self-proclaimed "best-ever Olympic games in history" is costing 37 billion US dollars alone. Thirty-one of the 37 competition venues are located in Beijing, and 12 of these are being built from scratch. Perhaps the most eye-catching is the 100,000-seater National Stadium, known as the "giant bird's nest" on account of its mesh of interlocking steel bands. In stark contrast to the last-minute panics of Athens in 2004, construction on all venues will be finished well before the end of 2007.

best face. Concerned at residents' tendency to spit, push in line and drop litter, Beijing's social guardians have launched a series of campaigns to improve manners. The 11th day of each month is now officially "anti-queue-jumping day", for example.

But success is by no means guaranteed. Beijing mayor Wang Qishan hinted at desperation in early 2007 when he felt moved to remind citizens of their obligations. "More than 30,000 reporters are coming to cover the Games and they are going to cover every detail of Beijing in their articles," he warned. "We have to have a good Olympics, otherwise not only will our generation lose face, but also our ancestors."

Unruly citizens are not the only worry. The huge sums of cash at stake have already provided irresistible temptation to some. In June 2006, Liu Zhihua, vice mayor of Beijing and head of the Olympic construction projects, was dismissed on charges of moral and financial corruption.

"Officials must not be dissipated by wine and women, and should not visit entertainment venues after work," Liu Qi, Beijing's Communist Party chief, has said since.

When Beijing was announced as the surprise victor in the IOC vote in June 2001, millions of people across China immediately looked forward to 2008 as the inevitable tipping point when change

Best Behaviour

But the Olympics will be about far more than showing off China's new engineering prowess. With the international spotlight trained on the city, officials are at pains to present the nation's very

would become irresistible in Beijing's closed political system. However, despite the odd concession, there have been few signs of a sea-change in the thinking of the nation's leaders. Right now, most Chinese will probably settle for a spectacular 18-day party, a bit of summer sunshine and a place at the top of the medal table.

THE
Essential China Experiences

Ride the Maglev It may be ludicrously uneconomical to run but Shanghai's Magnetic Levitation train (left) – with its 431kph (268mph) top speed and steep bends – still takes the breath away.

Marvel at Qin Shi Huang's vast army of Terracotta Warriors This is imperial grandeur on a vast scale (below). It's world famous for a reason.

Climb one of China's nine sacred mountains The Buddhists have four, Taoists five, and they are all spectacular. Take your pick.

Sample a spicy Sichuan hotpot – Cantonese dim sum and Beijing duck run it close, but the Sichuan classic is the pick of a very fine culinary crop. Best tried in Chongqing.

Hike the Great Wall "He who hasn't climbed the Great Wall isn't a real man," said Chairman Mao. So don't be tempted to take the chairlift.

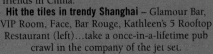

Sing karaoke at a KTV parlour Cast aside inhibition and get wailing. There's no better way of making friends in China.

Hit the tiles in trendy Shanghai – Glamour Bar, VIP Room, Face, Bar Rouge, Kathleen's 5 Rooftop Restaurant (left)...take a once-in-a-lifetime pub crawl in the company of the jet set.

Go gambling in Hong Kong or Macau Hong Kong boasts two fine horse-racing tracks, Macau has two dozen dazzling casinos. The Chinese, you'll note, like a flutter.

Enjoy an hour-long hair wash Indulgence doesn't get any cheaper than this. Just 10RMB (give or take) will inject new life into those tangled locks.

Hunt around the wholesale markets of Guangzhou You don't have to be an international trader to appreciate the prices, though it'll help.

Finding Your Feet

First Two Hours

The majority of long-haul flights from Europe and the USA land in Hong Kong, Shanghai or Beijing. All three cities have excellent modern airports, though standards of English are generally poor in mainland China. There are several other international airports, but these handle flights between China and its immediate Asian neighbours.

Arriving in Beijing

- **Beijing Capital International Airport** (PEK; www.bcia.com.cn) is around 25km (15.5 miles) northeast of central Beijing. There are six major Airport Bus routes (7am–11pm, individual times vary) which allow passengers to access most parts of the city inexpensively. By 2008, an elevated railway will connect the airport with the city centre metro system.
- There are two interconnected terminals. All international flights arrive at Terminal 2. A **third terminal** – tipped to be the largest in the world – is currently under construction and will be opened in 2008 to cope with the influx of Olympic visitors.
- With **40 million passengers** passing through each year, Beijing Airport is the busiest in China. Ironically, it's the least attractive and comfortable of China's major air hubs. Terminal 3 may well change that.
- A **taxi ride** to the north of the city can cost as little as 50RMB, but those going to the south or west of China's sprawling capital can expect to pay more than 100RMB. Prices increase after 11pm.

Arriving in Shanghai

- All long-haul international flights land at **Pudong International Airport** (PVG; www.shanghaiairport.com), a sleek, modern facility 40km (25 miles) east of the city centre. There are seven main bus routes to the city proper. Each operates between 7:30am and 11pm.
- Looking ahead to the Shanghai World Expo in 2010, the airport authority is adding a **second terminal** at Pudong. It's scheduled to open in 2008.
- The **Maglev** (Magnetic Levitation train) whisks passengers the 30km (18 miles) to Longyang Lu metro station in 8 minutes (7am–9pm). With a top speed of 431kph (268mph), it's the fastest train in the world. The one-way fare is 50RMB, but if you show your airline ticket you get a 20 per cent discount.
- **Taxis** to the city centre cost around 140RMB, though prices rise slightly after 11pm. It is possible to arrange set-fare travel to any given Shanghai district from the terminal.

Arriving in Hong Kong

- **Hong Kong International Airport** (HKG; www.hongkongairport.com) regularly shows up on travellers' lists of favourite airports in Asia. It was opened in 1998 on reclaimed land north of Lantau Island, around 40km (25 miles) from Hong Kong Island.
- The **Airport Express train** speeds passengers to Kowloon or Hong Kong Island (Central) in just over 20 minutes.
- There are three separate **taxi ranks** at the airport itself. Blue taxis go to destinations on Lantau Island, green taxis cover the New Territories and red taxis go to Hong Kong Island and Kowloon.
- If you want to skip Hong Kong completely, it's possible to take boats and buses direct from the airport to the nearby **mainland cities** of Shenzhen, Dongguan and Zhongshan, as well as Macau.

Tourist Information Offices

- Stores signed "Tourist Information" are often **private companies** interested mainly in signing you up for a guided tour or pointing you in the direction of their friends' hotels. Both Shanghai and Beijing airports have a series of small **hole-in-the-wall tourist offices** whose staff will likely call out as you pass. Treat any unsolicited approach with suspicion and any information with cynicism. In complete contrast, **Hong Kong has superb tourism information** facilities and official Tourism Board representatives may well proactively approach you at the airport.

Beijing

- The recent emergence of the **Beijing Tourism Information Centre** network is a step in the right direction. However, English-language skills are patchy and information is not always reliable. The centres are notable for their turquoise facades and there's an office in Beijing Capital International Airport's Arrivals Hall (tel: 010 6459 8148). The 24-hour **Beijing Tourism Hotline** (tel: 010 6513 0828) has an English-language service.

Shanghai

- Shanghai also has a number of Tourist Information and Service Centres though staff are **generally unhelpful**. There are no information offices in Pudong International Airport. The local **Tourist Hotline** (open 10–9) is on 021 6355 5032 and has a reasonable English-language service.

Hong Kong

- There are **Hong Kong Tourism Board Visitor Information** counters at Transfer Area E2 and Buffer Halls A and B at Hong Kong International Airport. Staff operate the desks between 7am and 11pm, though tourist literature and access to the i CyberLink computerized information network is available at all times. There is also a multilingual tourist information hotline, tel: 852 2508 1234 (open 8–6). Check out www.discoverhongkong.com

Getting Around

China's major cities have excellent public transport systems. New underground and elevated metro systems are helping smooth the passage of vast numbers of commuters. Getting between cities has also never been easier: Air transport is safe and relatively inexpensive; intercity buses run regularly; and, though trains are slow, the rail network is extensive. On the downside, standards of English are poor, trains and buses can be extremely crowded and traffic is heavy. Self-drive is not possible in China, though – given the abominable driving standards – this is not necessarily a bad thing.

Urban Transport
Taxis

- **Fares range** from 5RMB in small cities to 11RMB in Shanghai, and cover a basic distance of either 2 or 3km (1.2 or 2 miles). Prices go up after 11pm.
- All drivers should have a **licence number** and photograph prominently displayed in the front of the taxi, along with a complaints telephone number. Drivers are obliged to **use the meter** at all times.
- Taxi drivers **rarely speak English**. Moreover, the English name of your destination may be quite different to the original Chinese name, so pointing

at written text will not always work. Drivers may not even recognize written **pinyin** (the Romanized form of Chinese script). If possible, have someone **write your destination in Chinese**.

- The law that states all passengers must **wear a seat belt** is best seen as a commendable "theory". Don't be surprised if a driver interprets your desire to belt up as an affront to his driving skills.

- If there is any **argument or confusion** at the end of a taxi ride, ask the driver for a *fa piao*. These printed receipts give details of your journey, identify the driver and can be used in later complaints. They'll generally discourage drivers who might be tempted to squeeze you for extra cash.

- Taxis that loiter outside train and bus stations at night **may refuse a fare** if the distance isn't great enough. Walk a few hundred metres in any direction and normal service will resume.

Buses

- With taxis being inexpensive, few tourists use public buses. Signs are often written **only in Chinese**, though multilingual LED screens are becoming more common.

- If you do take a bus, be sure to have **plenty of change** before boarding. Some routes will have conductors, but most buses rely on passengers inserting the correct change into a slot.

- Except for Hong Kong and Macau (which have staggered pricing), **one fare** will cover the entire journey. Prices are usually 1 or 2RMB.

Metro

- Signs usually display the cost to reach any given station. Ticket attendants may not speak English, but you can **buy tickets by value** rather than destination. Automatic ticket machines usually give change.

- **Announcements** on platforms and trains are made in Mandarin and English (with added Cantonese in Hong Kong and Guangzhou).

- Trains can get oppressively **crowded**, especially at rush hour. The practice of letting passengers disembark first doesn't work in China and there's often a crush to get on/off a train.

On Foot

- Don't be fooled by the zebra crossings along virtually all busy roads. **Drivers will rarely stop** for pedestrians. Crossing a road is normally done in several stages with pedestrians having to pause between streams of traffic. If in doubt, head for the nearest set of **traffic lights**.

- Cars and motorbikes frequently **mount pavements** in search of short cuts.

Other Urban Transport

- Rickshaws may be a thing of the past but their modern equivalent – **pedicabs** – are common around tourist sights in smaller cities. Beijing is the only major city which still has a sizeable pedicab population. Many are found around the Shichahai "Lake District" behind the Forbidden City. Ensure you agree a price and length of journey before you set off.

- **Motorcycle taxis** are common in smaller cities. Though cheap, the dangers are obvious.

Intercity Transport
Driving

- It's not possible for travellers to drive in China, though you may rent a car with **a driver**. Avis (www.avischina.com) has offices in several Chinese cities, including Shanghai, Beijing and Guangzhou. A chauffered car costs from 530RMB per day, depending on the length of hire.

- China has an **appalling road safety record**. Intercity bus travel around mountainous western China can be a truly hair-raising experience.

Train

- Obtaining train tickets is a **real ordeal**. Depending on the route, tickets only become available between seven and four days before departure and then only in the city you want to travel from. It's cheapest to buy tickets at the station, but the crowds can be horrendous and very frustrating. For a small surcharge, you can **buy tickets through your hotel or travel agent**. The 5 to 10RMB commission is money well spent.
- Due to rampant **touting** (which has semi-official sanctioning), tickets can be scarce and all but impossible to buy around Chinese New Year.
- Tickets are divided into **four classes** – hard seats, soft seats, hard sleepers and soft sleepers. For most foreign travellers, the price difference will be so small that you may decide to buy a sleeper ticket even for a daytime journey. If you are prepared to take a risk, it's often possible to buy a seat (or standing) ticket and upgrade to a sleeper once on the train.
- **Hard sleeper beds** are not actually that hard. The main difference is that each berth has six beds (soft sleepers have four), but there's no door to guarantee privacy from passers-by.
- In the hard sleeper class, the bottom and middle bunks have good window views, **though the top bunk** is lodged right up in the ceiling.
- The **journey from** Beijing to Shanghai takes 12 hours; from Guangzhou to Shanghai or Beijing 24 hours; from Hong Kong to Guangzhou 2 hours.

Air

- China has **several reliable domestic carriers**. The best are Air China (www.airchina.com.cn), China Eastern Airlines (www.ce-air.com) and China Southern Airlines (www.cs-air.com).
- Though city-based travel agents can help buy tickets, it's possible to book independently **online** using web-based aggregators like www.ctrip.com or www.elong.com. Both have additional telephone operators who speak English. Prices are normally lower than when booking from the airline direct. The use of **e-tickets** means there's no need to worry about delivery.
- It *should* be possible to use your credit card to buy tickets, but there are often problems when paying with international plastic (China has its own domestic credit card system). It may be possible to **courier tickets** to your hotel where you can hand over payment in cash.
- The **flight from** Beijing to Shanghai takes 1.5 hours, from Beijing to Hong Kong is 3 hours, and from Shanghai to Hong Kong is 2 hours.

Intercity Buses

- There are **regular daytime departures** between most major cities. Tickets are easily obtained at short notice from the bus station. **Free drinking water** is usually provided aboard the bus, but seat belts are scarce.

Admission Charges
The cost of admission for museums and places of interest mentioned in the text is indicated by the following price categories:
Mainland China (RMB), Hong Kong (HK$)
Inexpensive under 30RMB/HK$30 **Moderate** 30–100RMB/HK$30–100
Expensive over 100RMB/HK$100

Accommodation

Hotels in China range from depressing flea-pit establishments to opulent glass palaces. The local brands can sometimes look jaded next to international lodgings. China is *the* big new market for the world's major hotel groups. There are no genuine bed-and-breakfasts, no novelty temple-stays and no campsites.

Hotels
Chinese Hotels

- You will be asked for your **passport** on check-in. All hotels are obliged to report the presence of foreign travellers to the Public Security Bureau.
- China's **domestic star-rating system** provides a useful way to compare hotels, but should not be relied upon implicitly. That said, four- and five-star outfits will invariably be comfortable and there are a handful of superb hotels.
- **Room tariffs** are nearly always negotiable. For walk-in customers, ignore the prices listed on the board behind the reception desk and ask for the cheapest price. Ask to look at the room before agreeing to stay.
- You'll find **throwaway slippers** in your room. Use them. The Chinese spitting habit knows no limits and carpets are often filthy.
- In lower grade hotels it's likely your **toilet** will be of the hole-in-the-floor variety. Four- and five-star hotels will normally have sit-down toilets.
- All hotels provide **thermos flasks** with boiling water for making tea.
- Breakfast is **often included** in the tariff. This will usually comprise a Chinese buffet.

International Hotels

- The two guarantees will be staff who speak (enough) English and international food in the restaurant. The ethics of globalization aside, international-brand hotels provide a **familiar environment** for Westerners in what is a very unfamiliar country.
- **Accor:** This expanding **French group** owns the five-star Sofitel (17 hotels) and mid-market Novotel (11 hotels) brands, plus several budget hotels, including Ibis (7 hotels), Grand Mercure (5 hotels) and Mecure (1 hotel). Check out www.accorhotels.com
- **Banyan Tree:** This luxurious **Singaporean hotel group** is big on sustainable tourism. It currently has two resort-style hotels in Yunnan province. Check out www.banyantree.com
- **Hilton:** This **American company** has swish hotels in Shanghai, Beijing, Chongqing, Sanya and Hefei, as well as a super-luxurious Conrad hotel in Hong Kong. Check out www.hilton.com
- **Intercontinental:** The expanding **British group**'s four China brands – Intercontinental (7 hotels), Crowne Plaza (16 hotels), Holiday Inn (36 hotels) and Express by Holiday Inn (6 hotels) – cover most budgets. Sixty new hotels are planned by the end of 2008. Check out www.ichotelsgroup.com
- **Kempinski:** This trendy **German chain** has large properties in Beijing, Chengdu, Dalian, Shenyang, Shenzhen and Urumqi, as well as a beach hotel in Sanya and the boutique Commune by the Great Wall resort. Check out www.kempinski.com
- **Marco Polo:** Up-market group with namesake hotels in Beijing, Xiamen and Shenzhen and three more in their hometown, Hong Kong. Check out www.marcopolohotels.com

- **Marriott: American group** which includes two luxury brands – JW Marriott (3 hotels) and Ritz-Carlton (3 hotels) – as well as the smaller Renaissance (8 hotels) and Courtyard (5 hotels). Check out www.marriott.com and www.ritz-carlton.com
- **Shangri-La:** This expanding, luxurious, **five-star brand** with hotels across Asia has 23 Shangri-La hotels in China and four mid-market Traders Hotels. Check out www.shangri-la.com
- **Starwood:** The **American hospitality behemoth** owns the five-star Sheraton (23 hotels), Westin (3 hotels), St Regis (2 hotels) and Le Meridien (3 hotels), and also has two mid-market "Four Points by Sheraton" hotels. Check out www.starwoodhotels.com
- **Wyndham Hotel Group:** Wyndham has four **major brands** in China – the five-star Howard Johnson (13 hotels) and Ramada (19 hotels) hotels and the budget Super 8 and Days Inn. By 2008 Super 8 will have reached more than 60 cities. Check out www.hojochina.com, www.daysinn.cn, www.super8.com and www.ramada.com

Budget Hotels

- Deliberately marketed **"budget" hotels** are a recent phenomenon. The most conspicuous of these is Super 8 and Holiday Inn.
- Wherever you are there will be at least a handful of extremely cheap Chinese hotels to choose from, though **standards can be low**.

Youth Hostels

- There are many hostels throughout China, though most would perhaps be better described as cheap hotels. **YHA membership is not essential** and not all have self-catering facilities. Check out www.yhachina.com

Guest Houses

- **Popular tourist places** such as Lijiang, Yangshuo and Pingyao have plenty of simple guest houses located in the old part of town. The large numbers of foreigners mean staff usually speak reasonable English.
- **Hong Kong's guest houses** are usually converted apartments and can be found in residential areas. They can be claustrophobic, but are normally clean and offer value for money in China's most expensive city.

Camping

- Technically you need the **permission** of the Public Security Bureau to camp in China. It's not a popular option and, accordingly, there are no official camp sites or camping facilities.

Making Reservations

- **Websites such as** www.ctrip.com and www.elong.com have excellent hotel reservation services, but specialize in Chinese hotels.
- Most of the major hotel chains offer **online booking**.

Prices
Expect to pay per double room per night, including breakfast and taxes:
Mainland China
$ under 400RMB $$ 400–1,200RMB $$$ 1,200–3,000RBMB
$$$$ over 3,000RMB
Hong Kong
$ under HK$500 $$ HK$500–1,500 $$$ HK$1,500–3,000
$$$$ over HK$3,000

Food and Drink

It is difficult to imagine a people who spend more time thinking about, talking about and (finally) eating food. Dining is at the heart of Chinese culture. The restaurant is where friends gather to socialize and it's where nearly all business deals are sealed. Every street corner boasts some form of eatery, from hole-in-the-wall joints to mammoth banquet halls. Nowhere is China's "otherness" more obvious than at the dinner table, but nowhere is this "otherness" more easily enjoyed – provided you are prepared to take a few risks and throw yourself into the experience.

Eating Out

- The Chinese **take time** over their food. You will never be encouraged to hurry, no matter how late or how many people are waiting for a table.
- Chinese observe **regular meal times**, earlier than eating hours in the West. Breakfast starts around 6am, lunch begins at 11:30am, while dinner gets under way at 5:30pm. Even if there are no customers, however, restaurants rarely close so it's usually possible to get a meal any time of the day.
- **Late-night feasting** is popular and the Cantonese have an actual word for it: *siu ye* is essentially the fourth meal of the day.
- **Dress codes** are rare, though customers tend to dress up to visit the more expensive restaurants (especially around the Bund in Shanghai).
- It's wise to carry around a **packet of tissues** with you at all times. Restaurant toilets, like public ones, rarely supply toilet paper.

Chinese Restaurants

- The Chinese eat around large circular tables, allowing everyone access to the food, placed in the middle. **All dishes are shared**.
- Exclusive use of the **wok** means food is cooked quickly and arrives at the table with astonishing speed.
- **Tea** is usually free, although some restaurants levy a small charge.
- If you are not confident with **chopsticks**, bring along your own cutlery.
- Skin and bones may not be removed during food preparation. Chinese diners will normally **spit out** undigestibles onto the table.
- **Tipping** is not expected and attempts to do so will likely be refused.
- **Non-smoking areas** don't exist. Chinese men are dab hands at smoking with one hand and eating with the other.
- Restaurants are often raucous places. If the noise and smoke become too much, ask for a **private room**. Most restaurants have them and there's normally no extra charge.
- Considering restaurant staff are appallingly paid and hugely overworked, **service** in China is extraordinary. Nothing is too much trouble for waiting staff. However, they will not come to your table without being called.
- Because freshness is highly prized, many restaurants (especially in Cantonese areas) display **live produce**.
- **Free fresh fruit** is often brought to the table at the end of the meal. However, the Chinese rarely eat dessert.
- There are plenty of **dos and don'ts** when eating out. See page 17.

Menus

- Menus are often **written in Chinese only**, especially in smaller restaurants. When you find something you like, ask someone to write down its Chinese name. Safe and popular choices include:

- Beef/pork/chicken fried rice: *niurou/zhurou/jirou chaofan*
- Sizzling beef/lamb: *tieban niurou/yangrou*
- Tomato and fried egg: *fanqie chaodan*
- Fried broccoli: *chao xilanhua*
- Boiled/fried lettuce: *yanshui/chao shengcai*
- Fried sliced potato: *tudou si*

Western Food

- Most towns and cities (and hotels) have **"Western" restaurants**, which are usually Chinese-owned and staffed. The food is generally unexceptional, but you can get a passable spaghetti/pasta dish or pizza.
- Western restaurants may include a **service charge** in the bill.
- Beijing, Shanghai and Hong Kong have lots of genuinely Western-owned restaurants where you can get **bona fide Western food**, albeit at premium prices.
- **KFC** and **McDonalds** outlets are all over China.

Vegetarian Food

- There are plenty of options for vegetarians: tofu, green vegetables (galore), rice, noodles, dried fruits and so on. Cooking methods may be unacceptable to the strictest of vegetarians as chefs pan-cook everything and **meat traces** can sometimes be found.

Tea and Coffee

- **Coffee shops** are the big new thing in China, and Starbucks has run rampant. Homegrown brands like Shangdao Coffee and UBC offer comfortable surroundings with decent hot food menus, though the coffee itself is nothing special.
- Surprisingly, specialist **teahouses** are not easy to find. Sichuan's capital, Chengdu, has fine tea-supping traditions, and tea shops (where you can sample before you buy) are everywhere. However, there are many more coffee shops than teahouses.

Alcohol

- Most Chinese enjoy the **occasional tipple**, but drinking to excess is rare. Ironically, the one time you're guaranteed to find Chinese people blind drunk is at formal meals, where near-constant toasting with 50 per cent proof wine is de rigueur.
- Germany's colonial influence in the early part of the 20th century left China with great **beer-brewing traditions**, especially in Shandong province where beer is often sold in plastic bags from streetside kegs. China's only internationally recognized brand, Tsingdao, is common, but there are several other reliable varieties. Harbin Beer is one of the best.
- **Red wine**, like coffee, is gaining middle-class approval. Domestic brands (Changyu, Dynasty and Great Wall) are cheap, but uninspiring. Big city supermarkets stock imported wines but these are usually very expensive.
- **Rice wine** is China's traditional spirit. It's frighteningly strong and best sampled on a full stomach and with a soft drink chaser to hand.

Prices
Expect to pay for a meal for one, excluding drinks and service:
Mainland China
$ under 50RMB $$ 50–150RMB $$$ over 150RMB
Hong Kong
$ under HK$100 $$ HK$100–200 $$$ over HK$200

Shopping

China's shopping districts are remarkable both for their fabulous prices and fake products. Many of the imitations are of a reasonable quality, but real caution is required when buying anything that purports to be "genuine". Check, check and check again. The other major rule of shopping in China is bargaining. Never buy anything without asking if it can be cheaper than the advertised price. This applies equally to major malls and market stalls.

Malls

- Malls in China come in **two basic varieties**: shiny new emporia, filled with individually branded shops with glistening window displays; and jumbles of open-fronted stalls or desks. The first are very similar to the kind of malls you will encounter back at home; the second are essentially markets with roofs.
- Payment can be confusing in some malls. Having selected your purchase, you may be given a label to take to a **cashier**, who will process payment before handing you another **receipt** to take back to the shop assistant. You'll then finally get your goods.
- One of the more obvious indicators of China's low wages is the number of **shop assistants**. Often, every single aisle has its own member of staff. Few speak English and the sales tactic normally involves wandering from product to product, mutely pointing.
- **VAT** should be included in the price, but it's often possible to forfeit the tax receipt to get a cheaper price. By doing so you will lose your guarantee.

Markets

- **Outdoor markets** are best for the very cheapest goods. The quality of the products may be variable, but there are some terrific bargains to be had.
- As a **foreigner** you will be hugely overcharged. Start your haggling at a third of what is being asked and aim to pay no more than half.

City Specifics

- Most cities have entire **neighbourhoods** that are famous for one kind of product, with a series of stores selling identical goods. Ask at your hotel for the best spots for shoes/jewellery/cameras/computers and so on.
- **Hong Kong** is a shopper's paradise, with something to tempt every taste and budget. In the many malls you can buy originals of every brand at substantial discounts – all the big-name Western shops are represented. Hong Kong has long been famed for its cheap electrical products and prices remain very competitive. Mainland malls have even lower prices, but you'll forfeit the guarantee.
- **Shanghai** is the home of chic shopping in mainland China. Nanjing Donglu, the Bund and Huaihai Zhonglu all have fabulous malls and (genuine) designer stores. Shanxi Nanlu is great for shoes, while the Old Town will take care of your souvenir and knick-knack needs. Xujiahui has cheap electrical goods.
- **Beijing** comes into its own for kitsch Mao memorabilia. All the major sites have Mao stalls. Liulichang, a street south of the Hepingmen metro station, has some great curios and souvenirs, while Wangfujing Dajie is the capital's snazziest shopping drag.
- **Guangzhou** has China's largest trade fair (held twice a year in April and October) and is great for wholesale markets. Shoe City, Leather City and

Watch City are close to the main train station. Fabric City is opposite Zhongshan University, while Computer City is in the Tianhe district. All goods can be bought either as single items or wholesale.

What to Buy
Traditional Products

- **Jade:** Jade is a common gift between Chinese friends and family members, said to bestow luck and good health on the wearer. Only nephrite (soft, oily and fibrous) and jadeite (hard, waxy and glasslike) qualify as jade. When held to the light, jade should be translucent, without blemishes or scratches.
- **Pearls:** Freshwater pearls are farmed in the south of the country and in lakes around Shanghai. They may be sold loose or on strands. Check for lustre, colour and cracks, and roll pearls on a flat surface to make sure they are round and evenly sized.
- **Porcelain:** Jingdezhen, in Jiangxi province, was former home to the Royal Kilns and remains China's most famed porcelain centre. Foshan, in Guangdong province, is a more easily accessible historic porcelain city.
- **Paintings:** Some of the most provocative modern art in Asia is emanating from China. Traditional watercolour paintings are also widely sold. There is an interesting trade in high-quality reproductions of Western classics, with painters working in factory conditions to produce brushstroke-perfect "original copies".
- **Tea:** China's national drink comes in three main varieties: green tea (*lu cha*), red tea (*hong cha*) and semi-oxidized oolong (*wulong*). Like a good wine, tea improves with age. All tea stores have a try-before-you-buy policy.
- **Seals:** Carved seals engraved with the owners' initials have been used for thousands of years as a means of signing official documents or marking authorship. Stores can help translate your name into Chinese. Don't leave without the accompanying red ink.
- **Antiques:** Genuine antiques are **hard to find** in mainland China. Most are high-quality reproductions of Ming- and Qing-era furniture. No item made before 1795 may be sold or exported, while those dating from 1795 to 1949 are defined as "cultural relics" and may not be taken out of the country without an **official seal** and a government export licence. Note that a seal does not guarantee a genuine antique. Antiques laws do not apply in **Hong Kong**.

Fake Products

- In most street markets you can buy **fake** anything. Most popular are T-shirts, football kits, purses, watches, ties, scarves and handbags, all at silly prices.
- For stylish fakes of big-name goods, expect to be taken to a **back room** to browse. Some market stalls display a brochure of their back room products.
- As a foreigner, expect random strangers to whisper the word "DeeVeeDee" as you pass. The secrecy is not really necessary. All DVD shops in China sell **pirated discs**. There are intermittent crackdowns, but stock is merely moved to back rooms. Most are of a good quality and cost between 10 and 15RMB.

Warning

- **Software piracy** is rampant in China. Illegal versions of everything from computer games to fully flegded operating systems are available. However, discs often contains viruses.

Entertainment

In Shanghai, Beijing and Hong Kong you'll find everything from acrobatic shows to multistorey nightclubs. There's a glut of free English-language listings magazines, which can be picked up in bars and restaurants. Alternatively, check the *China Daily* newspaper. Entertainment in smaller cities is rather stale and generally limited to eating, drinking and karaoke.

Traditional Performing Arts

- **Acrobatic** shows are regularly staged in the big cities and mix gymnastics with circus acts and vaudeville.
- Traditional **Chinese opera** is massively popular and makes for a fascinating spectacle, even if the melodies challenge the Western ear.

Festivals

- **Chinese New Year** is a time to avoid being in China. Prices increase dramatically, crowds are heavy and fireworks will keep you awake.
- The Tibetan festival of **Monlam** is held around two weeks after the lunar New Year. Fascinating temple events mix celebration and spirituality.
- The **Dragon Boat Festival** (usually in June) sees outdoor races on lakes and rivers throughout China.
- The **winter festivals** of the Dongbei region feature remarkable snow and ice sculptures; the most famous is in Harbin every January and February.
- Each of China's 55 minority groups holds **indigenous festivals**. These are more interesting for outsiders than the Han festivals of eastern China.

Spectator Sports

- **Football:** China has a competitive domestic league and obtaining tickets is easy. Shanghai and Dalian have the biggest teams. English Premiership football matches can be watched live on domestic TV.
- **Basketball:** China has a successful basketball league which attracts overseas players. NBA games are often screened live.
- **Golf:** The European Tour sometimes holds competitions on Hainan Island. Shanghai's HSBC Champions Tournament is held in November.
- **Motor racing:** Shanghai's Formula 1 Grand Prix is held every October. Macau's Formula 3 Grand Prix takes place in November.
- **Badminton, table tennis, volleyball:** China is a world beater at each of these sports.

Cinema

- China's **domestic film industry** is on the up, but finding mainland cinemas which show English subtitles is difficult. Check listings.
- The government sets a strict quota on the number of **Hollywood films** shown each year. The decision over which to admit is often political.

Music

- China's **live music scene** has come a long way in a very short time. There is always something going on in the bar districts of the bigger cities.

Nightlife

- **Bars and clubs** pack China's big cities. Shanghai, Beijing and Hong Kong are the biggest party places, but Guangzhou, Xi'an and Nanjing are not too far behind. You'll find everything from super-clubs to Irish bars.
- **Karaoke parlours** generally feature a few English songs.

Beijing and the Northeast

Getting Your Bearings 44 – 45
In Five Days 46 – 47
Don't Miss 48 – 57
At Your Leisure 58 – 59
Where to... 60 – 64

Getting Your Bearings

China's capital has not just been touched by the hand of history; it has seized that hand in a firm grasp, shaken it vigorously and made a deal for a lifelong supply of drama and tragedy. From Genghis Khan's Mongol marauders to Chairman Mao's mass rallies, by way of 600 years of imperial grandeur, Beijing tales are tall ones.

With its scores of historic sights and cultural attractions, Beijing is where visitors can best conjure up the "costume-drama" China portrayed in novels and movies – mighty emperors, grand palaces and so on. As the nerve centre of the Chinese Communist Party, Beijing retains an imposing, Soviet-styled atmosphere, though recent Olympic preparations have added a modern sheen.

The map of China is often compared to a rooster, with Beijing situated – appropriately enough – right on the jugular. Unusually for a capital, Beijing lies close to neither river nor sea. With development unconstrained by natural obstructions, the city has grown into a sprawling metropolis. Its size is mitigated by orderliness: Beijing is structured around wide, straight boulevards and a series of giant ring roads that radiate out from Tiananmen Square.

Northeast of Beijing is the rooster's head. This area is best known in the West as "Manchuria" – a place of frighteningly cold winters and wild, forested landscapes. It's also China's historic industrial heartland and explains the many attempts by China's neighbours to wrest the region from its grasp. Indeed, the Russian, Korean and Japanese influences evident today give this area its unique character.

★ Don't Miss

❶ The Forbidden City ➤ 48
❷ Tiananmen Square ➤ 50
❸ Beijing's Hutong ➤ 52
❹ Temple of Heaven ➤ 54
❺ The Summer Palace ➤ 55
❻ The Great Wall ➤ 57

Chengde **❿**

The Great Wall **❻** **❽** Ming Tombs

798 ✦ Art District

The Summer Palace **❺** **❾** BEIJING

Tangshan

Langfang

Tianjin Bo Hai

Page 43: Marble bridge leading to the Gate of Heavenly Peace, Tiananmen Square, Beijing

Right: Fishing boats, Laohutan Bay, Dalian

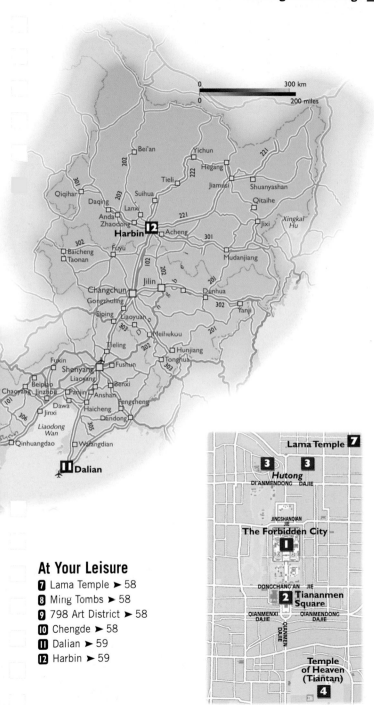

300 km
200 miles

Bei'an
Yichun
Hegang
Tieli
Jiamusi
Shuanyashan
Qiqihar
Daqing
Suihua
Qitaihe
Anda
Lanxi
Zhaodong
Harbin 12
Acheng
Jixi
Xingkai Hu
Baicheng
Fuyu
Taonan
Mudanjiang
Changchun
Jilin
Dunhua
Gongzhuling
Siping
Liaoyuan
Yanji
Meihekou
Tieling
Hunjiang
Fuxin
Tonghua
Shenyang
Fushun
Liaoyang
Benxi
Beipiao
Chaoyang
Jinzhou
Panjin
Anshan
Dawa
Fengcheng
Jinxi
Haicheng
Dandong
Liaodong Wan
Qinhuangdao
Wafangdian

11 **Dalian**

At Your Leisure
7 Lama Temple ➤ 58
8 Ming Tombs ➤ 58
9 798 Art District ➤ 58
10 Chengde ➤ 58
11 Dalian ➤ 59
12 Harbin ➤ 59

Lama Temple 7
3   3
Hutong
DI'ANMENDONG   DAJIE
JINGSHANQIAN JIE
The Forbidden City
1
DONGCHANG'AN   JIE
2 **Tiananmen Square**
QIANMENXI DAJIE
QIANMENDONG DAJIE
QIANMEN DAJIE
Temple of Heaven (Tiantan)
4

Beijing is a sprawling city and, though most of its major attractions lie within the first ring road, getting between the sights takes time. The Summer Palace and the Great Wall are farther out of town and each demands a whole day.

Beijing and the North in Five Days

Day One

Morning

Rise early to watch the well-drilled PLA soldiers raising the national flag over **2 Tiananmen Square** (right, ➤ 50–51) at sunrise. Join the gathering throng at the **Mausoleum of Mao Zedong**. Having doffed your cap to the "Great Helmsman", head over to the **Great Hall of the People** and tour China's political HQ with one of the English-language guides.

Afternoon

There are many restaurant options at the south of Tiananmen Square. Having refuelled, walk north to the **Gate of Heavenly Peace** (Tiananmen) and climb the balcony where Chairman Mao announced the foundation of the People's Republic of China in 1949. Spend the whole afternoon exploring the **❶ Forbidden City** (➤ 48–49). Exit via the north gate (Shenwumen), and cross to **Jingshan Park** to enjoy the views back across the rooftops. If time allows, take a sunset stroll around nearby **Beihai Park**.

Evening

Take a taxi to **Wangfujing Dajie** (➤ 63). Beijing's premier shopping street comes alive after dark. After browsing the boutiques, grab a bite in one of the many restaurants.

Day Two

Day

Take a boat to the **5 Summer Palace** (➤ 55–56). Spend the morning walking around Kunming Lake (left) and visit the handsome buildings in the north of the park towards the end of the day, when the crowds are likely to have thinned out.

Evening

Head to the Lao She Teahouse (➤ 51) for the nightly variety show of Chinese performance arts. Before bed, take a short stroll east to **Qianmen** at the southern end of the brilliantly illuminated Tiananmen Square.

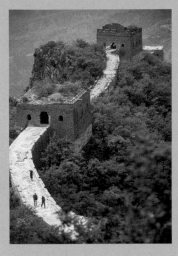

Day Three

All Day

Visit the **6 Great Wall** (left, ➤ 57). If time is short, taked the combined tour of **Badaling** and **Dingling** (one of the **8 Ming Tombs**, ➤ 58). Buses depart the Tourist Bus Station at the southwest corner of Tiananmen Square and the 160RMB cost includes entrance tickets and a meal. Those wanting to escape the tourist hordes should visit **Simatai**, a three-hour ride out of the city. At Badaling, avoid the worst of the crowds by turning right (for some reason, nearly everyone heads left).

Day Four

Morning

Rise early and join the tai chi practitioners at the **4 Temple of Heaven** (➤ 54). Wander through the parkland areas before beginning your tour of the temple complex at the Round Altar.

Afternoon

Take a bus or taxi to the **Drum and Bell towers** and walk around the *hutong* neighbourhoods (below) either side of Qianhai Lake (➤ 174–176). If time allows, stop by the **7 Lama Temple** (➤ 58, 174).

Evening

Assuming the weather is warm enough, dine outdoors on the Qianhai waterfront.

Day Five

All Day

Take a train to **10 Chengde** (➤ 58). You might like to use this as the first step of a trip into the northeast of China. Alternatively, spend the night in Chengde and return to Beijing the following day.

❶ The Forbidden City

As the largest and best preserved cluster of ancient buildings in China, the Forbidden City (Gu Gong) should be at the top of your to-do list in Beijing. This walled compound in the middle was once the impenetrable heart of the empire – a place so separated from the mortal realm that those who worked here were rarely permitted to leave. It remained off-limits to commoners for more than 500 years and, though the rules have loosened a little, a rarefied atmosphere remains.

The Forbidden City is accessible from either the north or south gates. For dramatic effect, most people enter from the south, passing under the giant portrait of Mao Zedong as they go. Note that the Forbidden City does not begin at the famous picture of the "Great Helmsman". This is Tiananmen (Gate of Heavenly Peace) and, though there is a ticket booth here, it merely buys you entrance to the gate's upper balcony. To reach the Forbidden City proper, pass under the portrait, through the tunnel and walk north for about 400m (440 yards) until you reach the imposing **Meridian Gate**.

With 980 buildings, 9,000 rooms and much else in between, the Forbidden City is vast – so allow plenty of time. A stroll through the central corridor of courtyards and palaces offers a great insight into the grandeur of dynastic rule and only requires a couple of hours. However, it's worth allowing half a day to better explore the delightful mini-museums, pavilions and gardens that lie to the east and west.

Stone lion guarding the 15th-century Gate of Heavenly Peace

Ming City

Very few of Beijing's buildings date further back than the 13th century, when the city formerly known as Zhongdu was razed to the ground by Mongol warlord Genghis Khan. His grandson, Kublai, returned in 1260 and made it his capital. By 1279, it had been reborn as the First City of the world's largest empire. In 1368, Hongwu – first emperor of the succeeding Ming dynasty – relocated to Nanjing, only for Emperor Yongle to return a few years later. The Forbidden City, built between 1406 and 1420, was the culmination of Yongle's plan to sweep away all traces of the earlier Mongol rulers.

Inside the Audience Hall of the Palace of Heavenly Purity

Heading north from the Meridian Gate, the first building you'll encounter is the **Gate of Supreme Harmony**, which overlooks a courtyard large enough to host an imperial audience of 100,000. Just to the north is the Forbidden City's centrepiece – a series of three ceremonial halls raised on a marble terrace. The first, the **Hall of Supreme Harmony**, was the most important and would have been used for coronations. Behind is the **Hall of Middle Harmony**. The **Hall of Preserving Harmony**, the final building on the terrace, was used for imperial banquets.

The size of the Forbidden City means that renovations are continuously being carried out on some part of the complex. The wholesale beautification of Beijing ahead of the Olympic Games has cranked up the pressure further. Those visiting before the Games start in August in 2008 should expect some of the buildings to be under scaffolding.

TAKING A BREAK

There is a **service area** southeast of the Hall of Preserving Harmony which sells drinks, snacks and souvenirs. This ornate building once housed a Starbucks outlet, but the US coffee giant decided to leave in July 2007 after being told it would have to share the space with domestic vendors, who now ply their trade there.

➕ 210 B2 ✉ Xichang'an Jie, Dongcheng District ☎ 010 8511 7311; www.dpm.org.cn ⏰ Apr–Oct daily 8:30–5; Nov–Mar daily 8:30–4:30 💰 Adult moderate 🚇 Tiananmen Xi, Tiananmen Dong

FORBIDDEN CITY: INSIDE INFO

Top tip A new **automated audio guide** can be hired from the tourist centre beside the Meridian Gate. It features an electronic map of the complex, with red lights indicating where audio explanations are available.

Must see After leaving the Forbidden City from its north entrance/exit, cross the road and pay the 2RMB to enter **Jingshan Park**. The hill in the middle of the park was built from earth excavated during the creation of the Forbidden City outer moat. Climb to the top for great views across the imperial rooftops.

2 Tiananmen Square

If the Forbidden City captures the glory of the imperial past, Tiananmen Square symbolizes the strength of Communist control over modern China. In the West, the name may be associated with the 1989 massacre of pro-democracy demonstrators. However, to the tens of thousands of Chinese tourists who visit daily, it's primarily a place of pilgrimage, for this is where Mao Zedong's embalmed body lies in state.

Wide Open Space

Vast concrete plazas are a peculiarly Chinese conceit. In terms of size, scale and history, none can compete with Tiananmen Square. In 1919, it was the focal point of the "May the Fourth Movement", a protest against political infighting and colonial exploitation that ultimately inspired the creation of the Chinese Communist Party. Here Mao Zedong announced the creation of the People's Republic of China in 1949 and, later, orchestrated mass rallies during the Cultural Revolution. Tiananmen Square, with an area of

400,000sq m (4.3 million square feet) – is the largest public square in the world.

In its design, it mimics the shape and layout of the Forbidden City. Like its northerly neighbour, the square has traditional gates at the top and bottom and a series of halls to the side.

Above: The Mausoleum of Mao Zedong, illuminated at night

The Square's Buildings

The imposing edifice to the west of the square is the **Great Hall of the People**. Built in the late 1950s, it is home to China's parliament,

Left: Outside the Great Hall of the People

the National People's Congress. You can take a guided tour of the 5,000-seat banquet hall and 10,000-seat auditorium, though access is restricted at times.

In the middle of the square is the **Monument to the People's Heroes**. Despite the name, the obelisk isn't only dedicated to the working-class champions of the Communist era. A bas-relief at the monument's base shows Chinese sailors setting fire to a consignment of British opium in 1839, the incident which sparked off the First Opium War (➤ 22–23).

The enormous **Mausoleum of Mao Zedong** rears up towards the south of the square. Though vilified in the West, Mao Zedong is credited in China with freeing the country from feudalism and foreign exploitation and most locals display deep reverence when confronted with the sarcophagus.

Qianmen is the gate just to the south of the square. It dates from the Ming dynasty, when it formed part of a huge wall separating the inner city from the outer. You can climb it for great views back across Tiananmen Square. For a similar view from the opposite direction, visit the balcony at **Tiananmen** (Gate of Heavenly Peace).

TAKING A BREAK

The **Lao She Teahouse**, just west of the palatial KFC on Qianmen Xidajie, is a popular haunt. There are daytime performances of folk music and Beijing opera. Or visit at 7:30pm for the daily variety show of music, magic, acrobatics and opera.

Gate of Heavenly Peace
🚹 210 B2 ☎ 010 6309 5630 ⏰ Mar–Oct daily 8:30–4:30; Nov–Feb daily 8:30–4 💷 Inexpensive 🚇 Tiananmen Dong

Great Hall of the People
🚹 210 B1 ☎ 010 6309 6156 ⏰ Daily 8:30–3 💷 Inexpensive 🚇 Tiananmen Xi

Mausoleum of Mao Zedong
🚹 210 B1 ☎ 010 6513 2277 ⏰ Tue–Sun 8:30–11:30am (also Tue, Thu 2–4) 💷 Free; small charge to deposit bags and cameras 🚇 Qianmen

TIANANMEN SQUARE: INSIDE INFO

Top tips If you can bear the early start, it's worth watching the **flag-raising ceremony** in the relative quiet of sunrise. The PLA soldiers are back at sunset to take the flag down, but by this time the crowds have normally gathered.
• Visible behind the Great Hall of the People is the **National Grand Theatre**. This structure has been dubbed the "giant egg" because of its domed glass roof.

Must see Come back to see Tiananmen **by night**. Though the square itself is closed to pedestrians the buildings are impressively lit.

❸ Beijing's Hutong

Beijing's historic treasure is not only showcased in its grandiose palaces and temples. The narrow alleys and cramped courtyard dwellings of the capital's *hutong* neighbourhoods reveal more about the fabric of the city than any throne, altar or porcelain jar. Many have disappeared during China's ceaseless modernization drive, but those that remain are as charming as ever.

Traditional Residences

Towering apartment blocks and wide boulevards may be the penchant of modern city planners, but Beijing wasn't always this organized. This sprawling city was once a mass cluster of rambling, occasionally ramshackle, neighbourhoods known as *hutong*. They first appeared in the wake of Genghis Khan's destructive visit in 1215. After the burning came the rebuilding, the entire city being redrawn into a matrix of parallel east-to-west alleys. Around these sprang up *siheyuan* (literally "four sided courtyard") houses, which gradually merged together and multiplied. As time went on, *hutong* became defined both by width and proximity to the Forbidden City. Generally speaking, the higher class the neighbourhood, the wider were its lanes and the closer it was to the centre. Many were named according to the trade of their occupants. Wet Nurse Lane, for example, housed young mothers charged with breast feeding the imperial offspring.

By 1949 there were nearly 6,000 distinct *hutong* – "as many as the hairs on a cow", as a popular saying has it – but they began to disappear rapidly as China's new communist government pursued its love of faceless apartment blocks. Only fairly recently has there been a concerted effort to protect certain areas in an attempt to preserve this aspect of Chinese cultural history. Most

Opposite: Cyclist in Nanluogu Xiang Street in the Dongcheng District

Left: Courtyard in the Doufuchi Hutong District

modern *hutong* date from the Qing dynasty, but a few survive from the Ming era. Particularly noteworthy or historic *hutong* have a white plaque near their entrance identifying them as being protected.

There are many fine *hutong* well within reach of the Forbidden City. The best way to enjoy them is simply to stroll. There's plenty to enjoy on either side of **Qianhai Lake**. To the west, on Liuyin Jie, is **Prince Gong's Residence**. Prince Gong was uncle of the Last Emperor, Puyi, and – appropriately – the house is one of the grandest examples of a *siheyuan* still visible in Beijing.

For a look at how the more common man might have lived, head east. Immediately southeast of Beijing's famous **Drum Tower** lies a huge block of delightful *hutong*. Nearly all of the east-to-west lanes that run between Dianmen Waidajie and Jiandaokou Nandajie are *hutong* of one variety or another. Running north to south through the centre of this block is **Nanluogu Xiang** (Drum and Gong Alley), well known by locals for its collection of coffee houses and street-side cafés. This is a great spot to while away an afternoon in atmospheric surrounds (► 174–176)

TAKING A BREAK

Nanluogu Xiang alley is one of Beijing's most famous café zones, filled with tempting places to stop for refreshment. Try the **Passby Bar** (No 108) or **Xiaoxin Café** (No 103; ► 62).

Prince Gong's Residence
🏠 210 A5 ✉ 14 Liuyin Jie (close to Qianhai Xijie), Xicheng District ☎ 010 6616 8149 🕐 Daily 8–5 💵 Inexpensive 🚇 Gulou (then bus 60)

BEIJING'S HUTONG: INSIDE INFO

Top tips Those who want to get a taste of *hutong* life while staying in Beijing can check into one of the **hotels** that occupy a *siheyuan* plot. Consult the accommodation listings for details.
• Most of the pedicab drivers who approach tourists with offers of *hutong* tours end up in the vicinity of the Drum and Bell towers. The *hutong* here are fairly sprawling, but there's no reason not to **explore by yourself**; by foot or by bicycle.

❹ Temple of Heaven

Unlike Beijing's other great tourist draws, the Temple of Heaven (Tiantan) is renowned less for its size and scale than for the perfection of its design. Each temple, altar and walkway has intricate ceremonial significance.

The Temple of Heaven originally functioned as a vast stage for a solemn ceremony practised by the emperor. Every winter solstice the "Son of Heaven" – accompanied by a huge entourage – would travel down from the Forbidden City. Dressed in ceremonial silk garb, the emperor would leave his courtiers and walk along the bridge, known as the **Red Stairway**, to the **Hall of Prayer for Good Harvests**. There he offered ritual sacrifices and delivered a state of the nation address for the benefit of celestial ears.

The triple-eaved Hall of Prayer for Good Harvests

The vibrantly colourful Hall of Prayer for Good Harvests was destroyed by fire in 1889, and this faithful reproduction was erected a year later. Its intricate design typifies the geometric planning that went into the construction of the entire site. The four central pillars represent the seasons, the 12 secondary pillars represent the months and the final circle of pillars represent the 12 "watches" of each day.

TAKING A BREAK

There are **Chinese restaurants** close to the Western gate.

🚩 210 B1 (off map) ✉ Tiantan Donglu ☎ 010 6702 8866 🕐 Temple Buildings: Apr–Oct daily 8–6, last ticket 4:30; Nov–Mar daily 8–5, last ticket 3:30. Park: daily 6am–9pm 💰 Temple Buildings: moderate high season, inexpensive low season. Park: inexpensive 🚇 Chongwenmen, then bus 60 or 38

5 The Summer Palace

The Summer Palace (Yiheyuan), around 16km (10 miles) northwest of the Forbidden City, effectively functioned as a country retreat for the cosseted emperors of the Qing dynasty. The lakeside parkland provided China's royalty with respite from both the political stresses and the sweltering summer heat of their urban environs. It survived two vicious assaults by foreign troops in the 19th century and remains the largest landscaped garden in China.

The Summer Palace's size and suburban location mean that you should consider giving over an entire day to a visit. Most of the major sights are concentrated in the easily navigable northern part of the park and this is where the tourist throngs flock to. However, if you want to avoid the crowds it's best to pack a picnic and head out along the willow-lined pathways that skirt and dissect Kunming Lake.

Kunming Lake takes up around three-quarters of the entire area of the Summer Palace. It was effectively made to order by around 100,000 labourers working for the Emperor Qianlong, ruler of China for most of the 18th century. Despite his impressive military prowess, Qianlong is perhaps best known as the man who rebuffed European advances for trade, dismissing the British ambassador and his entourage as "barbarians". Nearly 70 years later, in 1860, the British took their revenge when they destroyed many of the Summer Palace's buildings in the wake of the Second Opium War. They ransacked the palace for a second time in 1900.

All this means that the buildings visitors see today are fairly recent restorations. It doesn't, however, diminish their splendour. Close to the most popular

The Temple of Buddhist Virtue

THE SUMMER PALACE: INSIDE INFO

Top tips The emperors of old usually travelled to the Summer Palace **by boat**. In summer tourists can do the same. Between March and October there are departures from the Bayi Lake Pier, inside Yuyuantan Park, and the Shijitan Pier, just east of the park. A one-way ride is 60RMB, return is 80RMB.
• If you can't make it out to the Summer Palace, **Beihai Park** is a worthy city centre alternative, offering a similarly restful atmosphere.

Must see The photogenic **17 Arch Bridge** crosses the 150m (490-foot) span between South Lake Island and the eastern bank of Kunming Lake. There are 544 carved stone lions along the railings, each one unique.

entry point – the East Palace Gate – is the **Hall of Benevolent Longevity**, which houses a hardwood throne where the palace's most celebrated sponsor, Empress Dowager Cixi, held court.

Running for 728m (2,388 feet) along the northern bank of Kunming Lake is the remarkable **Long Corridor**. This shaded walkway is decorated with around 10,000 individually painted murals. Paths lead from here to the temple complex atop **Longevity Hill**, which offers sweeping views across the lake and access to the lovely **Buddhist Incense Tower**.

The lake itself can be traversed in several ways. Large pleasure cruisers cater mainly for tour groups. For a more peaceful alternative, rent a rowboat or pedalo from the jetty at the western end of the Long Corridor. Like most of Beijing's watercourses, the lake freezes over in winter and can be crossed on foot – or with ice skates.

TAKING A BREAK

The **Tinliguan Restaurant**, in the Pavilion of Listening to Orioles, serves up imperial-style cuisine, but is pitched at tour groups, especially in the evening, when a minimum table charge of 3,000RMB applies. Between 11am and 2pm there are no such restrictions. Alternatively head to **Suzhou Jie**, close to the North Palace Gate, where there lots of fast-food outlets.

🚇 202 B5 ✉ Yihe Yuan Lu, Haidian District ☎ 010 6288 1144 🕐 Apr–Oct daily 6:30–6; Nov–Mar daily 7–5 💷 Adult moderate; includes admission to all attractions 🚇 Xizhimen, then bus 375 to North Palace Gate

Opposite: The Great Wall at Simatai, on the border of Hebei province and Beijing municipality

Left: Sailing on man-made Kunming Lake

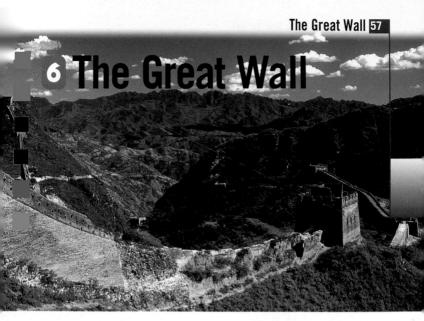

6 The Great Wall

Slithering its way up and down the undulating landscapes of northern China like a mythical dragon, the Great Wall is unquestionably one of the great wonders of the world.

The wall (Changcheng) has its roots in the Warring States period (475–221 BC) when the feudal kingdoms of the era built earthen ramparts to defend against nomadic invaders. It was only under the fearsome Qin Shihuang, the first emperor to unite China, that the wall began to take shape late in the third century BC. Some 300,000 men were conscripted to join existing sections into a single wall. The Great Wall was continuously repaired and extended by subsequent rulers, most notably the Ming emperors (AD 1368–1644).

Beijing is the most convenient base from which to launch your assault on the wall. Several impressive stretches survive in the northern reaches of the municipality. The most famous, and "developed", section is at **Badaling**. Regular buses make the trip from the tourist bus station, southwest of Tiananmen Square. Crowds are heavy, but it's still possible to get away from the tourist scrum, if you're willing to walk. **Simatai** is highly recommended for those who want a slightly less packaged trip. It too has ticket gates and cable cars, but the area is outstandingly beautiful. **Huanghua** is popular with those who like their walls crumbled slightly. It's still possible to climb here, but the wall is officially "closed for redevelopment" and access is awkward.

Badaling
✚ 202 B5 ✉ Yanqing County, 66km (41 miles) northwest of Beijing ☎ 010 6912 2222 🕐 Daily 7:30–5:30 💷 Moderate 🚌 919 from Deshengmen, close to Jishuitan metro station

Simatai
✚ 202 C5 ✉ Miyun County, 106km (66 miles) northeast of Beijing ☎ 010 6903 1051 🕐 Daily 8–5 💷 Moderate 🚌 980 or 970 from Dongzhimen bus terminus to Miyun, then taxi

Huanghua
✚ 202 B5 ✉ Huairou County, 64km (40 miles) north of Beijing 💷 Free (local villagers may try to impose their own pricing structure) 🚌 916 from Dongzhimen Waidajie. Change at Huairou for one of two buses to the wall, marked Sandaoguan or Xishuiyu; signs in Chinese only

At Your Leisure

7 Lama Temple

The Lama Temple (Yonghe Gong) represents a rare haven of peace in downtown Beijing. It is the most important Tibetan lamasery outside Tibet itself, and monks of the Yellow Hat sect live on site and can be seen scurrying through the clouds of incense. The five main prayer halls – each slightly bigger than the last – are typically Tibetan in their vibrant colours. The largest hall, the **Pavilion of 10,000 Blessings**, houses the world's largest Buddhist statue carved from a single block of wood. At 18m (59 feet) high, his head is right up in the rafters.

➕ 210 C5 (off map) ✉ 12 Yonghegong Dajie, Dongcheng District ☎ 010 6404 4499 🕓 Daily 9–4:30 💷 Inexpensive Ⓜ Yonghegong

8 Ming Tombs

Thirteen emperors of the Ming dynasty (AD 1368–1644) were buried in this valley to the northwest of Beijing, though only three of the tombs (Shisan Ling) are open to the public. Each comprises a series of gates, courtyards and halls, as well as a single "Soul Tower" and a burial mound. The **Chang Ling** tomb is the final resting place of one of Beijing's most important figures, Yongle, who commissioned the Forbidden City and the Temple of Heaven.

The burial mound itself is not open to the public but the enormous **Hall of Eminent Favours** is stunningly decorated and worth a look. The **Ding Ling** tomb is the burial place of Wanli and is of particular interest for its subterranean vaults. **Zhao Ling** is the least busy of the three and a pleasant alternative if you are looking to avoid crowds.

➕ 202 B5 ✉ Changping District, 48km (30 miles) northwest of Beijing ☎ 010 6076 1888 (Chang Ling), 010 6076 1424 (Ding Ling); www.mingtombs.com.cn 💷 Moderate 🕓 Apr–Oct daily 8:30–5:30; Nov–Mar daily 8:30–5 🚌 314, or designated "Tourist Bus" from Qianmen or Beijing Railway Station

9 798 Art District

Arguably the biggest paradox of modern day Beijing is that, despite the stifling political climate, the city has the most liberated and experimental art scene in China. The 798 Art District, in the northeastern suburbs, is one of its best showcases. This hotbed of creative talent is located on the site of "Factory 798", a disused electronics factory complex built by East German engineers in the 1950s. It's now home to scores of hip design studios, bohemian bookshops, trendy cafés and expansive galleries, many of which make inventive use of the cavernous factory interiors.

➕ 202 C5 ✉ 2/4 Jiuxianqiao Lu (close to Airport Expressway) ☎ 010 6437 6248 🕓 Daily 10–6 (approximately). Many galleries close Mon 🕓 Free Ⓜ Dongzhimen, then bus 401

10 Chengde

The Imperial Mountain Resort, just a few hours' drive from Beijing, was the summer retreat for the great Qing emperors Kangxi and Qianlong. The Imperial Summer Palace is the main

Prayer wheels at the Putuozongcheng Temple in Chengde

attraction, but equally worthy are the eight outer temples scattered at intermittent distances around a wild, rambling valley. Built in various styles – Han, Mongolian, Tibetan and Uyghur included – these temples represent 18th-century architectural shock and awe tactics, built to hammer home the message of China's size, strength and unity. Even if you are "templed-out" after Beijing, Chengde remains a great spot for walking and cycling in stunning surroundings.

➕ 200 B2 ✉ Hebei province ☎ 0314 203 7350 (Information Centre)
🎫 Imperial Summer Palace: mid-Apr to mid-Oct daily 7–5:30; mid-Oct to mid-Apr daily 7–4:30 💰 Imperial Summer Palace moderate 🚆 Regular trains from Beijing take around 3 hours

🔟 Dalian

With its multicultural melange and scenic surrounds, Dalian was voted the "second most livable city in China" in a 2005 survey by the *People's Daily* newspaper (bettered only by Shanghai). Its location at the southerly tip of the Liaoning Peninsula makes it tricky to get to (though there is a convenient overnight train from Beijing), but equally explains why the city is so attractive. Within the city limits there are rugged cliffs and beaches (the sand having been imported from Hainan Island); the huge port has been a conduit for Russian, Korean and Japanese cultural influences; north of the city there are some wonderful links golf courses; and then there's the succulent seafood.

The Church of St Sophia in Harbin

➕ 203 E4 ✉ Liaoning province
☎ 0411 96181 (Dalian Tourist Hotline)
🚆 Overnight train from Beijing leaves at 9:21 and arrives at 6:58 ✈ Dalian International Airport

🔢 Harbin

While boasting some fine Russian architecture, Harbin is notable mainly for the fabulous Ice Lantern Festival that brings the city to life every January and February. Despite temperatures as low as -30°C (-22°F), thousands make the trip north to marvel at the colossal snow sculptures displayed at Sun Island Park or the finely chiselled ice carvings at Zhaolin Park. The ice is taken from the Songhua River, carved into a variety of people, animals or replica buildings and studded with colourful neon. The temperatures do daunt many but, as the largest and most important city in the Dongbei (Northeast) region, Harbin has plenty of snug cafés and restaurants to retreat into when your toes start to numb.

China's best skiing resort, Windmill Village, is a three-hour train ride from Harbin at Yabuli.

➕ 201 D3 ✉ Heilongjiang province
🚆 Several trains from Beijing daily; journey takes 12 hours ✈ Harbin International Airport

Windmill Village Ski Resort
✉ Yabuli, Heilongjiang ☎ 0451 5345 5168; www.yabuliski.com 🚆 Trains from Harbin take around 3 hours

Where to... Stay

Prices

Expect to pay for a double room, per night including breakfast and taxes
$ under 400RMB $$ 400–1,200RMB $$$ 1,200–3,000RMB $$$$ over 3,000RMB

Bamboo Garden Hotel $$

A wonderfully restored courtyard mansion, the Bamboo Garden Hotel is located among the *hutong* that surround the Drum and Bell Towers. There are two Chinese restaurants, a café and bar and a spa service. Rooms are tastefully decorated with reproduction Ming furniture. Ask for a room overlooking the tranquil gardens.

✚ 210 B5 ☒ 24 Xiaoshiqiao Hutong, Dongcheng District ☎ 010 5852 0088; www.bbgh.com.cn

Beijing Raffles Hotel $$$

Just a few steps from the Wangfujing metro stop, Beijing's oldest hotel has been rejuvenated. Raffles took over management in 2006 and helped the quality of service keep pace with the stunning interior. The lobby retains a classical opulence, while visitors to the JAAN restaurant can see the old dance floor in its restored glory. Facilities include indoor swimming pool, squash and tennis courts.

✚ 210 C2 ☒ 33 Dongchang'an Jie, Chongwen District ☎ 010 6513 7766; www.beijing.raffles.com

Commune by the Great Wall Kempinski Beijing $$$$

This trend-setting resort, 40km (25 miles) north of Beijing, comprises 11 enormous villas – each designed by a different architect – and a series of less expensive suites. A section of the Great Wall lies within the estate's vast grounds.

✚ 202 B5 ☒ The Great Wall, Exit No 16 at Shuiguan Badaling Highway ☎ 010 8118 1888; www.kempinski.com

Grand Hyatt Beijing $$$

One of China's first "Five Star Platinum" hotels (the top tier of a new classification system), the Grand Hyatt is close to Tiananmen Square and the Forbidden City. The design is top notch, service exemplary and rooms very comfortable. There's an indoor pool and four superb restaurants.

✚ 210 C2 ☒ 1 Dongchang'an Jie, Chongwen District ☎ 010 8518 1234; www.hyatt.com

Red Capital Residence $$$

This quirky hotel has built its reputation on offering a unique "Maochic" experience. Its five rooms are packed with the kind of Liberationera memorabilia that wouldn't look out of place in a museum. An old bomb shelter beneath the central courtyard has been converted into a wine bar that shows propaganda films. You can even take a tour of Beijing in a limo that once belonged to Mao's wife, Jiang Qing. The hotel is unmarked. Look for the red door with the number 9.

✚ 210 (off map east) ☒ 9 Dongsi Liutiao, Dongcheng District ☎ 010 6402 7150; www.redcapitalclub.com.cn

St Regis $$$

Like its sister hotel in Shanghai, the St Regis offers all the usual elegance of this super-exclusive Starwood brand. The hotel is in the heart of the embassy district in South Chaoyang and the standards of service and the opulent décor are impressive. The hotel's restaurants are major destinations in their own right.

✚ 210 (off map east) ☒ 0121 Jianguomen Waidajie, Chaoyang District ☎ 010 6460 6688; www.stregis.com

Where to...
Eat and Drink

Prices

Expect to pay for a meal for one, excluding drinks and service

$** under 50RMB **$$** 50–150RMB **$$$ over 150RMB

Baguo Buyi $

Baguo Buyi is one of the capital's most fun eating experiences. With an ornate, carved wood interior, the restaurant looks like a ye olde Chinese inn from a TV period drama. The restaurant is part of a chain, originating in Chengdu, and the food is appropriately Sichuanese. There is also a traditional Sichuanese "face-changing" performance at 8pm to keep the customers amused.

✚ 210 C4 ⊠ 89 Di'anmendong Dajie, Dongcheng District
☎ 010 6400 8888 ⊚ Daily 11–2:30, 5–9.30

Bellagio $$

Just to the west of the Workers' Stadium, the ever-crowded Bellagio offers a wide variety of classic Chinese dishes in cool surroundings. Its high glass windows give plenty of natural light, and the marble-topped tables and velvet chairs clinch the trendy mood. This Taiwanese-owned chain stays open till late and is a good option is you are feeling peckish after a night out in nearby Sanlitun, Beijing's premier bar district.

✚ 210 (off map east) ⊠ 6 Gongren Tiyuchang Xilu, Chaoyang District
☎ 010 6551 3533 ⊚ Daily 11am–5am

Be There Or Be Square $$

This Cantonese chain is an inexpensive pit stop, popular with Beijing's office workers. The food is served in a bustling fast-food environment and it's a great option if you are craving the simplicity of the Chinese takeaway back home. The *cha siu bao* (sweet pork-filled buns) and *chun juan* (spring rolls) are fantastic, as are the noodle and rice dishes. Unusually, there are smoking and non-smoking areas. There are other outlets in the Henderson Center (18 Jianguomen Neidajie) and the Landmark Tower (8 Dongsanhuan Beilu).

✚ 210 C2 ⊠ Oriental Plaza, 1 Dongchang'an Jie ☎ 010 8518 8518
⊚ 24 hours

The CourtYard $$$

One of Beijing's most celebrated restaurants, the Courtyard specializes in international fusion cuisine and priceless views. The interior is a sophisticated, spot-lit affair and some tables look out over the nearby Forbidden City and surrounding *hutong*. After dinner you can relax in a divan up in the cigar lounge upstairs or browse the contemporary art in the CourtYard's very own gallery.

✚ 210 C2 ⊠ 95 Donghuamen Dajie, Dongcheng District ☎ 010 6526 8883
⊚ Daily 6–10pm

Dongbei Ren $

This fabulous three-storey restaurant specializes in easy-to-eat Dongbei cuisine from China's far northeast. The raucous, colourful environment captures the essence of the Chinese dining experience. The squirrel fish is a Dongbei classic and the liveried waiting staff will sing and clap as it's brought to your table. The rice wine is served out of huge wooden barrels. The multi-coloured dumplings are also a little bit special.

✚ 210 (off map east) ⊠ A1 Xinzhong Jie, Dongzhimen Waidajie, Dongcheng District ☎ 010 6415 2588 ⊚ Daily 9am–11pm

Donghuamen Night Market $

This remarkable market, close to the shopping mecca of Wangfujing Dajie, is a veritable food zoo. The kebabs range from traditional lamb to crispy scorpion, while the pungent Inner Mongolian cheese and tofu make it a full-on sensory experience. Prices are hiked up slightly for the benefit of tourists, but with kebabs costing around 5RMB, it's relatively inexpensive.

✚ 210 C2 ⊠ Dong'anmen Dajie, Dongcheng District ⏱ Daily 3–10

Dong Lai Shun $

This Muslim hot pot restaurant on Wangfujing Dajie has plenty of tasty *halal* mutton and fragrant bubbling broths. Raw food is brought to the table and the diner dunks it in the tank – here, wonderfully old-fashioned coal-burning copper installations. This is one of the best located and most atmospheric hot pot options in Beijing. The restaurant is always busy with locals and offers great

insight into cosy feasting traditions of Beijingers, especially in winter.

✚ 210 C2 ⊠ 5th Floor, Xindong'an Plaza, Wangfujing Dajie, Dongcheng District ☎ 010 6528 0932 ⏱ Daily 11–9

Quan Ju De $$

No one does Beijing Duck better than this famous old chain. The duck is wheeled to the table and its crispy skin expertly sliced off. The prices are relatively high for what is a staple dish in these parts, but the imperial atmosphere and succulent meat make it well worthwhile.

✚ 210 B1 ⊠ 32 Qianmen Dajie, Chongwen District ☎ 010 6511 2418 ⏱ Daily 11–2, 4:30–9

Red Capital Club $$$

Located in a once-exclusive neighbourhood where notable Communist officials had their homes, the Red Capital Club draws on the atmosphere, ambience and appetites of Liberation-era leaders. The Chairman Mao Vegetarian Bean Curd Wrap is one of many dishes inspired by the former Politburo members' "humble" tastes. Every dish has a story and even the chairs are, apparently, the same ones used by the late leaders. The restaurant also has a cigar and cocktail lounge.

✚ 210 (off map east) ⊠ 66 Dongsi Liutiao, Dongcheng District ☎ 010 8401 8886 ⏱ Daily 6–11pm

Vineyard Café $$

This artsy bar/café/restaurant specializes in homestyle European cooking and is located among the *hutong* close to the Lama Temple. The bohemian ambience is enhanced by regular jazz nights and off-beat film screenings. The beer and wine lists are impressive by Beijing's sometimes limited standards. It also has the distinction of serving the best full English breakfast in all of China (probably).

✚ 210 (off map east) ⊠ 31 Wudaoying Hutong, Dongcheng District ☎ 010 6402 7961 ⏱ Food available 11:30–3, 6–10:30. Café closed Mon

Xian Bai Wei $

Xian Bai Wei is a simple family-run eatery whose plain décor disguises truly top-notch Shanxi cuisine. The house special is the delicious *roujiamo*, the original Chinese "hamburger", made with freshly kneaded naan-style bread and a flaky pork-and-onion filling. The restaurant also does fabulous *saozimian*, thin al dente wheat noodles.

✚ 210 (off map east) ⊠ 76 Yonghegong Dajie, Dongcheng District ☎ 010 6402 7070 ⏱ Daily 11–11

Xiaoxin Café $$

Xiao Xin is the name of the owner of this cosy café. The young Beijinger's pastries and cheesecakes are renowned among the capital's expat community. It is one of the most light and airy of the courtyard cafés in this famous old *hutong* alley, making it a great spot to while away an afternoon with a coffee.

✚ 210 C4 ⊠ 103 Nanluogu Xiang, Dongcheng District ☎ 010 6403 6956 ⏱ Daily 9am–2am

Where to... Shop

Beijing has a diverse range of shopping haunts, from mega malls and department stores, to roadside markets and itinerant hawkers. If you bargain hard, prices can be very cheap. In major stores the marked price is normally (though not always) final, whereas in the markets haggling is expected. Art, antiques and reproductions, silk, carpets, clothes, jewellery and tea are popular. Many tourist shops can arrange shipping overseas, but examine the costs and charges with the vendor in detail before going ahead with the purchase.

MALLS/DEPARTMENT STORES

Wangfujing Dajie is the capital's snazziest shopping drag. On the corner of the southern entrance to the street is the **Oriental Plaza** (1 Dong Chang'an Jie), a staggeringly large mall which includes big name fashion brands, hair salons, supermarkets and tea shops.

The **China World Shopping Mall** (1 Jianguomen Waidajie; tel: 010 6505 2288) is Beijing's trendiest address and houses Prada, Cartier and Louis Vuitton, among others. An ice rink caters for the kids.

There are no such gimmicks at **Dashilar**, an old-fashioned alternative to the department store experience. This *hutong* alley, running west from the top end of Qianmen, is an interesting jumble of department stores, medicine shops, teahouses and food and clothes specialists. Many of Beijing's oldest shops are here.

CLOTHES MARKETS

The **Sanlitun Yashou Clothing Market** (55 Gongren Tiyuchang Beilu) is one of the best spots in Beijing to buy clothes. The basement and first three floors contain virtually anything you might need. The fourth floor sells jewellery, with food available on the top floor.

The **Silk Market Plaza** (Xiushui Dongjie; tel: 010 5169 8800), on the northern side of Jianguomen Waidajie, just to the east of the Yonganli metro stop, is another popular spot. Recent high-profile lawsuits may (or may not) have stemmed the flow of good quality fake goods. Be sure to bargain hard.

ANTIQUES/REPRODUCTIONS

Bear in mind that antiques should have a red seal at the bottom indicating they are genuine (though even that isn't a foolproof guarantee). **Liulichang**, a quaint restored wooden street south of Hepingmen metro station, has some great curios and souvenirs. There are also plenty of old Chinese books and Cultural Revolution-era kitsch.

Panjiayuan, off Panjiayuan Lu close to the Third Ring Road, offers yet more collectables in a market atmosphere. It's also very strong on arts and crafts. With 50,000 visitors daily, you need to arrive early to catch the best bargains.

Just south of here is **Beijing Curio City**, a four-storey building that has great knick-knacks and souvenirs.

BOOKS/NEWSPAPERS

It's usually possible to buy a handful of international newspapers and magazines from the major five-star hotels. The **Foreign Languages Bookstore** on Wangfujing Dajie has English-language novels.

OTHER CITIES

Harbin has plenty of Russian-themed souvenirs stores (think Stalin hip flasks). Both Harbin and **Dalian** have fabulous multistorey underground malls that come into their own in winter when the outside temperatures plummet.

Where to...
Be Entertained

NIGHTLIFE

Sanlitun, also known as Bar Street, is home to a large number of expatriate bars but has become a place where many locals also go to unwind. Indeed, quintessentially Chinese tastes have filtered in: the bands play pop pop covers, there are magic and acrobatics shows, while the punters play dice.

The shores around **Houhai and Qianhai lakes**, and the former market street of **Yandai Xijie** (close to the Drum and Bell towers) are packed with café-bars. Similarly, many of the *hutong* cafés around **Nanluogu Xiang** have boozy bohemian evenings that can be great fun. The Beijing dance scene is thriving. A bevy of internationally acclaimed DJs occasionally

parades through town. The nightclubs tend to be huge – witness **Babyface** (6 Gongren Tiyuchang Xilu; tel: 010 6551 9081), **Banana** (22 Jianguomen Waidajie; tel: 010 6528 3636), **D-Power** (at the west gate of Chaoyang Park) and **Kiss Disco** (35 Xiaoyun Lu; tel: 010 8455 2361, ext 216).

KARAOKE

The Chinese have grown to love karaoke. **Melody**, **Cash Box** and **Tango** are the most popular places (and tend not to offer the girly services that many seedier establishments do). The first two spots have chains across the city, while Tango is in the basement of a disco of the same name, located at the south gate of Ditan Park.

CINEMA, THEATRE AND MUSIC

Beijing is the best place in China to watch live music. **Yu Gong Yi Shan** (1 Gongren Tiyuchang Beilu; tel: 010 6415 0687) is Beijing's best venue, with regular hip hop dance parties to boot. Other rock venues include **Nameless Highland** (Building 14, Area 1, Anhuili Yayuncun; tel: 010 6489 1613) and **Club 13** (161 Lanqiying; tel: 010 8262 8077).

Live jazz from Thursday to Saturday can be found at **CD Jazz Café** (Dongsanhuan Lu; tel: 010 6506 8288). There are regular concerts at the Beijing Concert Hall, the premier venue for traditional Chinese and classical Western music, though the wackylooking **National Grand Theatre**, located just to the west of the Great Hall of the People on Xi Chang'an Jie, will probably assume this mantle when it opens (scheduled to be summer 2007). A night at the movies in Beijing is expensive and

difficult to reconcile with the cheap DVDs that cost a fraction of the price of cinema entry. The **Star City Cinema** (tel: 010 8518 5399) in the Oriental Plaza on Wangfujing Dajie is a case in point, but has a convenient central location.

SPORTS

Golf has become massively popular among China's newly rich elite. The **Beijing International Golf Course** (tel: 010 6076 2288) has a great location in the valley of the Ming Tombs, north of the city. The **Beijing Golf Club** (tel: 010 8947 0245; www.beijinggolfclub.com) is another international-standard course, northeast of Beijing Airport. The **Nanshan Ski Resort** (tel: 010 8909 1909; www.nanshanski. com) is the largest ski resort in the Beijing area and boasts some of the most advanced facilities in the country. The 18 runs cater for all abilities, though the snow is very much man-made.

Shanghai and the East

Getting Your Bearings 66 – 67
In Five Days 68 – 69
Don't Miss 70 – 79
At Your Leisure 80 – 83
Where to... 84 – 90

Getting Your Bearings

If Beijing is China's distinguished elder statesman, Shanghai is his wayward mistress – a city that has lived fast, and may well die young. In only a few centuries she has grown from impoverished minnow, fishing for scraps at the mouth of the Yangtze River, to swaggering financial giant, dictating terms to the nation.

It was a drug-fuelled transformation. Prised open by British guns in the First Opium War, Shanghai became educated in the ways of the world by gangsters, bankers and political radicals. After a wild adolescence, she spent 30 years in rehab. Time stood still as Communism's puritanical impulse kept the "Paris of the East" in check. But almost the minute China opened up again, Shanghai was flashing her charms at the world. Once more, she grew rich on the attention.

The future should be bright for Shanghai, but beneath the glossy veneer she is slipping into depression. Every year she sinks further into the swamps upon which she was built. If that master of killjoys – global warming – has his way, Shanghai will be one of the first to find herself underwater.

But there's little sense of impending doom. Shanghai revels in danger and – thanks largely to the financial attractions – the finest minds in China are helping the grand dame to come to terms with her problems and grow ever stronger. In the meantime, she continues to seduce most who pass her way.

Waiting in the wings, meanwhile, are the rivals – Hangzhou, Suzhou and Nanjing. These cities of refined manner and classical beauty deservedly get their fair share of suitors. With the distances between them small and the roads easy, it would be remiss of any visitor not to play the field.

★ Don't Miss

1 The French Concession
➤ 70

2 People's Square ➤ 72

3 The Huangpu River ➤ 74

4 Yuyuan and the Old City
➤ 76

5 The Water Towns of
Jiangnan ➤ 78

6 Hangzhou ➤ 79

Page 65: Looking
down to the atrium
of the Grand Hyatt
Hotel, Shanghai

Opposite: The
Pudong skyline

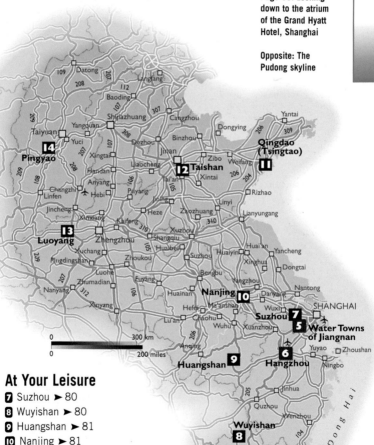

At Your Leisure

7 Suzhou ➤ 80

8 Wuyishan ➤ 80

9 Huangshan ➤ 81

10 Nanjing ➤ 81

11 Qingdao ➤ 82

12 Taishan ➤ 82

13 Luoyang ➤ 82

14 Pingyao ➤ 83

What Shanghai lacks in temples and palaces it more than makes up for in energy and excitement. It is a compact city compared to Beijing, and its elevated and subterranean metro represents the best public transport system in mainland China. For a change of pace, visit one of the many attractive cities just outside Shanghai.

Shanghai and the East in Five Days

Day One

Morning

Starting early at **Fuxing Park**, ease your way into Shanghai life with a stroll around the ❶**French Concession** (➤ 70–71, 177–179; Old China Hand Reading Room right). Pause for lunch at the Hengshan Moller Villa's Bonomi Café or try Xiao Nan Guo, a renowned Shanghainese restaurant in the grounds of the Ruijin Guesthouse (➤ 85).

Afternoon

Providing it isn't a weekend, visit ❹**Yuyuan** and the **Old City** (➤ 76–77). Afternoon tea is served in the Huxingting Teahouse.

Evening

Head to Xintiandi (➤ 89) for dinner and take an after-meal tipple in one of the trendy local watering holes. For classic Shanghai swagger, check out the Dr Bar. Those looking for something less ostentatious should take the short taxi ride to Cotton's (➤ 86), one of the most attractive and down-to-earth spots in town.

Day Two

Morning

Taking care to avoid the morning rush hour, ride the metro to ❷**People's Square** (➤ 72–73)and spend the entire morning in the **Shanghai Museum**. Enjoy a leisurely lunch at Kathleen's 5 (opposite top; ➤ 87) on the rooftop of the nearby **Shanghai Art Museum**.

Afternoon

Walk the meal off with a stroll down **Nanjing Donglu** (➤ 74). At the river-side, take a right onto the **Bund** and pop your head in the door of the

Pudong Development Bank at No 12. Cross the **3** **Huangpu River** (➤ 74–75) to enjoy an afternoon cocktail at the Grand Hyatt's 87th-floor Cloud 9 café (➤ 86). Time your visit to experience a (likely smoggy) Shanghai sunset and the neon-soaked night-time vista (left).

Evening

Head back to The Bund for your evening meal. Three of these colonial banking buildings have become temples to European fine dining. No 3 (➤ 87) has Laris, New Heights and Jean Georges. No 5 boasts M on the Bund (➤ 87), with its famous balcony view of Pudong, while No 18 can claim Sens & Bund. The Whampoa Club (at No 3) and Tai Wan Lou (at No 18) offer gourmet Chinese cuisine. All are spectacular, so take your pick.

Day Three

Take a morning bus to **6** **Hangzhou** (➤ 79) and spend the afternoon cycling around the picturesque **West Lake**. Stop by the Louwailou restaurant to try the famous sweet and sour West Lake carp.

Day Four

Head up to **5** **Wuzhen** (➤ 78), a delightful canal town in the north of Zhejiang province. Overnight in one of the waterside guest houses.

Day Five

Make the short bus ride to **7** **Suzhou** (below; ➤ 80). A single day will be sufficient to explore one of the famous classic gardens and take a boat trip through the ancient canals. Take the train back to Shanghai in the evening. Those with more time can continue on to **10** **Nanjing** (➤ 81), a couple of hours away to the northwest.

◘ The French Concession

With its marvellous mesh of stylish bars, colonial villas and leafy avenues, the French Concession (Faguo Zujie) is Shanghai's trendiest and prettiest district. It was starved of vitality (and customers) during Mao's reign, but has rediscovered its racy edge thanks to a cosmopolitan cohort of restaurateurs and publicans. This is *the* place to wine, dine and have a good time during your stay.

The French Concession was formed in 1844, shortly after the First Opium War. After defeat by the British, the Qing government accepted France's terms for control over a generous slice of the city. It was initially used as a trading base, but the area gradually developed its own, unique identity; plane trees were imported to line the newly built avenues; theatres, hotels and clubs sprang up; and residents became subject to the laws of the mother country. Among the notable figures who took advantage of the concession's separation from its surrounds was Mao Zedong. The Communist Party was formed here in 1921, right under the colonial rulers' noses.

The French Concession no longer has any formal administrative status. It is defined by ambience alone, but is a class apart thanks to the colonial villas in the area. They house

Above: Eating outside Sasha's, one of the best bar/restaurants in the French Concession

Right: Couples like to practice their ballroom dancing in Fuxing Park

many of the city's best bars and restaurants and provide the perfect architectural counterweight to the cloud-bursting excesses of other parts of the city.

Something for Everyone

Huaihai Lu clips the area into north and south sections. Built in 1900, the street is lined with malls and boutique stores and is one of the city's premier shopping districts. West of the junction with Changshu Lu are several old French mansions, though the only house open to the public is the **Former Residence of Song Qing Ling**, wife of Nationalist leader Sun Yat-sen.

South of Huaihai Lu is **Fuxing Park**. This hidden gem was acquired by the French in 1909 and designed as a Parisian-style garden. It was initially only open to French passport-holders, though now it's much more egalitarian. **Park 97**, one of Shanghai's trendiest restaurant-cum-nightclubs, is on the western edge. Nearby is the **Former Residence of Sun Yat-sen** (➤ 177).

Nearby **Xintiandi** (➤ 89) is Shanghai's most stylish funhouse. This old *shikumen* (stone-gate house) neighbourhood has been restored to its former beauty and is filled with bars, restaurants and clubs. The **Site of the 1st National Congress of the Chinese Communist Party** is in a corner of this fashionable enclave.

Those hunting for traces of Gallic bohemia should go along to **Lane 210**, just off Taikang Lu. Fashioned out of a former factory, this art district is home to a panoply of independent galleries, studios and stores.

TAKING A BREAK

The French Concession is packed with places to eat and drink. **Check out** *That's Shanghai*, *City Weekend* or *Shanghai Talk* for comprehensive details. They can be picked up free in many bars and restaurants.

Former Residence of Song Qing Ling
🔶 208 A2 (off map) ✉ 1843 Huaihai Zhonglu ☎ 021 6474 7183
🕐 Daily 9–4:30 💷 Inexpensive 🚇 Hengshan Lu

Former Residence of Sun Yat-sen
🔶 208 B2 ✉ 7 Xiangshan Lu ☎ 021 6437 2954 🕐 Daily 9–4:30
💷 Inexpensive 🚇 Shanxi Nanlu

Site of the 1st National Congress of the Chinese Communist Party
🔶 208 C2 ✉ 76–78 Xingye Lu, Xintiandi ☎ 021 5383 2171
🕐 Daily 9–4 💷 Inexpensive 🚇 Huangpi Nanlu

THE FRENCH CONCESSION: INSIDE INFO

Top tip The best way to experience the French Concession is simply to **wander on foot**. See pages 177–179 for a suggested route.

Don't miss The American-built, ivy-covered **Community Church** on Hengshan Lu has services in English at 2pm on Sundays. The grounds are only open when a service is on. The Catholic **St Ignatius Cathedral** is bigger, grander and more accessible, located close to the Xintiandi metro stop. Two **Russian Orthodox churches** are listed in the walking tour (see above).

② People's Square

Up until 1951, People's Square (Renmin Guangchang) was home to a British-built horse-racing track, but the new Communist government's antipathy towards gambling was as strong as its admiration of concrete. The area was paved over and used for marches and rallies. These days the square is layered in greenery. Below is a colossal subway interchange and subterranean shopping mall; above are three of the city's best museums and galleries.

Shanghai Museum

People's Square lies at the intersection of Line 1 and Line 2 of the metro and – if you avoid the rush-hour – this is the easiest way to arrive. The museum, standing alone in the southern half of the square, is a highlight of any visit. In terms of the quality and diversity of exhibits, only the Shanxi History Museum in Xi'an (► 164) comes close. For presentation and quality of English, it is peerless. Some 120,000 items are beautifully displayed in spot-lit and soundproofed galleries. Whereas most Chinese museums are organized chronologically, the exhibits here are arranged into themes. There are separate displays on bronzes, sculpture, ceramics, paintings, calligraphy, seals, jade, coins, furniture and ethnic minority art. Any of the halls that don't take your fancy, simply skip.

The **Ancient Bronzes Gallery** spans more than two millennia and features a remarkable collection of *ding* (cooking cauldrons), *zun* (bowls) and *jue* (wine pourers). The three-legged *ding* from the Western Zhou period (11th–8th century BC) is a highlight. It's shape provided the inspiration for the building's architect, Xing Tonghe.

The **Ancient Chinese Ceramics Gallery** has a fabulous collection of porcelain, much

Below: Detail of a delicately painted frieze in the Shanghai Museum

from the legendary royal kilns of Jingdezhen. Look for the blue and white oblate glaze pot of the early Ming dynasty. It's one of the earliest examples of a style that became synonymous with "China" in the West.

The **Chinese Painting Gallery** guides visitors past classic works of artists dating from the Tang dynasty (7th–10th century AD). Anyone who has visited any of China's sacred mountain peaks will be able to appreciate where many of these old masters got their inspiration.

The art deco tower (right) of the Shanghai Art Museum

The **Calligraphy Gallery** can only really be appreciated by expert readers of Chinese. Head instead to the **Minority Nationalities Art Gallery**, which explains the culture of China's 55 minority groups. The colourful face masks and folk costumes displayed here are still used at ceremonies today.

The Other Sides of the Square

On the west side of People's Square is the **Shanghai Art Museum**. It was once the racecourse clubhouse and the marble floors and brick fireplaces remain. The giant scale model of Shanghai circa 2020 is the focus of the **Shanghai Urban Planning Exhibition Center**, to the east of the square. The photographs of old Shanghai on the ground-floor mezzanine are also fascinating.

TAKING A BREAK

There are superb views of the whole square from **Kathleen's 5** (➤ 87), an al fresco drinking and dining spot atop the Shanghai Art Museum.

Shanghai Museum
✚ 208 C3 ✉ 201 Renmin Dadao ☎ 021 6372 3500; www.shanghaimuseum.net ◉ Daily 9–5 🎫 Inexpensive 🚇 People's Square

Shanghai Art Museum
✚ 208 C3 ✉ 325 Nanjing Xilu ☎ 021 6327 2829 ◉ Daily 9–4 🎫 Inexpensive 🚇 People's Square

Shanghai Urban Planning Exhibition Center
✚ 208 C3 ✉ 100 Renmin Dadao ☎ 021 6372 2077; www.supec.org ◉ Daily 9–5 🎫 Moderate 🚇 People's Square

PEOPLE'S SQUARE: INSIDE INFO

Top tips Shanghai Museum's **ground-floor shop** has some excellent books covering all aspects of Chinese culture and history.
• In the west of the square is the **Shanghai Grand Theatre**, China's first purpose-built opera house. Its 1,700sq m (18,300-square-foot) main stage is claimed to be the world's largest. There are guided tours on Monday mornings, or come for an evening performance.

3 The Huangpu River

The Huangpu River wends its way through Shanghai in an S-shaped curve. Rising in the east is Pudong, a landscape of brashly modern buildings and wide boulevards, built from scratch over the past 20 years. To the west is Puxi, the old city in its cluttered, colonial glory. Draw a circle around the whole and you get a perfectly formed yin-yang symbol: past and present, divided by a muddy waterway. The Huangpu is the pivot of China's remarkable balancing act.

Start your approach on **Nanjing Donglu**. Cantonese merchant Ma Yingbiao opened mainland China's first department store here in 1917. Out went hard bargaining and musty storage cupboards; in came smiling staff, fixed prices and till receipts. Located on the corner of Zhejiang Zhonglu, the store is singled out by its baroque, Greco-Roman tower.

Above: View across the Huangpu River to Pudong

The Bund

Let the crowds sweep you towards the **Bund**, where 25 of Shanghai's most resplendent colonial buildings stare haughtily down on the Huangpu River. "Bund" is an Anglo-Indian word meaning "embankment", and it was here that foreign banks and trading houses set up shop early last century. The neo-classical colonnades, domes and clock towers have survived the wars and revolutions that engulfed Shanghai.

It's possible to cross the river by three forms of public transport, none of them convenient. The closest metro stop is a 10-minute walk back down Nanjing Donglu. The ferry ports are also awkwardly located, departing at the most southerly extremity of the Bund and depositing passengers far from the attractions on the other side. The Bund Sightseeing Tunnel

Right: Floodlit buildings on The Bund

involves a pseudo-scientific train ride in which strobe lighting and clouds of dry-ice represent the geological layers of the earth. It goes beyond the "so-bad-it's-good" stage to being mind-bendingly awful. In defiance of logic, the **Museum of Chinese Sex Culture** at the tunnel's far end is remarkably good.

Across the River

Rising from the depths, you'll emerge at **Liujiazui**, a showcase of modern architectural exuberance. The **Oriental Pearl TV Tower** is the one that most visitors rush towards. The **Shanghai History Exhibition** in the basement can be combined with a trip to either the lower, middle or upper viewing spheres.

Those wanting to avoid queues should visit the **Jinmao Tower**. Rising to 88 floors, it's the tallest structure in mainland China and curves, bends and shimmers all the way to its 421m (1,380-foot) summit. The viewing platform is on the top floor, but for a more relaxed visit, head to the Grand Hyatt Hotel, which occupies floors 54 to 87. The hotel's **Cloud 9** café (➤ 86) has comfy chairs and cocktail menus with which to enjoy the vista.

TAKING A BREAK

The **Bonomi Café** on the second floor of Bund No 12 is well worth stopping at for a coffee. Or make a reservation at **M on the Bund** (➤ 87), in Bund No 5. The balcony views of the Pudong skyline are as sumptuous as the cuisine.

Oriental Pearl TV Tower
✚ 209 F3 ✉ 2 Liujiazui Lu ☎ 021 5879 1888 ⏰ Daily 8:30am–9:30pm 💰 Expensive for access to all three viewing platforms and history exhibition in basement, moderate for entry to history exhibition only 🚇 Liujiazui

Bund Sightseeing Tunnel and Museum of Chinese Sex Culture
✚ 209 E3 ✉ Accessible from subway opposite Nanjing Donglu ⏰ Daily 8am–10:30pm 💰 Tunnel, one-way: inexpensive; museum: inexpensive; combined ticket: moderate

Jinmao Tower
✚ 209 F2 ✉ 88 Shiji Dadao ⏰ Viewing Platform daily 8:30am–10pm 💰 Moderate for access to 88th-floor viewing deck. The 87th-floor Cloud 9 café has a minimum 138RMB per person table charge 🚇 Liujiazui

---

THE HUANGPU RIVER: INSIDE INFO

Warning By night, **Nanjing Donglu** is awash with neon and heavy with pedestrian traffic. Mingling among the throng will be peddlers of prostitutes, fake watches and hashish. As a foreigner, you are guaranteed to be approached.

Hidden gems The **Peace Hotel**, at the junction of Nanjing Donglu and the Bund, is Shanghai's premier historic hotel. The hotel closed for a major renovation in 2007, but the Gothic façade is still worth pausing for.
• The lobby of the **former HSBC building** (now the Pudong Development Bank) at Bund No 12 has stunning mosaics on the domed ceiling.

4 Yuyuan and the Old City

In a city whose chief attractions are shops, bars and relics of European empire building, Yuyuan garden stands apart as one of the few bona fide historic sights. Accordingly it's often full to bursting. Surrounding the garden is the claustrophobic Old City, much of which remains resolutely residential.

Southern Town

The district known as "Nanshi" – Southern Town – once operated as an independent city. Crisscrossed with canals and surrounded by a high wall and moat, it was the "Chinese" part of Shanghai. The wall was torn down shortly after the Qing dynasty fell in 1911 and the waterways filled in to create roads. Modern-day Renmin Lu and Zhonghua Lu trace the path of the moat. Look at any modern map and the circular shape of the Old City is clearly visible.

Yuyuan

In the northeast portion is **Yuyuan garden**. The beautiful pavilions, delicate rock pools and sturdy old trees represent one of the best surviving examples

of a classical Chinese garden. If you do not have time to visit nearby Suzhou (▶ 80) – also famed for its private gardens – a trip to Yuyuan is a must.

The garden is only accessible by first negotiating the **Yuyuan Bazaar**, which has its entrance on Fangbang Lu. The **Huxingting Teahouse** is located in the middle of an emerald pond and linked to the bank by a zigzag bridge. It served as the model for the 19th-century willow pattern porcelain that became popular in the West. The bridge, meanwhile, was designed by feng shui masters to steer bad luck off its nefarious course. The Chinese believe that evil spirits can't turn corners.

Left: Entrance to the Yuyuan Bazaar
Opposite: Covered walkway over the lake at Yuyuan garden

The garden itself was created by Pan Yunduan, a former governor of Sichuan. He spent 18 years nurturing the 2ha (5-acre) site to a state of perfection, finally achieved in 1577. Unfortunately, it was occupied and then ransacked by British invaders during the First Opium War. It took another battering during the Taiping Rebellion, 13 years later.

Yuyuan has been restored to its former glory and is now protected by a 10m-high (30-foot) wall which blocks out the cries from the surrounding markets. Unfortunately, the megaphone commentaries and camera clicking from within mar what was intended as a space of Zen-like serenity. For improved (though not complete) peace and quiet, avoid weekends.

Get away from the commotion by wandering into the traditional *longtang* neighbourhoods (the local equivalent of Beijing's *hutong*) that fill the Old City. Less tranquil is the scene on Fangbang Zhonglu. This street marks the pathway of one of the canals that flowed through the old walled city, and was filled in when the city walls were dismantled around 1912. Now it contains the overspill from the bazaar. The **Temple of the City Gods** is nearby, though you can give it a miss if time is short.

TAKING A BREAK
Try to grab a window seat at the **Huxingting Teahouse**, next to the entrance to Yuyuan Garden.

Yuyuan garden
🏛 209 E2 ✉ 218 Anren Jie ☎ 021 6355 5032 ⏰ Daily 8:30–5 (last ticket 4:30pm)
💷 Inexpensive

YUYUAN AND THE OLD CITY: INSIDE INFO

Top tip Haggling in the bazaar can be fun, but if you are determined to get the best price, root around in the smaller shops on **Fangbang Zhonglu**. As always, the fewer the number of passing tour groups, the lower the prices.

Hidden gem The bizarrely named **Shanghai South Bund Soft-Spinning Material Market** is great for inexpensive bespoke outfits. It's at 399 Lujiabang Lu, close to the intersection with Nancang Jie, just southeast of the circular Old City.

5 The Water Towns of Jiangnan

The area known as Jiangnan straddles the boundaries between Shanghai and its two neighbouring provinces, Jiangsu and Zhejiang. The region is renowned for its quaint "water towns", each a charming mix of burbling brooks, arched bridges and whitewashed houses.

The best of Jiangnan's Water Towns are Tongli, Wuzhen and Zhouzhuang. **Tongli** – the smallest of the three, is just south of Suzhou. **Wuzhen** is only one hour from Zhejiang's capital, Hangzhou. **Zhouzhuang** is the nearest to Shanghai. All three are small enough to explore in a day, though the best way to enjoy the atmosphere is to overnight in a waterside guest house.

The houses of Jiangnan have been built on the river, supported by stone buttresses or columns which rise from beneath the waterline. The canals functioned as pathways, taking vessels from door to door and outwards into the wider matrix of canals and streams that linked all of the region's towns. Every river ultimately connects to the 2,000-year-old Grand Canal that once flowed from here all the way to Beijing.

Each town has its share of regular pathways too. The slab stone-paved streets that run between timber-frame houses are a delight to wander. When fatigue sets in, rest awhile in one of the many waterside teahouses, from where you can watch gondolas glide by the window.

Boats cruising Zhouzhuang's canals

Tongli
✚ 205 E4 ✉ 18km (11 miles) south of Suzhou, Jiangsu province ☎ 0512 6333 1140
👜 Moderate (includes all attractions) or inexpensive (basic entry to old town) 🚌 Daily buses from Shanghai Sightseeing Bus Center (inside the Shanghai Stadium)

Wuzhen
✚ 205 E4 ✉ Near Tongxiang City, 80km (50 miles) northeast of Hangzhou, Zhejiang province ☎ 0573 873 1088 👜 Expensive (includes all parts of town and all attractions) 🚌 Regular buses from Hangzhou's East Bus Station. Two buses daily from Shanghai's South Bus Station

Zhouzhuang
✚ 205 E4 ✉ 38km (24 miles) southeast of Suzhou, Jiangsu province ✉ Daily buses from Shanghai Sightseeing Bus Center (inside the Shanghai Stadium) ✉ 0512 5721 1654; www.zhouzhuang.net ✉ Expensive (includes all attractions)

6 Hangzhou

Marco Polo declared Hangzhou to be the world's most splendid city when he passed through in the 13th century. There have been a few changes since then but he would still be able to recognize the city today, thanks to the eternally idyllic West Lake. Surrounded by towering pagodas and misty mountains, it is China's most revered body of water.

From the end of the 6th century AD, the Grand Canal began its 1,700km (1,055-mile) journey to Beijing from here. For hundreds of years, Hangzhou was a key port in the transfer of grain, silk and tea from the fertile south to the dry, barren north. The city took on even more significance during the Southern Song dynasty (12th–13th century) when it enjoyed a brief tenure as China's capital. These days it is the administrative capital of Zhejiang province and a tourist magnet.

This is due entirely to **West Lake**. Like nearly all of China's best-known sights, it too is man-made. Originally a humble lagoon, it was dredged in the 8th century and later dyked. It's located in the south of the city and is one of the few attractions in China that you won't need to pay for the pleasure of viewing. It takes the best part of a day to circumnavigate the lake on foot, so consider renting a bicycle.

TAKING A BREAK

Louwailou, 30 Gushan Lu, has great views over West Lake and offers solid interpretations of all of Hangzhou's signature dishes, including "Vinegar Fish", served in a sauce with the colour and consistency of tooth-rotting treacle.

Hangzhou
➕ 205 E3 ✉ 175km (109 miles) southwest of Shanghai, Zhejiang province 🚌 Buses depart Shanghai's Hengfeng Lu Bus Station (close to Hanzhong Lu Metro Station) and take 2.5 hours

Water lilies on West Lake (Xihu)

At Your Leisure

7 Suzhou

One of China's prettiest urban destinations, Suzhou is famed for its cobbled streets, ancient canals and genteel gardens. The latter are very much in the mould of what you might have seen at Yuyuan in Shanghai (► 76–77) – miniature vistas of rocks, ponds, screens, bridges and pavilions. These carefully contrived environments were intended to be viewed by a handful of scholars or officials, but are now swamped by the tourist masses. The biggest, best and most crowded gardens are the **Forest of Stone Lions Garden** and the **Humble Administrator's Garden**. Take a good book and a cushion – and perhaps some earplugs. Suzhou is also the most renowned of China's former silk-producing hubs. Drop by the **Suzhou Silk Museum**, which details this UNESCO-listed city's pivotal role in creating the world's oldest globalized industry.

205 E4 Jiangsu province 0512 6751 6376 (Suzhou Tourist Center) Suzhou has excellent road and rail links with Shanghai. The journey takes less than 2 hours

Silkworm cocoons at the Suzhou Silk Museum

8 Wuyishan

Tucked up close to the provincial borders of Fujian, Jiangxi and Zhejiang, Wuyishan is a jewel in China's impressive array of silent-river/misty-mountain landscapes. For those planning trips to the likes of Guilin or Zhangjiajie, Wuyishan may be overkill. However, travellers opting to hug China's east coast should definitely consider a visit. Created from the geological spasms of the dinosaur age, the region has a special place in China's cultural history. Important Taoist and Buddhist temples and Confucian academies once dotted the area. Eighth-century emperor Xuan Zong was the first to give the reserve national protection, forbidding fishing and logging. The conservationist instinct has continued and the **Wuyishan Scenic Reserve** is now one of China's 33 UNESCO World Heritage Sites.

With a subtropical climate and relatively low elevation, the mountains are great for year-round hiking. A bamboo raft ride through the 10km-long (16-mile) **"Nine Bends River"** gorge is also a must. Lazy swirls of mist lie low on the river and you'll be able to gaze up at subtropical forests, hanging from rocky mountain slopes. Wuyishan is also famed for its Yan tea, considered to be the best of China's many Oolong varietals.

205 D2 Wuyishan, Wuyishan City, Fujian province Entry to Wuyishan Scenic Reserve: expensive (add 10RMB for subsequent days); Bamboo Raft Cruise along Nine Bends River: expensive Airport just to the south of Wuyishan City has links to most major cities

9 Huangshan

Huangshan (Yellow Mountain), one of China's impressive array of mountains, tops most people's lists. Famous for the sea of clouds that often forms between its craggy peaks, Huangshan was long a romantic escape from urban stress for poets, painters and emperors of old. Located in southern Anhui province, an overnight train ride (or short flight) from Shanghai, the scenic area boasts a total of 72 peaks with three separate cable cars ferrying guests up, down and across the mountain range. As you gain height, an occasionally thrilling network of pathways disperses the crowds and draws visitors towards the best lookout points. Stunted pine trees, contorted into perplexing shapes, sprout from similarly gnarled rocks. Throw in a wispy cloud or two and you have all the ingredients for a classic Chinese landscape painting.

➕ 205 D3 ✉ Anhui province, 69km (43 miles) north of Huangshan City (Tunxi) 💲 Expensive. Cable car:

Rock formations at beautiful Huangshan

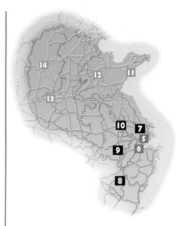

moderate one-way 🚆 Overnight train departs Shanghai at 10:02pm and arrives at 8:50am ✈ Huangshan City airport

10 Nanjing

Once the capital of six dynasties and headquarters of the Guomindang (Kuomintang) during Nationalist rule, Nanjing's star faded badly after the Chinese Communist Party emerged victorious in the Chinese Civil War of the mid-20th century. The name of one of China's most historic cities has been further sullied by its enduring association with the brutal massacre of civilians by Japanese invaders in 1937–38. It's a shame, because this laid-back, attractive city deserves deeper scrutiny.

The **Nanjing Museum** is a highlight, as are the remains of the 14th-century **City Wall**. This once stretched 32km (20 miles) around the city, making it the longest in China. To reach it, climb up from the verdant **Xuanwu Park**. When night comes, head to the bar-hub of **1912**. This restored neighbourhood attracts many of the urban sophisticates who are leading current Nanjing's economic resurgence.

➕ 205 D4 ✉ Jiangsu province 🚆 There are scores of direct trains from Shanghai. The journey takes between 2 and 5 hours

11 Qingdao

Kaiser Wilhelm II may have spent less than two decades in charge of this seaside Shandong city, but it was long enough to leave a lasting legacy. The mother-country's defeat in World War I saw resident Germans colonialists return home, but locals continued to brew their much-loved Qingdao (Tsingtao) beer, even if they did take the rather un-Teutonic step of selling it in plastic bags. Similarly, the imposing Gothic churches remained full of worshippers and the Bavarian-themed villas became much-cherished homes of Chinese families. Even Chairman Mao couldn't quite bring himself to allow the destruction of the **Xinhaoshan Ying Binguan**, built as the former Governors' residence. It was one of Mao's favourite summer retreats and visitors can now sit on the Great Helmsman's former bed. This famously sunny city – scheduled to hold the 2008 Olympic sailing events – also draws throngs of holidaymakers to its sheltered bays and sandy beaches. The best time to be in town is during the **International Beer Festival** in mid-August. Enjoy a frosty glass of Tsingtao beer at the **Coastal Café** on Taiping Lu. In front of you, stretching towards the middle of the bay, is the **Zhanqiao Pier**, immortalized on the Tsingtao label.

🛇 203 E3 ✉ Shandong province ☎ 0532 8561 6161 (Qingdao Tourist Information Center) ✈ Shandong's large airport has links with most major Chinese cities

12 Taishan

Taishan, right in the heart of Shandong province, is the holiest of China's five Taoist mountains. In Chinese terms, the 1,545m (5,070-foot) summit is hardly a monster, but it's surrounded by relatively flat lowlands, making the view from the top all the more spectacular. As the highest peak in the politically powerful eastern part of China, Taishan was regarded by the ancients as the point at which heaven and earth met and, until Beijing's Temple of Heaven

Taishan – the holiest of China's holy Taoist mountains

was built in the early 15th century, this was where the emperor made his annual sacrifices to the Gods. Like many of China's scenic reserves, minibuses and cable cars combine to help visitors cover the entire mountain in a day. Dedicated pilgrims can climb the 6,600 stone steps, spread over 7km (4 miles). The mountain is generously sprinkled with temples and teahouses where you can rest during your personal pilgrimage.

🛇 202 C3 ✉ Tai'an, Shandong province 💰 Expensive (high season), moderate (low season) 🚉 Railway station in Tai'an, at the foot of the mountain ✈ Jinan airport is a 90-minute bus ride away

13 Luoyang

Luoyang, capital of nine dynasties and with a history that stretches back 5,000 years, is one of China's most ancient conurbations. Sadly, the industrial face of modern Luoyang is far from inspiring and the city is perhaps best used as a base from which to explore the magnificent **Longmen Caves**, located beside the Yihe River 12km (7.5 miles) south of town. Cave carving was, like Buddhism itself, an idea imported from India. The devout rulers of the Buddhist Northern Wei dynasty (AD 386–534) were the first to commis-

**The Heavenly Guard and the Demon
Warrior at the Longmen Caves**

sion this art form, but a miscellany
of projects continued right up until
the Qing dynasty (1644–1911).
According to the Longmen Cave
Research Institute, there are 2,345
niches, 2,840 inscribed tablets, 60
pagodas and around 100,000 stone
statues. The site also boasts lush
mountains and ridges with springs
and waterfalls.

The **White Horse Temple**, just
east of Luoyang city, might be the
oldest Buddhist temple in China.
Founded in the first century AD, its
historic and cultural importance is
second to none.

➕ 197 F1 ✈ Airport 10km (6 miles)
from downtown Luoyang
Longmen Caves
✉ Longmen Village, Luoyang, Henan
province 🕐 Daily 8–6 🎟 Moderate

🔟 Pingyao

A beautifully preserved Ming-dynasty
town, Pingyao has become a firm
favourite for those seeking a bit of
old-world Chinese charm. Reached
via a convenient overnight train ride
from Beijing, the city is composed
of a network of narrow streets,
ensconced within a 12m-high (40-
foot) **perimeter wall**. It's well worth
spending a couple of hours strolling
around the top of the fortification,
gazing down upon the bustling
streets below. Few buildings rise
above two floors and many are
adorned with attractive roofs, latticed
windows, hand-painted glass
lanterns and ornate wooden pilasters.
The 18.5m-high (60-foot) **Town
Tower** on Nan Dajie offers great
views over the town. Pingyao also
hosts one of China's most important
**International Photography
Festivals** every September.

➕ 197 F2 ✉ Shanxi province 🎟 Free
entry to city proper; expensive for
access to all sights, including the wall
🚆 Direct overnight train departs
Beijing at 7:43pm and arrives at 6:56am

Where to... Stay

Prices

Expect to pay for a double room, per night, including breakfast and taxes

$** under 400RMB **$$** 400–1,200RMB **$$$** 1,200–3,000RMB **$$$$ over 3,000RMB

Grand Hyatt $$$$

Officially the highest hotel in the world, the Grand Hyatt occupies the top 34 floors of the Jinmao Tower. Standards are similarly lofty in terms of design, facilities and service. The atrium offers dizzying views all the way up to the roof and is worth seeing even if you aren't staying. The rooms have floor-to-ceiling windows to maximize the unrivalled vantage point; those facing the river (and Puxi, beyond) cost slightly more. It's often booked up, so reserve well in advance.

✚ 209 F2 ⊠ 88 Shiji Dadao ☎ 021 5049 1234; www.hyatt.com

Hengshan Moller Villa $$$

Many Shanghai hotels claim to be unique, but this is the only one that really lives up to the hype. It is like something out of a fairy-tale picture book, all conical turrets and pyschedelic brickwork. The interior is hardly less extraordinary, featuring an oak panelled staircase, crystal chandeliers, Persian rugs and satin sofas. The 11 rooms and suites in the original building retain some original furnishings and there are balcony views of the garden. Other rooms are available in the more modern block round the back.

✚ 208 A3 ⊠ 30 Shaanxi Nanlu ☎ 021 6247 8881; www.mollervilla.com

The Mansion $$$$

The Mansion Hotel has been fashioned from the abandoned shell of a French villa that once played home to one of Shanghai's most notorious gangsters. This charming five-floor building is now a 30-room boutique property. Each room has high ceilings and a large Jacuzzi. The rooftop has been renovated into a bar, which looks out over the low rooftops of the French Concession. The cost, needless to say, is on the expensive side of pricey.

✚ 208 A2 ⊠ 82 Xinle Lu ☎ 021 5403 9888

JW Marriott $$$

Ensconced within the twin-horned Tomorrow Square (probably the most eye-catching building in Puxi), this is Marriott's flagship hotel in China. It's located just to the west of People's Square, in close range of many of Shanghai's best museums and galleries and only a walk away from Nanjing Donglu and the Bund. The luxurious Mandara Spa offers southeast Asian-style treatments that will soothe any urban stresses that might arise during your stay.

✚ 208 C3 ⊠ 399 Nanjing Xilu ☎ 021 5359 4969; www.marriott.com

No 9 $$

You'd have to be fairly lost to stumble across the 9 by chance. This art deco villa is tucked away in a tangle of *longtang*. There is a classical elegance to the hotel: rustic northern-style furniture fills the communal sitting room, crickets cheep from little cages hung on a tree by the entrance and, in the evening, the halls and rooms are lit by soft lantern light. The upstairs rooms are the brightest.

✚ 208 A1 ⊠ No 9, Lane 355 Jianguo Xilu ☎ 021 6471 9950

Portman Ritz-Carlton $$$

The 50-storey Ritz-Carlton towers over Nanjing Xilu. The location may lack the charm of the French Concession or the buzz of People's

Square, but this is one of Shanghai's more stately locales. The adjoining Shanghai Center is home to a series of consulates, as well as some great cafés and shops. The hotel's lobby is ravishing, the service is superb and the rooms have everything you would expect of a five-star hotel. However, perhaps the greatest attraction is the nearby shopping. Plaza 66, one of Shanghai's premier malls, is just around the corner.

➕ 208 A3 ⊠ Shanghai Center, 1376 Nanjing Xilu ☎ 021 6279 8888; www.ritzcarlton.com

Pujiang Hotel $$

This decadent playhouse of high-society 1920s Shanghai was formerly known as the Astor House Hotel. It remains gloriously resistant to modernity. The lobby is a time warp, full of photos of famous guests like Charlie Chaplin, Bertrand Russell and Albert Einstein. The hotel now caters for all tastes. Those with a little more cash can enjoy the huge rooms with wooden floorboards and a variety of modern amenities. The location is fabulous, just north of the Bund.

➕ 209 F4 ⊠ 15 Huangpu Road ☎ 021 6324 6388; www.pujianghotel.com

Radisson New World $$

This reasonably priced five-star hotel soars 47 floors above Nanjing Donglu, just a stone's throw from People's Square, the Grand Theatre and Shanghai Museum, with the Bund only a 15-minute stroll away. It has five restaurants and bars, including the spectacular 45th-floor Epicure restaurant and the 47th-floor sky dome bar, in the giant bauble that sits on the roof of this standout building.

➕ 208 C3 ⊠ 88 Nanjing Xilu ☎ 021 6359 9999; www.radisson.com/shanghaicn_newworld

The Regent Shanghai $$$

The Regent Shanghai shuns the stately atmosphere of its eight sister hotels around the world, preferring a contemporary finish to its ever-elegant design. The striking new building stands 53 floors high over Yanan Xilu, with each of the 500 guest rooms offering expansive views of the Puxi skyline. Equally diverting is the 42-inch plasma TV in each room. Three restaurants, tennis courts, a spa and an infinity-edged swimming pool complete an impressive list of facilities.

➕ 208 (off map west) ⊠ Yanan Xilu ☎ 021 6115 9988; www.regenthotels.com

Ruijin Guesthouse $$

Within the former walled estate of colonial newspaper magnate H E Morris, the Ruijin Guesthouse consists of a series of converted 1920s villas surrounding a French Concession lawn garden. The elegant grounds represent a genuine retreat from Shanghai's relentless hustle and bustle. Also on the estate is one of Shanghai's classiest bars, Face, and Xiao Nan Guo, a top Shanghainese restaurant.

➕ 208 B2 ⊠ 118 Ruijin Erlu ☎ 021 6472 5222; www.shedi.net.cn/outedi/ruijin

The Westin $$$

Perhaps the hippest of Shanghai's internationally managed hotels, the Westin occupies most of the Bund Centre, a dazzling, tiara-topped building that looms behind the southern reaches of the Bund. East-facing rooms have spectacular views towards the Pudong skyline, while all have a comfortable, inviting elegance that contrasts with the too-cool-to-use interior design of this ever-trendy city. Where the Westin really rates is in its excellent dining options, featuring one of Shanghai's most celebrated Sunday brunches at The Stage, a café nestled amid the greenery and glowing neon of the gorgeous atrium. There are six other restaurants, plus the Banyan Tree Spa.

➕ 209 E3 ⊠ Bund Centre, 88 Henan Zhonglu ☎ 021 6335 1888; www.starwoodhotels.com

Where to...
Eat and Drink

Prices
Expect to pay for a meal for one, excluding drinks and service
$** under 50RMB **$$** 50–150RMB **$$$ over 150RMB

SHANGHAI

A Future Perfect $$
The wholesome approach here is evident in the menu of steaks, salads and smoothies. There are also funky cocktails, a reasonable wine list, and fair-trade coffee. This old place has a spacious walled garden with a leafy canopy.

✚ **208 (off map west)** ✉ **16 Lane 351 Huashan Lu** ☎ **021 6248 8020** ⏰ **Daily 7am–2am**

Barbarossa $$
Tucked away within the greenery of People's Park, Barbarossa comprises three floors of maharajah chic filled with North African antiques. Dining is on an open-air deck beside the lake and there are two floors of dimly lit interiors and cushioned lounges. Alternatively, head to the rooftop and try a cappuccino-flavoured sheesha pipe.

✚ **208 C3** ✉ **231 Nanjing Donglu** ☎ **021 6318 0220** ⏰ **Daily 11am–2am**

Bi Feng Tang $
This ever-popular chain has restaurants in various prize locations and serves up great value Cantonese dim sum dishes in a bright, festive environment. This flagship store is close to the Shanghai Center and has an outdoor bamboo shelter for al fresco dining. The menu is in English.

✚ **208 A3** ✉ **1333 Nanjing Xilu (close to Tongren Lu)** ☎ **021 6279 0738** ⏰ **Mon–Fri 10am–5am, Sat–Sun 8am–5am**

Cloud 9 $$$
On the top floor of the world's tallest hotel, Cloud 9 is a popular novelty splurge and a great spot to get 360-degree views of the Shanghai cityscape. While being super-trendy, it's mercifully tolerant of camera-toting tourists. Given Shanghai's muck and mist, getting the best perspective on the city often demands patience, so it's worth paying to have somewhere comfortable to wait for the perfect photo opportunity.

✚ **209 F2** ✉ **87th Floor, Grand Hyatt, 88 Shiji Dadao** ☎ **021 5049 1234 ext 8732** ⏰ **Mon–Thu 6pm–1am, Fri 6pm–2am, Sat 11am–2am, Sun 11am–1am**

Cotton's $$
Set in a heritage villa in a sleepy corner of the French Concession, Cotton's exudes both elegance and friendliness. There are four open fireplaces, richly coloured rooms and a fabulous backyard deck. Cotton, the Hunanese owner, serves up nostril-clearing dishes from her home province, including a chilli-drenched toast platter. The vibe is relaxed and friendly.

✚ **208 (off map west)** ✉ **132 Anting Lu** ☎ **021 6433 7995** ⏰ **Mon–Fri 11am–2am, Sat–Sun 11am–4am**

Dongbei Ren $
Offering the same deal as its successful sister outfit in Beijing, Donbei Ren specializes in fun peasant-style food. Order the Squirrel Fish and the staff will sing and clap as the food is brought to your table. The rice wine is consumed in huge quantities, making the atmosphere ever lively. There are other outlets around the city, notably on Shanxi Nanlu (close to Yanan Zhonglu).

📍 208 (off map west) 🗺 46 Panyu Lu (by Yanan Xilu) ☎ 021 5230 2230 🕐 Daily 10am–10:30pm

Kathleen's 5 $$$

Located on the rooftop of the Shanghai Art Museum, Kathleen's 5 is an elegant restaurant with a casual glassed-in terrace beneath the clock tower. The kitchen lives up to the superb views over People's Park.

📍 208 C3 🗺 5th Floor, Shanghai Art Museum, 325 Nanjing Xi Lu ☎ 021 6327 2221 🕐 Daily 11:30am–midnight

M on the Bund $$$

Booked out almost every night, the Bund's first world-class restaurant serves contemporary European fare. There's an outdoor balcony with wonderful views to the futuristic Pudong skyline. The adjoining Glamour Bar hosts panel discussions, musical recitals and Shanghai's annual writers' festival, among more regular champagne sessions.

📍 209 E3 🗺 7th Floor, 5 Zhongshan Dongyi Lu (entrance at 20 Guangdong Lu) ☎ 021 6350 9988 🕐 Daily 11:30–2:30, 6–10:30, weekend brunch 11:30–3, Sun afternoon tea 3:30–5:30

Old China Hand Reading Rooms $$

The Old China Hand Reading Rooms was opened in 1996 by photographer Deke Erh and doubles as a bookstore, with hundreds of books and magazines (both old and new). This charming coffee shop is the best place to buy Erh's fascinating series on colonial architecture in China.

📍 208 A1 🗺 27 Shaoxing Lu ☎ 021 6473 2526 🕐 Daily 10am–midnight

Sasha's $$

This three-storey bar, set in a big, red 1920s villa, offers a relaxed, colonial vibe, decent cocktails and wines, and an expansive courtyard with comfortable wicker chairs and a wood-fired pizza oven. The raucous Mexican-themed club Zapata's is just a few steps away.

📍 208 (off map west) 🗺 11 Dongping Lu (near Hengshan Lu) ☎ 021 6474 6628 🕐 Mon–Fri 11am–12:30am, Sat–Sun 11am–2am

Three on the Bund

Three on the Bund houses four of Shanghai's top dining destinations. **Laris** (6th Floor; tel: 021 6321 9922; open 11:30–2:30, 6–10:30, $$$) is set in a quarry of white marble and is the baby of celebrated Greek/Australian chef David Laris. The restaurant comprises six distinct spaces, ranging from social long-tables to exclusive private rooms. **Jean Georges** (4th Floor; tel: 021 6321 7733; open 11:30–2:30, 6–11, $$$) is the Michelin-star chef's only signature restaurant outside New York. The moody lounge is filled with club chairs and eel-skin benches leading through to a chic copper and cobalt dining area. The **Whampoa Club** (4th Floor; tel: 021 6321 3737; open 11:30–2:30, 5:30–10, $$) has extravagant light fittings and funny-shaped crockery with which to enjoy top-end Shanghai cuisine, prepared by Hong Kong super chef, Jereme Leung. **New Heights** (7th Floor; tel: 021 6321 0909; open 10am–2am, $$) is as much about drinking as it is about food, though it does serve some decadent Western and South Asian treats.

📍 209 E3 🗺 3 Zhongshan Dong Yilu ☎ 021 6323 3355

Yongfoo Elite $$$

Yongfoo Elite feels like an old-time members' club, which is no great surprise since it's based in the immaculately restored old British Consulate. It evokes the elegant and rarefied side of the Shanghai colonial era perfectly. After a Shanghainese meal, retreat to a canopy bed in the garden to sip cocktails.

📍 208 (off map west) 🗺 200 Yongfu Lu ☎ 021 5466 2727 🕐 Daily 11am–midnight

Where to... Shop

Shanghai is a freewheeling and free-spending city. The mall is probably the largest in China, but those hunting for one-offs may find something to tempt them in the market stalls of the Old City or the independent boutiques down on Lane 210, Taikang Lu.

Of Shanghai's major shopping hubs, **Nanjing Donglu** has the grandest buildings, the brightest neon and the most glorious history. The pedestrianized part of the street leading up to the Bund is filled with a mixture of giant emporiums (old and new) and quirky indie stores. **The Bund** itself is festooned with trendy boutiques, notably the first **Armani** store to grace China, located in the endlessly chic Three on the Bund. Nanjing Donglu is unfortunately rife with touts. Ignore any invitation that might come your way. There are more major malls on **Nanjing Xilu** (the western half of this huge street), notably **Plaza 66**, close to the Shanghai Centre, which features more than 100 designer brands.

The French Concession's **Huaihai Zhonglu** also hosts a raft of major brands, especially around the Shanxi Nanlu metro station. **Shanxi Nanlu** is the place to buy shoes, while nearby **Xinle Lu** and **Changle Lu** are stuffed with small boutique outfits. One of the best of these is **Torana House** (No 1, Lane 180, Shanxi Nanlu; tel: 021 5404 4886; www.toranahouse.com). It specializes in handmade wool rugs from Tibet and parts of the former Silk Road. It also stages occasional art and photographic exhibitions.

The district of **Xujiahui** is the last of Shanghai's major shopping zones. It's an essential trip if you are hunting for electrical goods. The **Pacific Computer City** (Taipingyang Dianmao Cheng), close to the huge crossroads, has great prices on computers and consoles.

The **Old City** is a completely different shopping experience and a top place for one-off souvenirs and knick-knacks. The nearby **Shanghai South Bund Fabric Market** (399 Lujiabang Lu; tel: 021 6377 5858) boasts a huge selection of textiles. This is a great place to get clothes made to measure, though prices will increase if you need them back quickly.

Lane 210, Taikang Lu, is often hailed as Shanghai's Soho and is full of stores, cafés and galleries. **Jooi Design** (2nd Floor, Building 3; tel: 021 6473 6193; www.jooi.com) has a range of silky scarves, elegant bags and designer pillows. **Harvest Studio** (Suite 118, Building 3; tel: 021 6473 4566) runs a line in colourfully embroidered Miao minority clothing. The **New Red Door Gallery** (No 5; tel: 021 6473 2593) has an excellent collection of Chinese artwork, while **Insh** (200 Taikang Lu; tel: 021 6466 5249), at the southerly entrance to Lane 210, is where local designer Helen Lee sells funky T-shirt prints with a Shanghai twist.

For something completely different, visit the **Propaganda Poster Art Center** (Basement, Building B, 868 Huashan Lu; tel: 021 6211 1845), which boasts a collection of Liberation-era posters. The collector who runs the store is happy to let you browse (for a charge of 20RMB), but only some of the posters are for sale.

Artsy types might consider a trip to **M50** (50 Moganshan Lu; tel: 021 5252 7856), a new cultural zone fashioned from former warehouse space. **Art Deco** (1st Floor, Building 7; tel: 021 6277 8927) sells furniture from the 1920s, while **ShanghART** (Building 16 and 18, 50 Moganshan Lu; tel: 021 6359 3923; www.shanghartgallery.com) has original painting, sculpture and photography by talented local artists.

Where to...
Be Entertained

Slick financial hub by day, Shanghai is transformed after dark. China's foremost party place is doing a fine job of reprising its 1930 reputation as one of the world's great sin cities. Pick up one of the city's many listing magazines (*that's Shanghai*, *City Weekend*, *SH*) for detailed information about what's on.

NIGHTLIFE

The *shikumen* neighbourhood of **Xintiandi**, site of the Communist Party's first clandestine meeting in 1921, has an array of glamorous (and expensive) delights.

Dr Bar (House 15, North Block; tel: 021 6326 8008) is a dark, sultry offering, owned by the architects behind the Xintiandi development,

Ben Wood and Carlos Zapata. Try the trio of vodka shooters served in a Chinese "cricket jar".

The **Paulaner Brauhaus** (House 19–20, North Block; tel: 021 6320 3935) offers novelty German ales and hearty culinary treats, including chewy sausages, pork knuckles and *apfelstrudel*.

Bar Rouge (Bund 18, 18 Zhongshan Dong Yilu; tel: 021 6339 1199), Shanghai's classiest cocktail lounge, features 33 hand-blown Venetian chandeliers, velvet couches and a fabulous outdoor roof terrace. The cost may be high, but this is the place to mingle with Shanghai's jet-set crowd. If you can catch the attention of the bartenders (who intermittently set fire to the bar – for fun) order one of the signature ginger melon martinis.

Located inside the western gate of Fuxing Park, **Park 97** (2 Gaolan Lu; tel: 021 5383 2328) is one of Shanghai's trendiest leisure emporiums, with dining, drinking and partying options.

Baci is an Italian restaurant with great thin-crust pizzas, and reasonably priced weekend brunches.

Lux serves drinks during the day and becomes a bar lounge at night.

California Club is a loud (in every sense) disco; while **Upstairs at 97** is a red and purple lounge bar that tones things down slightly with live jazz music.

Catering to all tastes, the **Julu Lu** strip features unabashed girly bars alongside sleek nightclubs.

Manifesto (748 Julu Lu; tel: 021 6289 9108) is one of the classier outfits with lofty ceilings and exposed piping. It tends to heat up only after 10:30pm, so get there early if you want to nab one of the seductive day beds.

The bars towards the Changshu Lu end of the street tend to be more

down to earth. **Goodfellas** (907 Julu Lu, near Changle Lu; tel: 021 6467 0775) plays blaring rock and attracts a (largely male) expatriate crowd.

The proprietors of **Tongren Lu**'s many bars pull in the punters with a mixture of booze, babes and beats. With a couple of notable exceptions, most are nestled between Yanan Xilu and Nanjing Xilu.

The most chic of those venues is **Blue Frog** (86 Tongren Lu; tel: 021 6247 0320), with smooth chill-out sounds and even smoother cocktails.

North of Nanjing Xilu are **Malones** (offering big screen sports and plenty of pool) and **Mint** (2nd Floor, 333 Tongren Lu, near Beijing Lu; tel: 021 6247 9666), one of Shanghai's more languid nightclubs.

Mexican-themed cantina-cum-club **Zapata's** (5 Hengshan Lu; tel: 021 6474 6166; http://zapatas-shanghai.com), housed in a French Concession villa within the same compound as Sasha's (▶ 87), attracts a youthful mixture of Shanghainese and Westerners. The music is usually chart and pop and the place gets packed on Mondays, when women can take advantage of free margaritas.

On Maoming Nanlu, another of Shanghai's famed bar drags, **Babyface** (180 Maoming Nanlu; tel: 021 6445 2330) is a small but pumping nightclub that attracts a largely Chinese crowd.

The classy **Madame Zung** (4 Xiangshan Lu; tel: 021 5382 0738) bar-cum-club has a long, slim, candlelit upstairs section at the street side and a thumping underground nightclub below. The club is only open Thursday to Sunday.

LIVE MUSIC

The **Peace Hotel Jazz Bar** (20 Nanjing Donglu; tel: 021 6321 6888; www.shanghaipeacehotel.com) offers big-band jazz from the 1930s golden era, played by musicians who just might be able to remember the good old days themselves. The band plays nightly to an almost exclusively tourist crowd. The cover charge is compounded by expensive drinks inside.

ARK Live House (House 5, North Block; tel: 021 6326 8008) is a bar, restaurant, concert hall and club. The interior is set up for serious performance, with a large raised stage and a professional PA system.

The intimate **JZ Club** (46 Fuxing Xilu; tel: 021 6431 0268; www.jzclub.cn), a French Concession venue, has benefited from a recent makeover and attracts a mixed, friendly crowd. The session musicians change on a regular basis, keeping things fresh. The music normally starts around 10pm. There are often three or four sets on weekends, the last of them reserved for the hardcore who remain into the small hours. There's no cover charge, but drinks are fairly expensive.

CINEMA

There are large multiplex cinemas scattered around town, including a UME in Xintiandi and a Studio City in the Westgate Mall on Nanjing Xilu.

The **Cathay Theatre** (870 Huaihai Zhonglu, on the corner with Maoming Lu; tel: 021 5404 2095), a gorgeous old art deco fixture, was Shanghai's first-ever cinema and continues to screen the occasional English-language film.

The **Shanghai Film Art Center** (160 Xinhua Lu; tel: 021 6280 4088) is the main venue for the Shanghai International Film Festival. Its outer appearance is fairly drab, but it shows a good range of movies. For Shanghai, the 50–60RMB tickets represent good value.

THEATRE

One of Shanghai's most interesting and historic theatres (Dame Margot Fonteyn danced here), the European-style **Lyceum Theatre** (57 Maoming Nanlu; tel: 021 6279 8663) shows a variety of high-quality performances, including acrobatics, ballet and Chinese opera. There's a small café in the renovated lobby interior and it's worth popping in, even if you aren't stopping for a show.

The low-key **Shanghai Dramatic Arts Center** (288 Anfu Lu; tel: 021 6433 5133) on the periphery of the French Concession stages Chinese and international productions (in both Mandarin and English). Check the listings magazines for what's on when you're in town.

The city's most popular acrobatics display takes place at the **Shanghai Centre Theatre** (1376 Nanjing Xilu; tel: 021 6279 8663) nightly, performed by the famous Shanghai Acrobatics Troupe. Performances start at 7:30pm. It also stages opera, ballet and symphony concerts.

Hong Kong and the South

Getting Your Bearings 92 – 93
In Seven Days 94 – 95
Don't Miss 96 – 105
At Your Leisure 106 – 108
Where to... 109 – 114

Getting Your Bearings

Hong Kong serves up an exotic entrée to the China experience. The years of colonial rule haven't diluted the city's overwhelmingly Chinese flavour. However, the social seasoning added by the sizeable foreign communities make Hong Kong the most palatable option for anyone tasting the Middle Kingdom for the first time.

Hong Kong grew out of the 19th-century drugs trade when the British seized the territory as a spoil of the First Opium War (► 22–23). Under colonial patronage, Hong Kong matured into a vibrant, cultured and wealthy city, attracting immigrants from across the region.

Since control was handed back to Beijing in 1997, Hong Kongers have maintained their commercial and cultural edge on their brothers across the well-guarded "mainland" border. Hong Kong remains the only place in China where English is widely spoken and where queuing etiquette is observed.

Hong Kong's geography is as unique as its melting-pot make-up. The territory comprises several mountainous islands and a chunk of "mainland" peninsula. Hong Kong

**Page 91:
Market stalls,
Tai Yuen
Street, Hong
Kong**

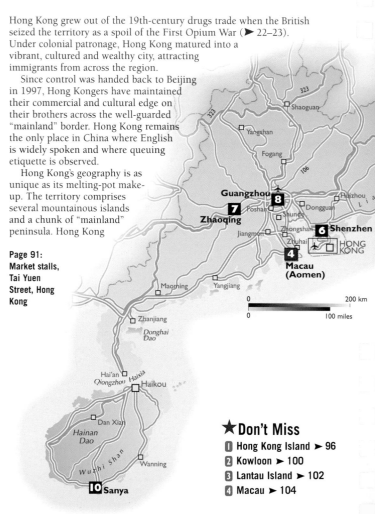

★Don't Miss

❶ Hong Kong Island ► 96
❷ Kowloon ► 100
❸ Lantau Island ► 102
❹ Macau ► 104

Island is the most densely populated part of the city, famed for its stunning harbour skyline. In contrast, parts of the Outlying Islands and New Territories offer rugged wilderness.

Above: A traditional sampan, an increasingly rare sight in modern China

North of Hong Kong is Guangdong province – the crucible of Cantonese culture and great food. There are several charming locales worth seeking out – even if air pollution often spoils the view. For clear skies, head to Hainan Island, China's most southerly province and beach-holiday hotspot.

Below: An evening view of Central Plaza from Victoria Peak, Hong Kong

At Your Leisure

5 Cheung Chau ➤ 106
6 Shenzhen ➤ 106
7 Zhaoqing ➤ 107
8 Guangzhou ➤ 107
9 Xiamen ➤ 108
10 Sanya ➤ 108

Hong Kong is a country in miniature and it's possible to go home without seeing any more of China, still feeling satisfied. To head into mainland China, simply walk across the border at Lo Wu or take a train or ferry from Kowloon.

Hong Kong and the South in Seven Days

Day One

Morning

Start with a classic Cantonese dim sum breakfast at Hong Kong's Maxim's Palace in City Hall. Go shopping in Central before riding the **Mid-Levels Elevator** to Soho for lunch along Elgin Street (➤ 182).

Afternoon/Evening

Return to sea level and take bus 6 from the Central Ferry Pier to **Stanley** (➤ 99). Wander around the market and beaches of this laid-back town. Take the funicular railway to **Victoria Peak** (➤ 98) just before sunset. Watch day turn to night over one of the world's most striking cityscapes before finishing the day in **Causeway Bay**, which bursts into life after dark.

Day Two

Morning

Head for the Star Ferry terminal for the trip across Victoria Harbour. In Tsim Sha Tsui, take the MTR to Diamond Hill to see the Chi Lin Nunnery.

Afternoon

Return to Tsim Sha Tsui and stroll along the TST East Promenade, exploring the museums and galleries en route. Cross Salisbury Road to take afternoon tea in the Peninsula Hotel.

Evening

Watch the Symphony of Lights (left) illuminate Hong Kong Island's skyline at 8pm before taking the MTR to the Temple Street Night Market.

Day Three

Morning

Take the MTR to Tung Chung and ride the **Ngong Ping 360** cable car up into the mountains of **3** **Lantau** (► 102–103). Visit the Tian Tan Buddha (below) and take lunch in the **Po Lin Monastery** opposite.

Afternoon/ Evening

Walk part of the **Lantau Trail** to Keung Shan Road from where you can jump on a bus to the fishing village of **Mui Wo**. Take a ferry across to **Cheung Chau** (► 106) for a seafood feast on the harbour front before going back to Hong Kong Island.

Day Four

Morning

Head to **4** **Macau** (► 104–105). From central Largo do Senado, stroll through the network of pretty alleys that lead past the **Macau Museum**, the **Monte Fort** and the **ruins of St Paul's Cathedral**.

Afternoon/Evening

Take a bus to **Taipa** and stroll through the village to Avenida de Praia. Drop in at the **Wynn Casino** for a flutter before having a waterside drink in the bustling bar district at the southern end of the **NAPE** area, before returning to Hong Kong.

Day Five

Fill in any blanks in your Hong Kong itinerary before taking the 2:20pm through-train to **7** **Zhaoqing** (► 107) from Hung Hom.

Day Six

Explore Zhaoqing's **Seven Star Crags** park in the morning. Take a taxi to **Dinghu Shan** in the afternoon.

Day Seven

Take the short bus ride to **8** **Guangzhou** (► 107). From here you can easily head back to Hong Kong or continue your trip into mainland China.

□ Hong Kong Island

What Queen Victoria once assumed to be a useless lump of uninhabited rock is now the high rise-studded symbol of Asian affluence. Hong Kong Island may only represent a fraction of the territory's overall bulk, but a great deal of money, power and people are packed into its limited confines. It's Hong Kong's business and political hub and has the lion's share of top hotels, restaurants and malls. Whatever your vice – food, fashion or high finance – Hong Kong Island guarantees an experience to remember.

Hong Kong Island can be crudely divided into two. To the north of the island's mountainous spine is a thin urban corridor, compact but heavily populated. The southern half, meanwhile, is green and hilly with a smattering of quaint seaside towns and sandy beaches.

Central

The district of Central is the land of luxury. Take a stroll from the **Star Ferry** terminal and celebrity names will announce themselves from behind polished glass façades – Gucci, Vuitton. Head along **Queen's Road** to view softly lit storefronts – Prada, Bvlgari. Rise from Central's seething MTR station straight into the glittering **Landmark Shopping Mall** – Dior, Dolce and Gabbana and more.

Much of the cash flow that sustains these enterprises is generated in the shimmering skyscrapers nearby. The 88-floor **Two IFC (International Finance Centre)** building is the jewel in the crown and has (another) excellent shopping mall at its base. Prior to the 2005 opening of the IFC complex, the 70-storey **Bank of China** building was the standout landmark in Hong Kong's forest of high-rises. There is a viewing gallery on the 43rd floor. Meanwhile, down below in **Statue Square** is the attractive **Legislative Council Building**, a relic of the colonial era and still the fully functioning seat of government.

Mid-Levels

Hundreds of international companies have their corporate HQ in Central. Many of the executives who keep things ticking over live in the finger-thin apartment blocks that sprout from the steep hillside behind. This area is known as the Mid-Levels and residents have their own conveyor belt – raised several metres above the busy streets – to help them make their daily commute. Fortunately for tourists, the **Mid-Levels Elevator** is not exclusive to locals and remains a great way to get an overview of Central (► 180–182).

Halfway up the hill, the elevator passes through **Soho**, an area known for its high-end art galleries, independent boutique stores and Western restaurants. A short walk to the east (and downhill slightly) is **Lan Kwai Fong**, Hong Kong's

Hong Kong's stunning skyline is particularly impressive at night when it is illuminated. Left to right: The Center, One International Finance Centre and Two International Finance Centre

premier bar district. There are better (and cheaper) watering holes in Hong Kong, but nowhere matches Lan Kwai Fong for crowds and style.

Night-time racing at Happy Valley Racecourse

Peak Tram

Further east again is the lower terminus of the Peak Tram, a creaking funicular railway that dates originally from 1888 and hauls tourists uphill in the direction of **Victoria Peak**. Passengers exit directly into the **Peak Tower**. The viewing platform is on the fifth floor, while kids will enjoy attractions like Madame Tussaud's (fourth floor) and Ripley's Believe It Or Not! Odditorium (third floor). Just across Peak Road is the **Peak Galleria**, home to several expensive restaurants and shops. The viewing deck (third floor) is larger than the one in the Peak Tower. Both lookouts take in sea, city and mountain views, though Hong Kong's smog means the trip is best made at night. For a taste of what the resident tycoons enjoy, tramp up moneyed **Mount Austin Road** all the way to the peak's 552m (1,811-foot) summit. The Victoria Peak Garden, formerly part of the governor's mountain lodge, remains open to the public.

East of Central

Sheung Wan, to the west of Central, is one of Hong Kong's most traditional districts, where shops sell herbal medicine and dried preservatives. **Wanchai**, east of Central, is the opposite. This district was once famed as Hong Kong's den of depravity (particularly during the Vietnam War). Plenty of escort bars remain, but the overall mood is now fairly salubrious. You can take a ferry here direct from Tsim Sha Tsui. The boat docks beside the Sydney Opera House-styled **Hong Kong Convention and Exhibition Centre**. As at Central, an elevated pedestrian walkway guides passengers into the urban jungle.

A few kilometres east again is **Causeway Bay**, a melting pot of neon-lit consumerism. The imposing **Times Square** building is a veritable skyscraper of a shopping mall, while **Island Beverley**, off Great George Street, is a warren of shops-cum-cubicles that sell knock-offs and one-offs straight off the truck. Nearby is the **Happy Valley Racecourse**. Evening meetings are held here most Wednesdays. **Central Library**, on the northern fringes of Victoria Park, has free internet and stunning views across Victoria Harbour.

HONG KONG ISLAND: INSIDE INFO

Top tip One of the best ways to experience the urban half of Hong Kong Island is to ride the **tram**, which begins in Sheung Wan and jangles its way through Central, Admiralty, Wanchai, Causeway Bay and beyond. The HK$2 fare will take you any distance.

Hidden gem Repulse Bay's sandy strand is popular for sunbathing and swimming. Like Victoria Peak, this area is an enclave for the rich, making it a good spot to people-watch. Have lunch in the **Verandah restaurant** (➤ 111) on the first floor of the Repulse Bay Hotel. Take bus 6, 6A, 6X or 260 from Central.

The South and West

The historic village of **Stanley** lies close to Hong Kong Island's most southerly point. This is one of the few areas populated prior to British rule and is now best known for its busy market. There is a pleasant beach close by and some great walking trails in the hills behind town. **Aberdeen**, across on the western side of the island, was once home to Hong Kong's floating junks. Numbers have dropped, but you can still take a sampan tour of the old harbor. **Ocean Park**, one of Asia's best marine parks, is located here.

TAKING A BREAK

For a really atmospheric experience, head to Causeway Bay. The open-air storefronts around **Jardine's Bazaar** are famed for hand folded *wonton*, fresh soymilk and roast duck. Or try **Tai Ping Koon** (➤ 111), one of the best.

✚ 207 D2
Peak Tram
✉ 33 Garden Road, Central (behind St John's Building) ☎ 852 2849 0818 🕒 Daily 7am–midnight 💲 Inexpensive (single), moderate (return) 🚌 15, 15B, 15C, 515

Ocean Park
✉ Ocean Park Road, Aberdeen ☎ 852 2552 0291 🕒 Daily 10–6 💲 Expensive 🚌 6A, 6X, 70, 75, 90, 97, 260

Jumbo Floating Restaurant, Aberdeen

❷ Kowloon

Kowloon is the area to the north of Victoria Harbour. With its historic buildings and modern museums, the peninsula's southern tip is arguably Hong Kong's most cultured locale. The maze of fragrant streets farther north is a different proposition. Gone is the slick sophistication of Hong Kong Island. What emerges instead is a riot of commercialism set against a backdrop of crumbling tenement blocks and crackly neon signs.

Tsim Sha Tsui

Kowloon begins at Tsim Sha Tsui, the district at the southern tip of the "mainland" peninsula. Stroll along the **Tsim Sha Tsui East Promenade**, a walkway that offers uninterrupted views of one of the world's most stunning cityscapes. This is the spot to take in the nightly **Symphony of Lights**, when 43 of Hong Kong Island's tallest buildings become a canvas to a series of synchronized searchlights and lasers. The show begins at 8pm.

The adjoining **Hong Kong Cultural Centre** was created in 1989 when city planners transformed Kowloon. The building, initially pilloried for its wacky design, is now considered a genuinely world-class venue for the performing arts. Near by is the **Hong Kong Museum of Art**, with to-die-for views and reliably good exhibitions. The **Hong Kong Space Museum and Theatre** has one of the largest planetariums in the world. The "Sky shows" in the IMAX theatre are great for the kids.

Just across Salisbury Road is the **Peninsula Hotel** (➤ 111), the grand old dame of British colonialism. Taking afternoon tea (2–7pm) in the white marbled lobby is a rite of passage for locals. For a less traditional experience, take the elevator to the **Felix Restaurant**. The famous toilet here offers male guests the singular pleasure of relieving themselves while looking down 28 storeys through a wall of glass.

Nathan Road and Surroundings

As you move north from the waterfront prepare to be assailed by incessant offers of tailor-made suits, "Rolex" watches and digital cameras.

The grand Peninsula Hotel

Nathan Road is the main vein that runs from the waterfront to the former mainland border at Boundary Road in Mongkok. The street has been virtually sealed from the elements by the number of overhanging hoardings. Top-end hotels and plush shops rub shoulders with hideous apartment blocks, like the **Chungking Mansions** (Nos 36–44). **Temple Street Night Market**, close to the Jordan MTR station, is Hong Kong's most famous night market and a great spot to pick up a bargain. It begins at 4pm and has a dizzying variety of street food.

Close to the Diamond Hill MTR station is the **Chi Lin Nunnery**, arguably the best temple in Hong Kong and certainly the best free temple anywhere in China. This Buddhist complex is not as ancient as it appears. It was built in the 1930s and restyled in wood as recently as 1998.

TAKING A BREAK

The supremely awful **Chungking Mansions** (36–44 Nathan Road) has a superb clutch of Indian restaurants.

✚ 207 D3
Hong Kong Museum of Art
✉ 10 Salisbury Road ☎ 852 2721 0116 🕙 Sun–Wed, Fri 10–6, Sat 10–8
🎟 Inexpensive (free on Wed) 🚇 Tsim Sha Tsui

Hong Kong Space Museum
✉ 10 Salisbury Road ☎ 852 2721 0226 🕙 Mon–Wed, Fri 1–9,
Sat–Sun 10–9 🎟 Inexpensive (free on Wed) 🚇 Tsim Sha Tsui

Chi Lin Nunnery
✉ 5 Chi Lin Drive, Diamond Hill ☎ 852 2354 1789 🕙 Convent: daily 9–4;
Lotus Pond Garden: daily 7am–9pm 🎟 Free 🚇 Diamond Hill

Top left: Wood-carving of Guanyin, the Goddess of Mercy, in the Museum of Art

Below: The Star Ferry Terminal

KOWLOON: INSIDE INFO

Top tips Take the super-cheap **Star Ferry** across Victoria Harbour for one of Hong Kong's defining experiences.
• Kowloon is the departure point for those entering mainland China. There are direct train services to Beijing, Shanghai and Zhaoqing (via Guangzhou) from **Hung Hom** station. Mainland ferries depart the China Ferry Terminal at **Harbour City** in Tsim Sha Tsui. The Kowloon-Canton Railway (KCR), meanwhile, ferries passengers to Lo Wu and the walk-through border with Shenzhen.

③ Lantau Island

With its mountainous interior and wild coastline, Lantau has long been popular with lovers of the great outdoors. It now also has mass appeal thanks to a series of man-made tourist developments. The unveiling of the so-called "Big Buddha" in 1993 kick-started the metamorphosis. Disneyland set up home here in 2005. Most recently, the Ngong Ping Skyrail – the world's longest cable-car ride – began operations. These days you'll need to find a good excuse not to visit, especially if you have kids.

Lantau is almost twice the size of Hong Kong Island, but has only around 5 per cent of its population, and is a great place to head for if you are looking for a bit of breathing space. The 70km-long (43-mile) Lantau Trail is perhaps the best hiking route in the region, taking in a series of soaring peaks, traditional villages and sandy beaches. It is well signed and easy to follow.

The **Tian Tan Buddha** ("Big Buddha") is near Lantau Peak and commands great views of the mountains and the sea. It is apparently the "tallest outdoor seated bronze Buddha in the world." At 34m (115 feet) in height, the statue on its base is easily seen from afar, but it's worth walking up the 260 steps to take a closer look. A combination ticket offers entry to the museum inside the Buddha's body and a meal at the **Po Lin Monastery**, just across the road. The large bell within the Buddha is controlled by computer and rings 108 times a day, a sobering reminder of the so-called 108 "troubles of mankind".

The Big Buddha is connected to Tung Chung – the biggest conurbation on Lantau – by road, pathway and the **Ngong Ping Skyrail** cable car. The 5.7km (3.5-mile) cableway makes its way over Lantau's mountainous landscape at thrillingly steep angles. Towards the end of the journey, the glass carriage dips down over the inlet which runs between Lantau proper and Chek Lap Kok Airport. Watching intercontinental airliners taking off *below* you is a real thrill.

A steep stairway leads up to the Tian Tan Buddha

Occupying yet more reclaimed land towards Lantau's eastern tip is **Hong Kong Disneyland** (► 114). The US$3.2 billion park is linked to Hong Kong Island by its own railway. Though much smaller, the resort has been closely modelled on the original 1950s Disneyland theme park and has virtually identical attractions to those in California. There have been a few concessions to local culture – ill-fortune is staved off by omitting the "unlucky" number four in the resort's two huge hotels.

TAKING A BREAK

The **Po Lin Monastery** has a huge on-site canteen that does a decent vegetarian banquet. The meal comes cheap if you have purchased a combination ticket to see the nearby Big Buddha and museum next door.

Buddhist trinkets for sale near the Po Lin Monastery

✚ 206 C2
Tian Tan Buddha
✉ Ngong Ping Village ☎ 852 2985 5669
🕐 Daily 10–6 💷 Free. Entry to museum and meal at Po Lin Monastery: moderate
🚌 2 from Mui Wo, 21 from Tai O, 23 from Tung Chung

Ngong Ping Skyrail
✉ Tung Chung ☎ 852 2109 9898; www.np360.com.hk 🕐 Mon–Fri 10–6, Sat–Sun 10–6:30 💷 One way: moderate, combo prices available for joint entry with other attractions 🚇 Tung Chung

Hong Kong Disneyland
☎ 852 1 830 830; www.hongkongdisneyland.com 🕐 Daily approximately 10–8 💷 Expensive
🚇 Disneyland Resort

LANTAU ISLAND: INSIDE INFO

In depth Hong Kong's **Big Buddha** may be the "tallest outdoor seated bronze Buddha in the world", but take out the word "bronze" and he immediately loses his crown: the (seated) Buddha of Leshan in Sichuan was carved from a cliff face and is 71m (233 feet) tall.

• Up until 1997, Lantau was accessible only by ferry. The opening of the **Chek Lap Kok Airport** changed everything. The 2.2km (1.4-mile) **Tsing Ma** bridge that links Lantau and Tsing Yi is now the world's longest rail-and-road suspension bridge and a true Hong Kong landmark.

One to miss The themed **Ngong Ping Village** at the top of the cable way has been built as a "traditional Chinese village", but comes complete with virtually every Western chainstore you care to name. The themed attractions, Walking with Buddha and Monkey's Tale Theatre, are both fun, though, if you have kids.

4 Macau

The former Portuguese enclave of Macau is a short boat ride across the Pearl River Estuary from Hong Kong. Older, smaller and far more relaxed than its neighbour, Macau combines sultry Mediterranean charm with a vibrant Cantonese culture. Thanks to the recent liberalization of the casino industry, this tiny territory is well on the way to being crowned the undisputed Las Vegas of the Far East.

When it was finally returned to Chinese control in 1999, Macau was the oldest slice of European-controlled territory in Asia. Portuguese merchants first set up shop here in 1557 and Macau flourished as a halfway house for trade between China and the Western world. With domestic traders forbidden from leaving Chinese territory and Europeans restricted from travelling on the mainland, Macau became a no-man's land where East and West mingled relatively freely.

Mediterranean Meets Orient
These days, Macau's cultural fusion is one of its abiding charms. The lovely pedestrianized **Largo do Senado**, surrounded by pastel-hued architecture, offers the best distillation of Macau's colonial ambience. Its most prominent building is the Leal Senado, former seat of the Portuguese administration. Starbucks and McDonalds are among the less historic buildings that have their home behind the neo-classical façades.

Top left: Tile-work at the Pousada de São Tiago hotel

Top right: St Francis Garden, on the peninsula

At the back of the square is the delightful Church of St Dominic and, a little farther up the hill, the stunning **ruins of St Paul's Cathedral**. Only the façade of this huge 17th-century church remains, but its visual impact has, if anything, been enhanced by the missing parts. Macau's precious collection of religious buildings are the legacy of the Jesuit missionaries who followed hot on the heels of the early Portuguese traders. It was the Jesuits who were also responsible for building the nearby **Monte Fort** as a means of protecting what had, by the early 17th century, become Asia's foremost bishopric.

Above: The impressive façade of St Paul's Cathedral

Entertainment Enclave
Macau's pious daylight personality takes on a different form by night. At the time of writing there were 29 casinos in Macau, most of them with hundreds of gaming tables spread across multiple floors. There's no shortage of customers. Macau has a resident population of only half a million and

yet, in 2006, an astonishing 22 million people visited the tiny peninsula. The vast majority came from nearby Guangdong and Hong Kong. The Chinese people's demonstrable love of gambling was the key factor in convincing several of Las Vegas' biggest names to expand their operations into Macau. The gloriously kitsch **Wynn Casino** is one of the most lavish in town.

Following Hong Kong Disneyland, Macau now also boasts its own multi-billion dollar theme park in the form of **Fisherman's Wharf**. This waterside project has a giant ferris wheel, state-of-the-art rollercoaster and a 40m-tall (130-foot), flame-erupting volcano. A series of restaurants and brand-stores ensures there's plenty to keep the grown-ups happy too. For those who need their sensory kicks slightly stronger, visit the nearby **Macau Tower**. The 338m-tall (1,109-foot) structure has a variety of heart-stopping sky walks and bungee rope-assisted rides.

Macau's Islands

Try to find time to head across one of the three long bridges from the Macau peninsula to one of the two outlying islands. Thanks to land reclamation, **Coloane** and **Taipa** have been merged into one but remain pleasant places to sample some Mediterranean-flavoured beach culture.

TAKING A BREAK

The **Clube Militar** (975 Avenida da Praia Grande; tel: 853 2871 4000) is one of Macau's most atmospheric dining halls, and is a good place to stop for lunch.

✚ 206 C2
Monte Fort
✉ Rua de Monte ☎ 853 2835 7911; www.macaumuseum.gov.mo 🕐 Daily 6am–7pm; Macau Museum Tue–Sun 10–6 🎟 Free; Macau Museum inexpensive

Macau Tower
✉ Largo da Torre de Macau ☎ 853 2893 3339; www.macautower.com.mo 🕐 Mon–Fri 10–9, Sat–Sun 9–9 🎟 Observation Deck moderate; Skywalk expensive

---

MACAU: INSIDE INFO

Top tips Users of PDAs can download a **free map of Macau**, including all the major sights, hotels, restaurants and bus networks, at http://marketing.macautourism.gov.mo./macaumap/en/intro_ppc.php
• Macau's Formula 3 **Grand Prix** is normally held the third week of November.

At Your Leisure

5 Cheung Chau

Loitering off the east coast of Lantau, the tiny island of Cheung Chau is the best bet for anyone looking to squeeze a beach holiday out of their stay in Hong Kong. The poor quality of the sand doesn't detract from the laid-back atmosphere that pervades the dumbbell-shaped island. The sleepy harbour front comes alive in the evenings when the long row of restaurants move business outdoors and set up beside the water. The seafood here is some of the best in town. Wander around the alleys behind **Praya Street**, where Hong Kong's "traditional way of life" actually becomes tangible. The island is a car-free zone, making it a great spot to clear the lungs, especially around the beautiful coastal pathways.

🚰 207 D2 🚢 Pier Five of the Outland Island Ferries Pier in Central has half-hourly services. The "fast ferry" takes around 30 minutes and the "slow ferry" 50 minutes (inexpensive–moderate)

6 Shenzhen

As a "Special Economic Zone", Shenzhen represents the oldest of China's experiments with capitalism. Its early exposure to Western entrepreneurs and its proximity to Hong Kong have made it the richest city in mainland China. It's far cleaner, prettier and more orderly

The China Folk Culture Village, Shenzhen

than Guangzhou, Shanghai or Beijing. While hardly bursting with tourist sights, Shenzhen has become a popular day trip for visitors to Hong Kong and offers an insight into life – and prices – enjoyed on the mainland. The districts of **Luohu** and **Futian** get most of the through-traffic and have their fair share of high-rises, malls and cheap massage parlours. The most interesting area is **Longgang**, which contains the **Dapeng Ancient City**. Dapeng is a well-preserved walled town dating back to the Ming dynasty (AD 1368–1644), built originally to protect the coast against pirates. The nearby **Hakka Enclosure** also has a number of fascinating Qing-era homes.

🚰 207 D3 ✉ Guangdong province
🚆 From Hong Kong take the Kowloon-Canton Railway train to the walk-through border at Lo Wu ✈ Shenzhen's Bao'an Airport has links with most mainland Chinese cities

7 Zhaoqing

Cradled by the Xijiang River to the south, sheltered by mountains to the north, and boasting a crag-studded lake at its heart, Zhaoqing is perhaps the most scenic urban sprawl in China – all the more impressive given that it's located in one of the most heavily industrialized land-scapes on earth. In few parts of the world will a city of half a million people convince you it's a quiet rural retreat, but in the teeming Pearl River Delta such illusions are not impossible.

The restful atmosphere is largely down to **Seven Star Crags** park, named after the limestone peaks that rise above the emerald Seven Star Lake. Walking trails take visitors away from the teeming streets and across the leafy causeways that dissect the lake. It's possible to climb each of the peaks, though the best views can be had from the 113m-high (370-foot) **Tianzhu Crag**. **Dinghu Mountain**, 20km (12.5 miles) east of the city, offers nicely shaded mountain trails that are strung around Taoist temples, towering trees, waterfalls and murmuring brooks.

✉ 206 B3 ✉ Guangdong province 🚌 Regular buses from Guangzhou and Shenzhen 🚉 Daily direct train to Hong Kong's Hung Hom station

8 Guangzhou

Guangzhou is the home of Cantonese culture. It was the first city to welcome Western traders to China back in the 16th century and was instrumental in leading the country's transformation from Communist powerhouse to Capitalist miracle in the 1980s. Consequently, it's one of the most progressive, developed cities in China. With heaving wholesale markets and legendary restaurants, Guangzhou will be irresistible to shoppers and foodies. However, the city's tourist sights are few.

The best is **Shamian Island**. This tiny plot of land is cleaved from the city by little more than a moat, but cross the footbridge and the moat could easily be an ocean. Traffic all but disappears, birdsong strikes up and Guangzhou's famously hectic mood evaporates. The central boule-vard, Shamian Dajie, runs nearly the 1km (half-mile) width of the island and makes for a pleasant stroll among the many examples of French and British architecture, leftovers from the 19th century, when Shamian was a western "concession". Great views across the Pearl River lure Tai Chi practitioners at dawn, while lovers take advantage of the many shady corners as the sun goes down. The luxurious – if incongruous – **White Swan Hotel** is in the southwest corner of the island.

🚏 206 C3 ✉ Guangdong province ☎ 020 8666 2325 (Guangzhou Tourist Information Centre) 🚉 Guangzhou has one of China's busiest railway stations with trains to all major cities, including Lhasa ✈ Guangzhou's Baiyun airport is one of the best connected airports in China with several international links

The tree-clad Seven Star Crags, near the town of Zhaoqing

9 Xiamen

Xiamen is a green seaside city with one of the best hot spring resorts in China – **Riyuegu** – as well as a fabulous slice of colonial history.

The tiny island of **Gulangyu**, a short ferry ride from the city proper, was once home to consulates of 13 different nations. Its modern charm lies in its steep, winding pathways, and the surviving handiwork of the 19th-century colonialists. Much of the British and French architecture has survived, now charmingly covered in creeping vines. Bicycles and electric buggies are the only form of transport allowed, making it a perfect spot to get away from the hustle and bustle of the mainland. The island is famed as a music-lover's paradise: there are 200 antique pianos lurking in homes and museums. *Gu lang* literally translates as "Drum Wave", and there's a rhythm of sorts on the east of the island where the waves pound the cliffs.

Nets drying on fishing boats in Sanya

🚶 207 F4 ✉ Fujian province 🚆 Daily trains from all major eastern cities ✈ Xiamen has its own airport with flights to China's main cities

10 Sanya

Right on the southern tip of the island province of Hainan, Sanya has become something of a playground for China's emerging jet set. With white sand beaches, whispering palm trees and top hotels, Hainan is avidly marketed as the "Hawaii of the Orient". The glamour of the natural surroundings is topped up

every November when 100-plus Miss World wannabes fly in to take part in the annual contest, held on a stunning 7km (4-mile) sweep of sand known as **Yalong Bay**. It's all a bit of a turnaround for an island that was, in dynastic times, dubbed the "Gates of Hell" on account of its hot climate and remote southerly location.

Hainan may not have Hawaii's fearsome breakers, but the tranquil ocean is perfect for windsurfing, jet-skiing, snorkelling and scuba-diving. Visitors will have plenty of space to stretch out, as the Chinese are generally not particularly keen on sunbathing. Hainan is also home to three of China's 55 minority "nationalities", and examples of their distinct culture can be found in the highland villages. A word of caution, though: the crass commercialization of minority culture – a problem throughout China – is particularly acute around Sanya. For a more authentic experience, head inland.

🚶 207 E1 (inset) ✉ Hainan Island 🚆 Train from Guangdong to provincial capital Haikou (the train is rolled onto a boat to cross the straits), then bus to Sanya ✈ Sanya has its own airport with flights to cities across China

Where to... Stay

Prices
Expect to pay for a double room, including breakfast and taxes, per night
$ under HK$500 $$ HK$500–1,500 $$$ HK$1,500–3,000 $$$$ over HK$3,000

HONG KONG

Four Seasons Hong Kong $$$
In the most claustrophobic part of the densely populated city, the new Four Seasons Hong Kong offers some much-needed breathing space. The rooms have views over Victoria Harbour from the floor-to-ceiling windows, while the outdoor swimming complex shares a similar outlook, allowing bathers to relish the tranquillity of the infinity-edged pool while marvelling at the bustling harbour beyond. The 399-room tower is part of the landmark International Financial Centre (IFC) complex, next to Hong Kong Island's Star Ferry terminal.

✚ 207 D2 ✉ 8 Finance Street, Central ☎ 852 3196 8888; www.fourseasons.com

Hong Kong Hostel $
The Hong Kong Hostel may occupy the lower end of the price spectrum, but in terms of location, it's almost unparalleled. Tucked away on the upper floors of a residential block right in the middle of Causeway Bay, the HK Hostel offers modest home comforts in one of the trendiest parts of Hong Kong Island. It's popular with backpackers, but with a smattering of clean – if cramped – twin rooms, also works well for couples on a tight budget.

✚ 207 D2 ✉ 3rd Floor, Block A, 47 Paterson Street, Causeway Bay ☎ 852 2392 6868; www.hostel.hk

JIA $$$
This 26-floor designer hotel shoots up like a blade of grass from the city melee. In addition to a slim figure, its stylish interiors were put together by design legend Philippe Starck. Mercifully, the rooms are warm and comfortable rather than über-cool, and there are stocked marbled kitchens and full entertainment centres, plus broadband. The lobby also functions as a living room, where guests share the continental breakfast at a common table.

✚ 207 D2 ✉ 1–5 Irving Street, Causeway Bay ☎ 852 3196 9000; www.jiahongkong.com

Landmark Mandarin Oriental $$$$
Pulled between the duty to be "Mandarin Oriental" reliable and the desire to be "Hong Kong" chic, the LMO blends the best of both worlds. This hybrid hotel is connected to the Landmark shopping mall in the heart of Central. What the rooms lack in views, they make up for with interior comforts. Dressed in off-white and ebony tones, they are spacious and decadent with a flat-screen TV built into the crescent-shaped wall which wraps around a spectacular bathroom. The socket that connects your iPod to the stereo system is a nice touch.

✚ 207 D2 ✉ 15 Queen's Road, Chung Wan (Central) ☎ 852 2132 0188; www.mandarinoriental.com

Salisbury YMCA $$
Don't be fooled by the name. The YMCA has some of the most sought-after rooms in Hong Kong, thanks to its superb location at the tip of the Kowloon Peninsula. Many (though not all) of the plainly furnished rooms have wonderful views towards Hong Kong Island. One YMCA trait that's well retained

Where to...
Eat and Drink

Prices
Expect to pay for a meal for one, excluding drinks and service
$ under HK$100 **$$** HK$100–200 **$$$** over HK$200

After School $$
This New York East Village-style café is run by an artist named Pokit, and is furnished with old school desks. It's a magnet to fashion editors, writers and designers.
✚ 207 D2 ⊠ 2nd Floor, 17 Yun Ping Road, Causeway Bay ☎ 852 2893 2130 🕐 Mon–Fri 7pm–midnight, Sat–Sun 3pm–2am

Baci (and Baci Pizza) $$
Ultra-modern décor is the order of the day at this Italian Lan Kwai Fong eatery. As in its sister restaurant in Shanghai, the thin-crust pizza is a show stealer and is available from the dedicated pizzeria below the main restaurant. The main restaurant itself has large windows overlooking Hong Kong's foremost drinking den.
✚ 207 D2 ⊠ 1 Lan Kwai Fong, Central ☎ 852 2801 5885; www.lankwaifong.com 🕐 Mon–Sat 12–2:30, 6:30–11, Sun 6:30–11

Café Deco $$$
The pan-Asian food served here is reasonable, but the real attraction is the spectacular view over Victoria Harbour. There's live jazz between 7pm and 11pm. Make reservations well ahead to be sure of snagging a window seat.
✚ 207 D2 ⊠ Level 1–2, Peak Galleria, 118 Peak Road, The Peak ☎ 852 2849 5111 🕐 Mon–Fri 11am–midnight, Sat 11am–1am, Sun 9:30am–midnight

Chunking Mansions $
This hideous heap of battered apartments houses the greatest concentration of cheap Indian restaurants in Hong Kong and can be a fun experience if you tire of the surrounding glitz and glam. C Block has a host of reliable eateries, including the **Delhi Club** (Flat C3, 3rd Floor; tel: 852 2368 1682; open daily 12–3, 6–11) and the **Swagat Restaurant** (Flat C3–C4, 1st Floor; tel: 852 2722 5350; open daily 12–10:30pm).
✚ 207 D3 ⊠ 36–44 Nathan Road, Kowloon

is the social buzz. As one of Hong Kong's least pretentious places, you won't find too many cool fashionistas here.
✚ 207 D3 ⊠ 41 Salisbury Road, Kowloon ☎ 852 2268 7888; www.ymcahk.org.hk

Pousada de São Tiago $$$
With similar prices, but a completely different atmosphere to the big casino complexes that now dominate the Macanese hotel scene, the Pousada de São Tiago is a traditional Portuguese-style inn on the grounds of the Barra Fortress, towards the tip of the Macau Peninsula. There are great balcony views over the Inner Harbour from each of the re-created, colonial-era rooms. The on-site Os Gatos restaurant is a destination in itself.
✚ 206 C2 ⊠ Fortaleza de São Tiago de Barra, Avenida da Republica, Macau ☎ 853 2837 8111; www.saotiago.com.mo

M at the Fringe $$$

One of Hong Kong's most celebrated restaurants, "Michelle's" is on the fringe of the Lan Kwai Fong area (hence the name) and has an ever-changing menu that is reliably tasty. Reserve ahead.

🕂 207 D2 ⊠ 1st Floor, South Block, Dairy Farm Builing, 2 Lower Albert Road, Central ☎ 852 2877 4000; www.m-atthefringe.com 🕒 Mon–Fri 12–2.30, 7–10.30, Sat–Sun 7–10.30pm

Maxim's Palace $$

No visit to Hong Kong is complete without a *yum cha* (literally, "drink tea") session. This important Cantonese social event is as much about the food as the tea. Steambasket dim sum snacks are wheeled around and you take them as they pass. Try the pork and shrimp *siu mai* or the glistening pork ribs. This dining hall in the heart of Central is a top spot in which to savour the very special atmosphere.

🕂 207 D2 ⊠ 3rd Floor, Hong Kong City Hall, 1 Edinburgh Place ☎ 852 2521 1303 🕒 Mon–Sat 11–3, Sun and public hols 9–3

Peninsula Hotel Lobby $$$

Experience the life of a British colonialist every afternoon in the lobby of Hong Kong's most historic hotel. Live orchestral music smoothes the way for cream tea and scones among the classical stone columns and creaking wooden furniture.

🕂 207 D3 ⊠ Peninsula Hotel, Salisbury Road, Kowloon ☎ 852 2920 2888; www.peninsula.com 🕒 Daily 2–7pm

Tai Ping Koon $

Tai Ping Koon is the pick of Causeway Bay's famed "soy sauce restaurants", which dress Western food up in a quintessentially Cantonese way. Dishes like eggs 'n' curry are served by grumpy waiters in white blazers and black ties.

🕂 207 D2 ⊠ 6 Pak Sha Road, Causeway Bay ☎ 852 2576 9161; www.taipingkoon.com 🕒 Daily 11am–11.45pm

The Verandah $$$

The restaurant of choice of Repulse Bay's moneyed residents offers European fine dining in an exotic seaside locale. The balcony area has fabulous views across the lawns towards Hong Kong's best sand beach, while the ceiling fans inside recall colonial days. The silver-service champagne brunch is particularly pleasant if you happen to be in town on a Sunday.

🕂 207 D2 ⊠ South Wing, Repulse Bay hotel, 109 Repulse Bay Road, Repulse Bay ☎ 852 2812 2722; www.therepulsebay.com 🕒 Tue–Sat 12–11pm, Sun 11–11. Closed Mon, except public hols

Water Margin $$$

The sleek antique wooden fixtures of Water Margin make a dramatic setting for Calvin Yeung's personalized takes on spicy tastes from Hunan and Sichuan.

🕂 207 D2 ⊠ Shop 1205, 12th Floor, Food Forum, Causeway Bay ☎ 852 3102 C088 🕒 Daily 12–3, 6–midnight

A Lorcha (The Sailboat) $$

This excellent Portugese restaurant, beside the A-Ma Temple, does great piri piri prawns and clams from the charcoal grill. The green- and white-checked tablecloths help to create a seaside Mediterranean vibe in this low-ceilinged, fishing village-style eatery.

🕂 206 C2 ⊠ 289 Rua do Almirante Sérgio ☎ 853 2831 3193 🕒 Wed–Mon 12:30–3, 6:30–11. Closed Tue

Casablanca Café $$

Enjoy a crisp green *vinho verde* wine at the Casablanca Café, an elegant watering hole with pictures of Hollywood and Hong Kong film icons decorating the walls. There are pool tables and cool jazz plays over the PA.

🕂 206 C2 ⊠ Ground Floor, Vista Magnifica Court Building, 1369–73 Avenida do Dr Sun Yat Sen ☎ 853 2875 1281 🕒 Daily 6pm–4am

Where to...
Shop

The Landmark (12–16 Des Voeux Road, Central; tel: 852 2525 4142; open daily 10:30–7:30), Hong Kong's trendiest mall, now houses nothing but five-star brands, including all the big names in luxury retail. It also boasts the first Asian branch of the London department store Harvey Nichols. Everything is gorgeous; everything is expensive.

Strung between the two huge International Finance Center (IFC) towers, the new **IFC Mall** (8 Finance Street, Central; tel: 852 2295 3308; open daily 10:30–10C) is open, spacious and has lots of natural light. Just about every major chain has an outlet here.

Lane Crawford, Hong Kong's answer to Harrod's, has its flagship store here. The Airport Express station is literally just downstairs.

The blue logo of **Sogo** (555 Hennessey Road, Causeway Bay; tel: 852 2833 8338; open daily 10–10) glows above the consumer throng on Hennessey Road. This Japanese-owned tower has 12 claustrophobic shopping floors, with an eclectic variety of largely independent stores, plus a relaxation zone at the top of the building.

The twin towers of **Times Square** (1 Matheson Street, Causeway Bay; tel: 852 2118 8900; open daily 10–10) rise to 46 and 39 storeys, the bottom 16 of which house a combination of international chains and local dealers. The stores are neatly organized by type. There are four floors of restaurants and a huge cinema complex, making it a popular all-round leisure destination

One of Hong Kong's newest attractive malls, **Festival Walk** (80–88 Tat Chee Avenue, Kowloon Tong; tel: 852 2844 2222; open daily 10am–midnight) is located immediately beside the Kowloon Tong metro interchange. It has the largest bookshop and cinema in town and a huge ice rink to boot.

The **Harbour City** shopping complex (3–9 Canton Road, Kowloon; tel: 852 2118 8666; open daily 10–9) comprises most of the western fringe of the Kowloon Peninsula and has four well-packed storeys. Something within the tangle is a ferry port where mainland-destined boats depart.

With around 300 stores spread over 15 storeys, **Langham Place** (8 Argyle Street, Mongkok; tel: 852 3520 2800; open daily 10:30am–11pm)is at the heart of an attempt to rejuvenate historically down-at-heel Mongkok. It attracts fewer tourists than some of the Hong Kong Island malls, but has a great energy. There is a branch of posh Japanese department store Seibu here, as well as a huge Muji store.

One of the most diverse and democratic of Hong Kong Island's malls, **Pacific Place** (88 Queensway, Admiralty; tel: 852 2844 8988; open daily 10:30am–11pm) has a variety of indie stores, including one owned by the Hong Kong-trained, New York-based designer Vivienne Tam.

Wyndham Street, Hollywood Road and **Upper Lascar Row** (aka Cat Street) have scores of antiques shops that sell everything from old typewriters and 1930s sunglasses to full-on Qing-dynasty furniture. The three-storey **Arch Angel** (53–55 Hollywood Road) is a trustworthy name. It stocks old mahjong sets, among a wealth of other goodies. **GOD** (48 Hollywood Road; tel: 852 2890 5555) has a catalogue that includes quirky notebooks printed with old Chinese archival photos. **Stanley Street** in Central is famous for its good-value and trustworthy photographic suppliers. For that extra bit of peace of mind, make the journey up to Mongkok to the reliable **Man Shing Photo Supplies** (106 Tung Choi Street; tel: 852 2396 2996).

Nathan Road and the surrounding streets in the southern part of Kowloon have the greatest concentration of tailors and jewellers in Hong Kong. Expect to be assailed by swish young Indian gentlemen as you wander along. **W W Chan and Sons** (2nd Floor, 92–94 Nathan Street; tel: 852 2366 2634) has an excellent reputation for bespoke suits, while **Pan Am Pearls** (9 Lock Road) is good for inexpensive pearls.

Bonham Strand West, stretching westwards from the Western Market in Sheung Wan, and nearby **Wing Lok Street** sell traditional roots and remedies, straight from the sack.

Youth culture breeds in the rabbit warren of stores at **Island Beverley**, close to Great George Street in Causeway Bay. It houses stacks of shop-cum-cubicles where up and coming designers ply their trade. For shoes and bags, check out **Lacoati** (Unit 829; tel: 852 2890 8628), while men might be more interested in nearby **No Name** (3rd Floor, Po Foo Building, 3–5 Foo Ming Street; tel: 852 2805 7728).

MARKETS

Western Market (New Market Street, Sheung Wan, open daily 10–7), dating from 1906 and the most "planned" of Hong Kong's many markets, has heaps of unique stores and a fun, festival atmosphere. The shops are more distinguished than your average market stall and there's plenty to interest the children.

Host to one of the most famous markets in Hong Kong, the former sleepy fishing village of Stanley throngs with tourists most days of the year. The scenic bus ride over the mountain is worth the trip alone. **Stanley Market** (open daily 9–6), meanwhile, is good for your standard Chinese knick-knacks and souvenirs, but it's difficult to find anything too precious here and it's very touristy.

Temple Street Night Market (near Jordan Road; open daily 4pm–midnight) is probably the most bustling flea market in Hong Kong and, unusually, geared almost exclusively towards men. You'll find a range of both new and used goods – everything from jeans and watches to DVD players. Fortune tellers and opera singers ply their trade at the southerly end of the market. There's also some great street food.

Often called the "Ladies Market" to distinguish it from the Temple Street Night Market which operates at similar times of the day, **Tung Choi Street Market** (Tung Choi Street; open daily 4pm–midnight) has a carnival atmosphere, with plenty of cheap clothes and fake designer goods, in addition to the usual cosmetics, jewellery and watches.

The **Jade Market** (Kansu and Battery streets; open daily 10–5) has some 400 stalls selling all manner of jade-inspired vanities. Many are licensed by the Hong Kong and Kowloon Jade Merchants Workers and Hawkers' Union Association, making it a reasonably safe place to buy. That said, you'll still need to bargain. Many stalls pack up as early as 3pm, so don't arrive too late.

Only a few metres from some of Hong Kong's trendiest shops are Li Yuen Street West and Li Yuen Street East, collectively known as **The Lanes** (open daily 10–7). These parallel alleys are a great place to buy knick-knacks and cheap clothing. The stalls are crowded, and you might well have to elbow your way to the front in order to properly rummage. If you're not planning a trip to mainland China, this is about the next best thing.

Where to...
Be Entertained

NIGHTLIFE

There are karaoke bars across Hong Kong, though – as on the mainland – many are fronts for prostitution. Causeway Bay has a couple of more classy outfits in the **Red Box** (9th Floor, Windsor House; tel: 852 2882 6188) and **Green Box** (8th Floor, Windsor House; tel: 852 2881 5088).

Hong Kong's most popular night-time hangout is the area around **Lan Kwai Fong** in Central. The fur-lined **C-Club** (Basement, California Tower, 30–32 D'Aguilar Street, Central; tel: 852 2526 1139) is a great place to head if you fancy a dance. All of the top hotels have smooth lounges. The **Champagne Bar** of the Grand Hyatt Hotel (Ground Floor, 1 Harbour Road, Wanchai; tel: 852 2588 1234, ext.7321) offers French fizz in sumptuous surrounds. There's live blues or jazz most evenings. The **Blue Bar** of the Four Seasons Hotel (IFC, 8 Finance Street, Central; tel: 852 3196 8888) is another low-lit and moody affair, with mosaic-tiled pillars and comfortable velvet-nipped lounge chairs and couches.

The **Fringe Club** (2 Lower Albert Street, Central; tel: 852 2521 7251; www.hkfringeclub.com) has some great alternative theatre, as well as dance and music events from local talent. The **Hong Kong Arts Centre** (2 Harbour Road, Wanchai; tel: 852 2582 0200; www.hkac.org.hk) is the strangely shaped building off Wanchai's shore. It has multiple auditoriums and a busy film and performing arts schedule. On the other side of the harbour is the **Hong Kong Cultural Centre** (10 Salisbury Road, Kowloon; tel: 852 2734 9009; www.hkculturalcentre.gov.hk), which stages regular music and theater performances.

CHILDREN'S ATTRACTIONS

Ocean Park (Ocean Park Road, Aberdeen, Hong Kong Island; tel: 852 2552 0291; www.oceanpark.com.hk; daily 10–6; expensive) is a huge aquarium and theme park. In addition to dolphins, sea lions and seals, there are four giant pandas.

Hong Kong Disneyland (Lantau Island; tel: 852 1 830830 for tickets; expensive; under-3s free) is a smaller version of the original Disneyland park in California. Tickets are valid for six months from the date of purchase and can be bought online and picked up at the gate. The park generally opens from 10am to 8pm, though times do vary.

The highlight of the Ngong Ping 360 (www.np360.com.hk) is the **Skyrail cable car** (Mon–Fri 10–6, Sat–Sun 10–6:30). The "Journey of Enlightenment Package" includes a return trip and entry to Ngong Ping Village's Walking with Buddha and Monkey's Tale Theatre attractions, close to the peak on Lantau Island. A return on the cable car costs HK$88; one-way HK$58. There are discounts for children under 12.

RACING

Hong Kong race meetings are held at **Sha Tin's New Territories** race-track most weekends (Sep–Jun). There are normally 10 races on the card, the first beginning around 1pm. The course at **Happy Valley** on Hong Kong Island is surrounding by glittering residential tower blocks. Meetings are held most Wednesdays. The first of eight races normally begins at 7:30pm. Entry to both is inexpensive (www.hkjc.com). **Macau** also puts on greyhound racing and less regular horse racing meetings.

The Southwest

Getting Your Bearings 116 – 117
In Two Weeks 118 – 119
Don't Miss 120 – 128
At Your Leisure 129 – 132
Where to... 133 – 136

Getting Your Bearings

Southwest China is where the factories end and the fun begins. Compared to the industrial landscapes and homogenous Han culture of the eastern half of China, the multicultural southwest comes as something of a revelation. The provinces of Guangxi, Guizhou, Hunan and Yunnan – as well as Chongqing Municipality – are home to soaring rice terraces, snowy mountain peaks, spectacular gorges and lush rain forests, as well as nearly all of China's 55 minority groups.

Guangxi's shining jewel is Guilin, a city hemmed in by a mesmerizing forest of karst limestone mountains – just one of the region's geological marvels. More than a third of the province's population is ethnically Zhuang, thus Guangxi is officially a "Zhuang Autonomous Region".

According to local legend, "It doesn't go for more than three days without raining in Guizhou and there's hardly a square metre of flat land". These testing conditions explain why the province has historically been dismissed as an irrelevant, impoverished backwater. But those same drawbacks for locals make it a spectacular find for tourists. Its mountains are raw and its rivers and waterfalls grateful for the downpours.

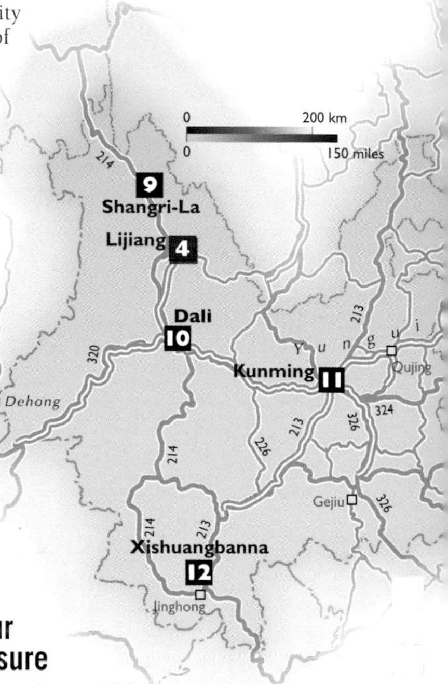

0   200 km

0   150 miles

214

9

Shangri-La

Lijiang **4**

Dali

10

320

Kunming **11**

Dehong

213

Qujiu

y   u   n   g

324

214

226

213

336

Gejiu

214   213

Xishuangbanna

12

Jinghong

336

★ Don't Miss

1 Guilin and Yangshuo
  ➤ 120
2 Wulingyuan ➤ 122
3 The Three Gorges ➤ 124
4 Lijiang ➤ 127

Page 115: Black Dragon Pool, with Jade Dragon Snow Mountain behind

At Your Leisure

5 Zhaoxing ➤ 129
6 Fenghuang ➤ 129
7 Chongqing ➤ 129
8 Dazu Rock Carvings
  ➤ 130
9 Shangri-La ➤ 130
10 Dali ➤ 131
11 Kunming ➤ 131
12 Xishuangbanna ➤ 132

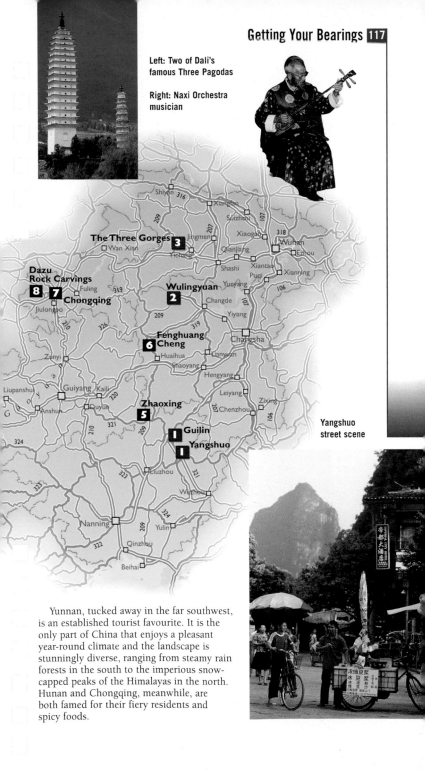

Left: Two of Dali's famous Three Pagodas

Right: Naxi Orchestra musician

Shiyan 316

Xiangfan

Suizhou

209 207 107

The Three Gorges **3**

Jingmen Xiaogan 318

Wan Xian Yichang Qianjiang Wuhan

Shashi Xiantao Ezhou

Dazu Rock Carvings **8** **7** Fuling 319

Yueyang Puqi Xianning

Wulingyuan **2** 106

Chongqing Changde

Jiulongpo Zunyi 209 Yiyang

326

Fenghuang **6** Cheng 319 Changsha

Huaihua Lianyuan

Shaoyang

Liupanshui Guiyang Kaili Hengyang

Anshun Duyun 320 Leiyang Zixing

321 Zhaoxing **5** Chenzhou 106

209 207

324 Guilin **1**

Yangshuo **1**

Yangshuo street scene

Liuzhou 321

Wuzhou

Nanning 209

322 Yulin

Qinzhou 324

Beihai

Yunnan, tucked away in the far southwest, is an established tourist favourite. It is the only part of China that enjoys a pleasant year-round climate and the landscape is stunningly diverse, ranging from steamy rain forests in the south to the imperious snow-capped peaks of the Himalayas in the north. Hunan and Chongqing, meanwhile, are both famed for their fiery residents and spicy foods.

Southwest China comprises a vast, mountainous area. The following is a suggested whistle-stop tour, but those travelling independently may want to take extra rest days in the scenic towns of Lijiang or Yangshuo.

The Southwest in Two Weeks

Days One and Two

From Hong Kong, Shanghai or Guangzhou, take an evening flight to Zhangjiajie (left) and rise early to take full advantage of **2 Wulingyuan's** (➤ 122–123) two-day entrance ticket. On day one, take the cable car to Huangshizhai peak, before walking the riverside path through the valley. On day two, ride the Bailong Lift up to Yongjiajie. Walk beside the canyon ridge before taking a bus to the park's highest point, Tianzi Shan, from where you can take a cable car back down to ground level.

Day Three

Take the train to **Yichang**. The No 1474 departs Zhangjiajie at 11:04am and arrives in Yichang just before 6pm. Consider buying a "hard sleeper" ticket, which allows you to stretch out and enjoy the countryside roll by. Avoid the upper berth, which has no window. Many Yangtze cruises allow passengers on board the evening before the trip begins. Check in advance.

Days Four, Five and Six

The first day is normally spent visiting the Three Gorges Dam (left), travelling through the giant lock system, and passing through the first of the **3 Three Gorges** (➤ 124–126). The remaining gorges are passed on day two. Day three is spent making a leisurely approach to **7 Chongqing** (➤ 129).

Day Seven

Explore Chongqing, then take an evening flight to **4 Lijiang** (➤ 127–128).

Day Eight

Take a morning stroll around **Black Dragon Pool Park** and climb Elephant Hill. Spend the afternoon and evening wandering around the canals of the **Old Town** before enjoying Xuan Ke's evening orchestral performance.

Day Nine

Scale **Jade Dragon Snow Mountain** via the cable car and donkey. If time allows, visit **Tiger Leaping Gorge** (right) in the afternoon.

Day Ten

Take the short flight to **10 Kunming** (➤ 131). Explore China's Spring City, then in the evening, watch the performance of **Dynamic Yunnan** (➤ 136).

Day Eleven

Fly to **8 Guilin** (➤ 120–121). Explore **Seven Star Park** before taking a boat to **Elephant Trunk Hill** in the afternoon.

Day Twelve

Take a day-long cruise to **9 Yangshuo** (➤ 121). Hang out on **West Street** in the evening.

Day Thirteen

Rent a bicycle to explore the countryside around Yangshuo (right). Check out the performance of **Impression Liu Sanjie** in the evening.

Day Fourteen

Bus it back to Guilin, stopping off at the **Yuzi Paradise** sculpture park. From Guilin you can take connecting flights or trains to Guangzhou, Hong Kong, Shanghai or Beijing, or explore the **minority villages** in **Guizhou**.

☐ Guilin and Yangshuo

An endless horizon of sugarloaf-shaped mountains is the visual treat awaiting visitors to this corner of Guangxi province. These conical clumps of karst limestone encircle the region's towns and cities, line the rivers and paddy fields and have left generation after generation baffled, bewildered and thoroughly enchanted.

Guilin was once a walled city, but destruction at the hands of the Japanese in World War II, and a drab modernization program, have left the city undistinguished amid its stunning mountain surrounds. The real sights are of nature's making.

Weird and Wonderful Rocks

Perhaps the most accessible of the karst towers is the 152m-tall (498-foot) **Solitary Beauty Peak** (Duxiu Feng), standing alone right in the middle of the city. A restored Ming-dynasty (AD 1368–1644) royal palace lies at the bottom of the steep stairway that leads to the top. **Folded Brocade Hill** (Diecai Shan), in the northeast of the city, is also easy to reach and offers sweeping views of the city and Li River. The hill has several pretty Buddhist altars, built between the 10th and 13th centuries, and the climb is slightly easier than Solitary Beauty Peak. Both peaks have a small entrance charge.

Seven Star Park (Qixing Gongyuan), just across the Li River from the city, has many attractive trails that wind around its seven peaks. The park's Seven Star Cave is one of many in the region. The stalactites and stalagmites are impressive, but the gaudy neon lighting tends to overwhelm the senses.

On the river just south of town is Guilin's most famous crag. **Elephant Trunk Hill** (Xiangbi Shan) is so named for the crag's resemblance to an elephant stooping to drink from the river water. Take a boat or bicycle from Guilin and – as always – expect to pay an entrance charge.

Slow Boat to Yangshuo

Perhaps the best way to enjoy Guilin's spectacular scenery is by taking a **Li River cruise** to Yangshuo, a backpacking magnet 60km (37 miles) south of the city. This once tranquil waterway is now more like a marine highway

owing to the number of tourist craft, but this in itself is quite a spectacle. The cruise traces a meandering route past bamboo groves, picturesque farms and karst peaks. Keep your eyes peeled around the village of **Xingping**. The view from the river bend here is the image on the back of the 20RMB note.

Tourist boats only run from Guilin to Yangshuo, with passengers taken back to Guilin by bus. It's worth stopping in Yangshuo. The town lies on a well-trodden backpacker trail through southern China and the town's café, restaurant and shop owners cater well for Western tastes. **West Street** (Xi Jie) is the place to enjoy the ambience. You can also rent a bicycle here and cycle around the surrounding countryside. Or jump into a hot-air balloon for a completely different perspective on the remarkable landscapes.

TAKING A BREAK

Yangshuo's **West Street** is full of funky cafés, bars and restaurants. The **Meiyou Café** at No 86 is great fun. Across the street is the **Le Votre** French restaurant (➤ 135).

Guilin
✚ 199 E2

Seven Star Park
✉ 1 Qixing Lu ☎ 0773 280 3000
🕐 Daily 6am–7:30pm 💷 Moderate
🚌 Buses 6, 10, 11, 14, 58

Li River Cruises
✉ Cruises begin at Zhujiang Pier, 20km (12.5 miles) southeast of Guilin ☎ 0773 282 5502 💷 Very expensive (includes lunch on boat). Buy tickets in advance at the ticket office on Fuwang Jie (close to the Zhongshan Hotel). Tickets including return transport can also be booked from your hotel 🕐 Departures at 8:40am, 9:20am and 10:10am

Above: Rice fields below Yangshuo's rocky cliffs

Right: Elephant Trunk Hill (Xiangbi Shan)

Yangshuo
✚ 199 E2

GUILIN AND YANGSHUO: INSIDE INFO

Top tips If you stay overnight in Yangshuo, don't miss the amazing **Impression Liu Sanjie** performance. This Cirque du Soleil-style extravaganza takes place in a spectacular open-air venue on the Li River close to Yangshuo.
• There are several simple **guest houses** along the riverside promenade at the bottom of West Street in Yangshuo. Many have fantastic balcony views.

Hidden gem Longsheng township, a few hours north of Guilin, is home to some amazing rice terraces and minority villages. It's worth a day trip.

② Wulingyuan

Wulingyuan – or Zhangjiajie, as it is colloquially known – is the natural reflection of China's high-rise cities. Thousands of rock columns rise precipitously from a deep valley, each a gravity defying compression of slate decorated in patches of green. This stunning national park in northwest Hunan has claims on the top spot in China's formidable list of geological oddities. Unfortunately the park's uniqueness is reflected in the price – it's the most expensive reserve in the land.

The ticket buys two days' entry to Wulingyuan, as well as free use of the bus network inside the park. As with many of China's paid-for parks, locals receive a free entry permit. If an entrepreneurial resident offers you a temporary loan, refuse. The electronic fingerprinting machines at the ticket gates weed out ticket dodgers easily.

Wulingyuan is divided into three sections: Zhangjiajie Forest Park in the south, Tianzi Mountain in the north and Suoxi Valley in the west. Each has its own ticket gate and town. **Zhangjiajie** is the largest area and the entire park is often referred to by this name. To add to the confusion, the town at the **Suoxi Valley** is now known as "Wulingyuan." Each of the three areas is connected by pathways, while shuttle buses ferry visitors between the lookout points and entry gates.

Top right: Zhangjiajie Forest Park

Above: The multiple peaks of Tianzi (Heavenly Mountain)

The Pinnacles Close up

Though the park can get seriously busy, hiking trails allow you to get away from the crowds. The walkway along the luxuriant valley floor is an absolute must. The paved trail follows the pathway cut by the **Jinbian Stream** (Jinbian Xi) and every so often a gap emerges in the forest canopy presenting a dizzying view up towards the mountain peaks.

Stone staircases allow fitter visitors to climb to the peaks, though there are mechanized alternatives. The **Bailong Lift** (Bailong Dianti) is an unmissable novelty. Cited in the *Guinness Book of World Records* as the largest outdoor elevator in the world, it whisks you up 326m (1,070 feet) in 118 seconds and provides jaw-dropping views. From here it's a

short bus ride to the spectacular cliffside walkways of **Yuanjiajie**, where there are more vertiginous views. One of the man-made bridges makes use of a grilled walkway through which hikers can stare 300m (1,000 feet) down to the valley floor. Farther on is the **Highest Natural Bridge in the World** (Tiansheng Qiao), a 40m (130-foot) arch which connects the canyon wall with one of the freestanding outcrops

Buses run from Yuanjiajie all the way to the highest point in the park, the **Tianzi Mountain** (Tianzi Shan). The lookouts here take in a sea of peaks, but there are no sheer drops and – in many ways – the views lower down are more spectacular. A cable car ferries visitors from Tianzi back down to ground level.

Thanks to the internal transport, it's possible to explore virtually the entire park in two days. As at all of China's most spectacular scenic locales, you must try to outsmart the weather. The peaks look radiant against a clear blue sky, but unfortunately they are often smothered in low-lying fog and mist.

TAKING A BREAK

Hunan food is famously spicy. Simple family-run restaurants are clustered around each entrance to the park. Food inside the park is scarce, so consider packing a **picnic**.

Wulingyuan Scenic Reserve

➕ 199 E3 ✉ Park entrance is 30km (18 miles) from Zhangjiajie city, Hunan province ☎ 0744 571 2595 ⏰ 24 hours 🎫 Expensive (two days' entry); cable cars and lift moderate for one-way trip 🚌 Regular public buses to park entrance. Taxis moderate 🚆 Zhangjiajie city ✈ Zhangjiajie city

Huanglong Cave

✉ 10km (6 miles) east of Wulingyuan town ☎ 0744 561 2132 ⏰ Daily 8–5:30 🎫 Moderate 🚌 Tourist bus runs between Tianzi Mountain, Wulingyuan town and Huanglong Cave

---

WULINGYUAN: INSIDE INFO

Top tips The guides who lead the tour groups rarely leave meals to chance and by 5pm most have begun their search for their evening sustenance.
• Anyone aching for a private moment with the mountains should stay inside the park until **dusk**, when the groups have gone.

Hidden gem Yellow Dragon Cave (Huanglong Dong), a few kilometres east of Wulingyuan town, is reckoned to be one of the 10 largest caves in China. The stalagmites decorating the cavernous interiors are spectacular.

❸ The Three Gorges

Lying in the mid-reaches of the third longest river on earth, the Three Gorges have been shortened by more than 80m (262 feet) since the Yangtze was controversially dammed in 2003. Nevertheless, these natural corridors of sheer rock faces and towering mountains remain spectacular, and a cruise past them is the perfect remedy for anyone feeling the effects of eastern China's ceaseless hustle and bustle.

There are scores of different cruise ships that sail the Yangtze River, each with individual itineraries. Some boats sail all the way from Shanghai to Chongqing, though most ships now limit themselves to the more spectacular passage between the Three Gorges Dam, near Yichang, and Chongqing. The following description assumes you begin your cruise at the Three Gorges and head upriver.

Engineering Feat

The **Three Gorges Dam** is the largest hydroelectric dam in the world and a worthy sight in itself, so ensure your cruise allows plenty of time for a shore excursion. Construction finished in May 2006 and tourists can now walk along the top of the 185m-high (605-foot) structure. It's also worth heading up to the **Tanziling Ridge**, between the southern river bank and the lock system, from where you can take in the entire Three Gorges Dam panorama – earth and sky, steel and concrete.

The ride through the colossal **lock system** has become one of the most popular aspects

Longmen, one of the Daning River's Lesser Three Gorges

Sampans

For a long while, sampans were the only vessels that could cope with the Three Gorges shallow waters and rapids. When the going got tough, these ragged, rib-sailed boats were hauled by hand over the rocks by "trackers" who made use of walkways carved into the rock face. These old carved pathways have since disappeared under the rising water.

of any Yangtze cruise. Smaller boats make use of the one-stage vertical lift, but most tour boats still scrum for room alongside the cargo ships in the main series of five locks. Taking in the industrial ambience from the deck of your ship is an oddly pleasing experience.

Through the Gorges

The dam lies roughly in the middle of the 75km-long (47-mile) **Xiling Gorge**, thus making a "Three Gorges Cruise" something of a misnomer as it's actually two-and-a-half. As the river widens towards the gorge's end, the boat passes over the submerged village of **Xintan**. This was once the location of the Three Gorges' most fearsome rapid.

Some distance upriver is the **Wu Gorge**. At 40km (25 miles) in length, it straddles the border between Hubei province and Chongqing Municipality. Its beauty is very much in its bleakness. Forested slopes rise to form jagged mountain peaks with little if any trace of human habitation. The Chinese have a great love of weaving legends around natural phenomena and, consequently, have singled out 12 mountains around which stories have been strung. Look for **Goddess Peak**. It soars more than 900m (2,950 feet) above the river and is surmounted by a 7m-high (23-foot) stone column, said to be the figure of a kneeling maiden.

> ## THE THREE GORGES: INSIDE INFO
>
> **Top tip** There are **four distinct classes** of local cruise tickets. A fourth-class berth comprises a bed in a large (often smoky) dormitory. A first-class ticket buys a bed in a twin room with TV, air-conditioning and ensuite facilities. Standards on these local vessels are lower than on the more expensive cruise ships that cater mainly for foreign tourists, but for the budget-conscious, the vastly reduced costs may make it a worthwhile sacrifice.

The city of **New Wushan** is at the confluence of the Daning River and the Yangtze ("old" Wushan is now underwater). It's worth pausing here for a tour of the Daning's **Lesser Three Gorges**, a narrower, more compact version of the (Greater) Three Gorges. In the second gorge (Bawu), look for one of the famous "hanging coffins" placed on a ledge high in the rock face by a member of the now-extinct Ba tribe. Tour guides often say the coffin is 2,000 years old, though sceptics reckon it may have gone up as late as the 16th century, when the history of the Ba people peters out. The final "lesser" gorge (Dicui) is notable for its population of **rhesus monkeys**, visible on the riverbank.

At just 8km (5 miles) long, the **Qu Gorge** is the shortest but most spectacular of the Three Gorges, with some mountain peaks more than 1,000m (3,280 feet) above the river. As you exit the Qu Gorge, be sure to glance back over your shoulder. This view is the image that adorns China's 10RMB note.

The river now becomes wider and less dramatic. Some 200km (124 miles) upriver is the **Shibaozhai** (Precious Stone Fortress) Temple, a 12-storey, red pagoda that dates from the reign of Emperor Qianlong (18th century). By now, it too should be partly underwater, but it has been protected by a dyke. Further west is **Fengdu**, or the "Ghost City". Most of the city was torn down ahead of the dam construction, but a single temple remains. This spot serves as a poignant reminder of the 1.3 million people who have lost their homes to the Yangtze's rising water.

TAKING A BREAK

Food is normally available on **board**, and on the most expensive boats, it is often included in the price of the tour.

✚ 199 E4 ⊚ Downriver from Chongqing to Yichang takes 3 days/2 nights; upriver from Yichang to Chongqing takes 4 days/3 nights. Times vary according to which shore excursions are made ⊌ Very expensive

A boat leaving the Three Gorges Dam

④ Lijiang

Lijiang's Old Town divides opinion. The high concentration of coffee shops, pizza parlours and resort-style bars make it a comfortable place to wind down after experiencing the raw Chinese hinterland. Others say these "attractions" prove Lijiang has sold out to the tourist dollar. What remains beyond doubt is the breathtaking beauty of both town and surrounds. Located in the lee of the mighty Jade Dragon Snow Mountain and constructed in timber around a network of murmuring brooks, Lijiang is about as picture-perfect as China gets.

Lijiang is in northwest Yunnan, close to Tibet and Myanmar (Burma). The city is divided into old and new sections, the larger New Town being as forgettable as the 800-year-old **Old Town** is beautiful. Dominating both is the looming presence of the 5,600m (18,400-foot) **Jade Dragon Snow Mountain** (Yulong Xueshan), a rugged, snow-capped peak which rises with Himalayan grandeur from the sweeping valley.

View over the rooftops of Lijiang's Old Town

Naxi City

Lijiang is home to the Naxi, one of China's most fascinating minority groups, whose written language uses one of the few pictographic scripts still in existence. Despite its international flavour, the Old Town is brimming with Naxi charm from its traditional paper-making factories to the many craft shops. The **Dayan Naxi Concert Hall** on Dong Dajie sees local Naxi legend Xuan Ke host daily concerts of traditional orchestral music. Shows begin at 8pm.

Lijiang remains lively at night. The riverside **Xinhua Jie** is designated "bar street". At night, groups of Naxi girls sing, clap and giggle as they entice customers into their particular watering hole. The sound of running water harmonizes with the singing and the whole scene is bathed in a soft red light.

A short walk from the Old Town is **Black Dragon Pool Park** (60RMB). The view of the pool, pavilion and snow-capped peak beyond is one of the most photographed perspectives in China. Near by is **Elephant Hill**. The climb is testing but the view of Jade Dragon Snow Mountain from the peak pavilion is truly outstanding.

Jade Dragon Snow Mountain

A trip to the mountain itself should not be missed. There are two cable cars. The first takes you roughly half way up the mountain where the road intersects with a horse trail. To continue from here, either take a second chairlift – the highest in Asia – or hire a donkey. Both will deliver you to stunning **Yak Meadow** (Maoniuping). From an elevation of 4,500m (14,765 feet), the 13 snowy peaks seem almost within touching distance.

Just north of the mountain is **Tiger Leaping Gorge** (50RMB), a 16km-long (10-mile) canyon carved by the Nordic-blue waters of the Yangtze. Buses drive

deep into the gorge to a car park above the most famous of the canyon's huge boulders – the point at which the eponymous tiger is said to have leapt across the water to escape a hunter. Jade Dragon Snow Mountain lurks menacingly behind the row of cliffs.

TAKING A BREAK

Mishi, at 52 Xinyi Jie, has a great choice of snacks, from pizza to deep-fried insects.

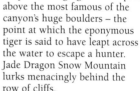 198 B3 Old Town: free, moderate ticket allows combined entry to main tourist sights Lijiang's airport is around 25km (15.5 miles) outside town

Jade Dragon Snow Mountain
 35km (22 miles) north of Lijiang
 0888 516 2707 24 hours. Cable cars 8–5:30 (approximately)
 Expensive Public buses from Lijiang. Taxi expensive

Tiger Leaping Gorge

At Your Leisure

5 Zhaoxing

Zhaoxing is the largest of the many Dong villages that pepper the rice-terraced hills of Guizhou's southeastern fringe. The village is divided into five sections, each belonging to a different Dong clan and each with its own wooden drum tower and Wind and Rain Bridge. These attractive bridges function as lively outdoor social clubs, capable of standing up to anything Guizhou's temperamental weather can throw at them – hence the name. Under the ornately designed roofs, old men tell long, slow stories and play fast games of chess. Evening cultural performances feature choral singing and *lusheng* bamboo pipe music. Tourism is still in its infancy in this part of Guizhou so there is less of a stage-managed feel to these villages than elsewhere.

➕ 199 E2 ✉ Guizhou province
🚌 Fast buses connect Guiyang with Kaili and Guilin with Sanjiang. Slow local buses then make the onward trip to Zhaoxing ✈ Nearest airports are in Guiyang and Guilin

6 Fenghuang

Phoenix Town, in west Hunan, is a great spot to sample the traditional way of life of China's Miao minority. Traditional stilted dwellings rise like mist from the emerald-green Tuojiang River, where women squat to wash clothes and men fish with hand-woven nets. The huge, yellow-hued **Rainbow Bridge** marks the centre of town, while a network of pretty alleys radiates outward. These are filled with shops, cafés and restaurants similar to those in Yangshuo or Lijiang. The local specialist handicrafts include hand-made silver jewellery and tie-dyed, printed or batik cloth. A short bus ride west of town is the **Great Wall of South China**. This remarkable 150km-long (93-mile) wall was built into the hilly countryside in the 16th century. It's not quite as grand as the real thing, but not too shoddy either.

➕ 199 E3 ✉ Near Jishou, Hunan province 🚌 Local buses take 90 minutes to reach Fenghuang from the nearest station at Jishou ✈ Nearest airport is Zhangjiajie

7 Chongqing

On paper Chongqing (Chungking) is home to some 30 million people, making it the biggest city in the world. What the statistics don't say is that the "municipality" is actually the size of a small province. The urban centre of this huge tract of land has been built into the steep hillsides around two huge waterways – the Yangtze and the Jialing. Two **cableways** connect the riverbanks and offer great views of the downtown high-rises, stacked up on a narrow peninsula at the rivers' confluence.

Looking back towards Chongqing from a ferry boat on the Yangtze

As the main launching point for Yangtze cruises, Chongqing receives a huge number of visitors, but few linger. This is a pity, because despite the lack of major sights this high-octane city is one of the best places to observe the contrasts of modern China. As the economic powerhouse of the southwest, the city absorbs millions of migrants who spend their nights in the ghoulish grey tenement blocks and their days building towering skyscrapers. Most of the visible history concerns World War II, when Chongqing acted as capital of the anti-Japanese coalition. The **Stillwell Museum** honours the American soldiers who helped to repel Japan's regular air raids.

Don't leave town without trying the local culinary speciality. Chongqing's chilli-infused hot pot has achieved national notoriety for its tongue-numbing kick.

➕ 199 D3 ✉ Chongqing Municipality

8 Dazu Rock Carvings

This extensive network of Buddhist grottoes is 100km (60 miles) north-west of Chongqing, right on the municipality's border with Sichuan. This protected UNESCO world heritage site has a total of 50,000 carvings dating from the Tang and Song dynasties (AD 618–1279), which unfold over an idyllic landscape of rolling hills and red earth. Of the two major sites, **Beishan** is the most accessible from Dazu city. Located 2km (1.2 miles) north of town, the site has 290 separate grottoes. Many of the statues have deteriorated badly, but there are a few that remain in good condition.

Baodingshan, 15km (9 miles) northeast of Dazu, requires more of an effort but the reward is a far superior collection of statues. The highlight is the 31m-long (100-foot) "Reclining Buddha". You may decide a trip is unnecessary if you have already visited the older cave carvings in Dunhuang or Luoyang. However, unlike those sites, the carvings here are singularly Chinese in style and represent the development of China's own unique Buddhist culture.

➕ 199 D3 ✉ Chongqing Municipality
🚌 Daily buses from Chengdu and Chongqing

9 Shangri-La

The brand-conscious Chinese have a history of renaming towns, cities and even whole districts in the hope of increasing tourist turnover. The most high profile example is the town-formerly-known-as-Zhongdian, which suddenly became "Shangri-La" some time around 2000. Claimed to be the inspiration for James Hilton's classic novel *Lost Horizon*, Shangri-La is an ethnically Tibetan outpost 3,200m (10,500 feet) above sea level in the far north of Yunnan province. Surrounded by grand Himalayan peaks, it's notable for the 17th-century **Songzanlin Lamasery**, a crucible of Tibetan Buddhism modelled on the Potala Palace in Lhasa.

Following Lijiang's successful example, Shangri-La has also built itself a new **"Old Town"**. Hewn from timber, the area has become a Tibetan-themed leisure park presided over by a cosmopolitan community of bar-owners and restaurateurs. Nevertheless, like Lijiang, development has been tasteful and the mood remains evocative.

A few kilometres outside town, close to the Banyan Tree Ringha hotel, is the **Dabao Temple**, a place of pilgrimage for locals blighted by illness. It's believed the release of a prize goat or lamb here will relieve suffering. The temple has a wonderful riot of prayer flags strung between surrounding pine trees.

🔢 198 B3 ✉ Yunnan province
✈ Shangri-La has a small airport with regular flights to Kunming and a handful of weekly flights to Tibet

you'll be able to enjoy the sumptuous sartorial results of the locals' embroidery and tie-dying skills. Dali's most famous landmark is the **Three Pagoda Temple**. Originally built during the peak of the 9th century Nanzhao Kingdom, these soaring structures, just north of town, were destroyed by fire in the 19th century and rebuilt in 1978.

Five kilometres (3 miles) east of Dali is **Caicun**, a small port on the banks of Lake Erhai. From here, local ferries criss-cross the lake.

🔢 198 B2 ✉ Yunnan province
🚌 A bus from Kunming to Dali takes up to 10 hours ✈ Xiaguan has a small airport with daily flights to provincial capital Kunming

🔢 Kunming

It may not be the most inspired city in China, but Kunming is almost certainly the "nicest" of the country's provincial capitals. Its orderly streets and green parks are a far cry from the cluttered chaos of the eastern metropolises. Known as the "Spring City" thanks to its mild

🔟 Dali

Before being conquered by the Mongol armies of Kublai Khan in the 13th century, Dali was the capital of the powerful Nanzhao Kingdom. This ancient land included Yunnan and larges swathes of modern-day Myanmar and Laos. Little remains to remind visitors of this turbulent, glorious past. On the contrary, Dali is best known as China's original hippy hangout – a quiet town at the base of the Cangshan Mountain Range. Like Lijiang and Shangri-La, Dali has an **old town** with the requisite cobbled streets and chill-out cafés. The "new town", meanwhile, is a soulless place, alternatively known as Xiaguan or Dali City.

Old Dali is a great base from which to explore outlying traditional Bai villages such as **Xizhou**, where

The entrance to Kunming's Taoist Golden Temple (Jin Dian)

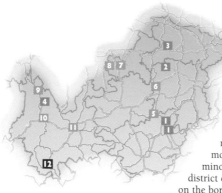

310 7859 ⌧ Excellent domestic air connections and international flights to Singapore, Bangkok and Seoul

12 Xishuangbanna

With their gold-capped teeth, wild tattoos and gaudy make-up, the Dai may well be one of the more distinctive of China's 55 minority nationalities. The district of Xishuangbanna, located on the border with Myanmar (Burma) and Laos, is home to around 400,000 of these colourful people, who live among lush forests and exotic wildlife. The regional capital, **Jinghong**, is a picturesque and easily accessible tourist hub that provides the focus for the Thai-influenced **Water Splashing Festival** that takes place 13–15 April.

For more authentic local flavour, head out to one of the Dai villages that surround Jinghong. **Ganlanba**, the most accessible of these, has examples of traditional stilted houses that have been built above the brown waters of the Lancang (Mekong) River, the lifeblood of the region.

✚ 198 B1 ⌧ Yunnan province
⌧ Several daily flights between Jinghong and Kunming

winters and temperate summers, Kunming is chiefly seen as a launch pad for trips to Yunnan's mountainous north or subtropical south. However, it's worth spending a day or so relaxing in the city. **Green Lake Park** is a lovely spot, famed for its resident poplation of white doves. There are some excellent cafés on the periphery of the park, well patronized by Kunming's large population of international students.

One of the highlights of any visit is a trip to the Kunming Huitang theatre to watch Dynamic Yunnan (► 136), a song and dance performance of amazing energy and captivating grace that portrays the indigenous traditions of the province's 26 minority groups (Mon–Sat 8pm, tickets expensive).

✚ 198 C2 ⌧ Yunnan province
☎ Tourist Information Centre: 0871

Yunnan women selling colourful traditional crafts and fabrics

Where to... Stay

Prices
Expect to pay per double room per night, including breakfast and taxes
$** under 400RMB   **$$** 400–1,000RMB   **$$$ over 1,000RMB

CHONGQING

Hilton Chongqing $$
The Hilton Chongqing offers a slice of Shanghai class in the middle of the Chinese hinterland, with spacious rooms (some with views of the river), top-notch restaurants, a spa and an indoor pool.
➕ 199 D3 ⊠ 139 Zhongshan Sanlu, Yu Zhong District ☎ 023 8903 9909; www.hilton.com

GUILIN

Hotel of Modern Art (HOMA) $$
This extraordinary hotel is located within the grounds of Yuzi Paradise, China's first dedicated showcase for modern art, and houses 200-plus sculptures by a number of international artists. The pyramid-shaped hotel at its centre has been renovated. The expansive grounds have great cycling and hiking routes.
➕ 199 E2 ⊠ Dabu Town, Yanshan District (midway between Guilin and Yangshuo) ☎ 0773 386 5555; www.relaischateaux.com

Lijiang Waterfall Hotel $$$
This huge hotel in the middle of Guilin boasts one of China's more peculiar hospitality gimmicks – the world's largest man-made waterfall. Every evening water tumbles 45m (28ft) from the roof, passing guest windows on the way down. More prosaically, there's a rooftop fitness room and four decent restaurants.
➕ 199 E2 ⊠ 1 Shanhu Beilu, Guilin ☎ 0773 282 2881; www.waterfallguilin.com

LIJIANG

Zen Garden Hotel $
This charming Old Town hotel has a teahouse for a lobby. There are two floors of rooms which overlook a tranquil courtyard and, from the top level, guests can look out over the roofs of the Old Town. There's no air-conditioning, but electric blankets are provided in winter.
➕ 198 B3 ⊠ 36 Wuyi Jie, Xingren, Old Town, Lijiang ☎ 0888 518 9799; www.zengardenhotel.com

SHANGRI-LA

Banyan Tree Ringha $$$
This magical resort was built from the recycled wood of old Tibetan farmhouses that were dismantled and reconstructed, log by log, to create a series of stand-alone villas, high in the mountains of northern Yunnan. The interiors of the 32 suites and lodges are decorated with contemporary Tibetan art. There's guided hiking in the mountains and one of China's best spas (some of the staff are Thai).
➕ 198 B3 ⊠ Shangri-La, Hang Po Village ☎ 0887 828 8822; www.banyantree.com

WULINGYUAN

Xiangdian International Hotel $$
This comfortable hotel, one of the best in Wulingyuan (Zhangjiajie), lies a few minutes' walk from the southern entrance to Hunan's famous scenic reserve. Rooms are based around a series of peaceful courtyards and the glass-domed roof of the Chinese Restaurant has views of the mountain peaks.
➕ 199 E3 ⊠ Zhangjiajie Forest Park, Wulingyuan ☎ 0744 571 2999; www.xiangdianhotel.com.cn

Where to...
Eat and Drink

Prices

Expect to pay for a meal for one, excluding drinks

$ under 50RMB $$ 50–150RMB $$$ over 150RMB

Xiao Tian E (Little Swan) $

This is one of Chongqing's finest all-you-can-eat hot pot chains. The huge dining hall can become very lively at meal times with (loud) Sichuanese singing and "face changing" performances staged between 7 and 8pm. There are menus in English and private rooms in case the atmosphere gets too overwhelming.

✚ 199 D3 ☒ 6th Floor, Xin Chongqing Guangchang, 22 Minzu Lu ☎ 023 6378 8811 ⚙ Daily 8:30am–11pm

Blue Papaya $

Tasty Italian, Chinese and vegetarian dishes are the staples of the Blue Papaya. The owner speaks good English and also runs a Tibetan antiques business on the side. There's a store beside the main dining room. The associated Blue Papaya Cultural Exchange Academy works to promote greater understanding of local Dongba (Naxi) culture and has lectures and lessons in yoga, tai chi and meditation.

✚ 198 B2 ☒ 50 Guan Men, Old Town ☎ 0888 661 2114; www.thebluepapaya.com ⚙ Daily 8:30am–11pm

Café de Jack $

A Dali institution, Café de Jack has been in business since 1989. Steaks and pizzas features prominently on the menu, but the local Bai hotpot is worth trying. You can have it less spicy if you wish.

✚ 198 B2 ☒ 82 Boai Lu, Dali Old Town ☎ 0872 267 1572 ⚙ Daily 8am–midnight

Sakura Café $$

This Korean-owned restaurant has been pulling in (mostly) Asian diners since 1997 and is especially lively at night time. It serves Korean and Japanese dishes, as well as local Naxi meals, such as Naxi *baba* (cake bread) with honey or ham and Western dishes. A bottle of the local Tibetan wine costs 130RMB.

✚ 198 B2 ☒ 123 Cuiwen Hutong, Old Town ☎ 0888 518 7619 ⚙ Daily 8am–4am

Dushilong Teahouse $

This comfortable teahouse in Zhangjiajie City is a good place to pass the time if you are waiting for your train or plane. It serves a variety of Chinese teas in private booths and there are some cheap and tasty noodle and rice dishes.

✚ 199 E3 ☒ 8 Renmin Lu ☎ 0744 829 5678 ⚙ Daily 8:30am–2am

Café China $$

Boasting Yangshuo's only rooftop dining terrace, Café China is a romantic spot to watch the sun set over the nearby karst mountains. In keeping with Yangshuo's best traditions, the restaurant does great Western dishes such as lasagne and pizza, but also has local clay pot specials.

✚ 199 E2 ☒ 34 West Street, Yangshuo ☎ 0773 882 7744 ⚙ Daily 8am–11pm

Where to...
Shop

CHONGQING

The **Jiefangbei Pedestrian Street** is the centre for shopping in Chongqing. Clusters of modern shopping malls and exclusive shops line the street, and there's even an Armani store thrown into the mix. The **Chaotianmen Market**, on Jiefang Donglu, is the biggest street market in Chongqing, selling a great variety of clothing at decent prices.

Chongqing is also one of the most foremost centres for painting in China. The art gallery above the entrance to the spectacular **People's Hall** (on People's Square) is particularly interesting, with a lot of local contemporary art, some good small pieces of sculpture and examples of calligraphy.

GUILIN AND YANGSHUO

The **Guilin International Commodity Market** in the southern section of Guilin has a big selection of handicrafts. **Zhongshan Zhonglu** is also lined with souvenir stalls. Popular items include buffalo horn combs, scrolls, painted fans and ethnic Zhuang clothing.

Most of the shopping (like the eating and drinking) in nearby Yangshuo takes place on **West Street**. Many vendors in this touristy part of town speak English and goods are named in both English and Chinese. There are scores of shops and stalls selling souvenirs, including antiques, ornaments, calligraphy and painting, as well as the usual gimmicky tourist T-shirts. The **Dong Xi Fang Folk Handicraft Product Shop** (88 West Street, Yangshuo) is one of the classiest stores on West Street and has a well presented range of jewellery, batik, clothing and cute Miao minority dolls.

LIJIANG

Lijiang is one of the most fun shopping experiences in China. The Old Town is full of handicraft and antiques shops, where you can shop for local produce, embroidery and silverware. The local Naxi minority craftspeople make delightful **Dongba batiks**, using the fascinating pictographic characters of the local Dongba langauge. Also look for **Lijiang Snow Tea**, which grows on nearby Jade Dragon Snow Mountain. Its name comes from its white colour, and it is also used in Chinese medicine. **Sifang Jie Square**, the major market area in the Old Town, is the best place for buying exotic local specialities. One shop deserving of particular note is **Bunong Bells** (Dashi Qiao (Big Stone Bridge), Old Town; open 8:30am–1:30am), which sells engraved bronze bells, like those used by itinerant traders along the old Yunnan–Tibet tea trading trail to announce their arrival.

Le Votre $$$

Located in an attractive wooden dining hall on Yangshuo's most famous street, Le Votre specializes in French cuisine, but runs a nice side line in deep-fried snake, among other local treats. Near the top of Yangshuo's most famous street, it's also a popular place to party come sundown. There's a sizeable outdoor dining area for the summer months and the restaurant also has its own micro-brewery.

➕ 199 E2 ⊠ 79 West Street, Yangshuo ☎ 0773 892 8040
🕐 Daily 8am–midnight

Ming Yuan (The Best Coffee) $

This charming café midway along West Street does first-class espresso. After grabbing one of the English-language books, retreat to the cosy upstairs area, which has atmospheric creaking floorboards and a low wooden ceiling.

➕ 199 E2 ⊠ 50 West Street, Yangshuo ☎ 134 5736 9680
🕐 Daily 8am–midnight

Where to...
Be Entertained

YANGSHUO

You can hardly go wrong heading down Yangshuo's West Street (Xi Jie). Many of the bars lining the street have foreign owners and cater well for Western-style social drinking. During the day, you might consider renting a bicycle for an independent tour of the stunning countryside surrounding Yangshuo. Many of the stores along West Street rent bikes for around 15RMB per day.

The Cirque Du Soleil-style spectacular **Impression Liu Sanjie** (Li River Mountain-Water Theatre, tel: 0773 881 1982; www.yxlsj.com; performances begin promptly at 7:40pm and last 70 minutes, expensive) has a cast of 600 who perform elegantly staged routines on a floating set at the confluence of the Li and Yulong rivers. The backdrop is 12 karst limestone peaks, lit dramatically by spotlights. There is now a similar show in Lijiang, though the backdrop in Yangshuo remains untouchable.

The **Yangshuo Cooking School** (Chaolong Village, tel: 137 8843 7286; www.yangshuocook-ingschool.com; open 9:30am, with an additional 3:30pm start Mar–Nov; expensive) offers half-day lessons in a village farmhouse. Lessons begin with students shopping in a local market to learn about ingredients, and then being taught to cook five specific dishes. You get to keep the recipes.

Flights with the **Guilin Flying Balloon Club** (Hudie Quan, Yangshuo, tel: 0773 882 8444; 134 7139 5531) are expensive by Chinese standards, but generally less than you would pay back home. There is the added knowledge that there's nowhere in the world quite like Yangshuo. The price includes hotel pick-up and insurance. Tethered flights are also available, though these are not half as much fun as soaring over the region's beautiful karst limestone pinnacles.

LIJIANG

Wander down Xinhua Jie ("Bar Street") in the Old Town of Lijiang and you can take your pick from any number of bustling bars. The local "reps" are generally Naxi girls who deliver choral singing performances in an effort to entice punters into their particular establishment.

Local musical legend Xuan Ke plays to packed houses with his fellow musicians of the **Naxi Orchestra** (Naxi Music Academy, Dong Dajie, Old Town, tel: 0888 512 7971; daily 8–10pm; expensive). This charismatic local figure gives lively (but lengthy) introductions to each piece in both Mandarin and English and is delighted to chat with foreign visitors after the show.

KUNMING

Dynamic Yunnan

The remarkable **Dynamic Yunnan** show (Kunming Huitang Theatre, tel: 0871 3134 218; www.dyci.cn; Mon–Sat 8pm; expensive) was directed by Yang Liping, one of China's most celebrated dancers, who rose to national fame in the 1980s for her celebrated "Peacock" dance, performed in silhouette against an iridescent moon. This is reprised here, along with some sumptuous choral routines of amazing energy that portray the indigenous traditions of the province's 26 minority groups.

Sichuan and Tibetan China

Getting Your Bearings 138 – 139
In Two Weeks 140 – 141
Don't Miss 142 – 149
At Your Leisure 150 – 152
Where to... 153 – 156

Getting Your Bearings

If eastern China can sometimes feel like a different planet, Tibet takes that sense of separation to an altogether different level. The "Roof of the World" is a bleak but beautiful land, its spirituality as beguiling as its remarkable geography.

Though the snowy peaks of the Himalayas mark its southern border, Tibet lies on a vast plateau, and its landscape is better characterized by barren, undulating plains. The average elevation is more than 4,000m (13,100 feet) above sea level which makes for big, fathomless blue skies and fierce sunshine – so don't forget the sunscreen. Altitude sickness is also common among the uninitiated and any itinerary should include acclimatization time.

Though immigration and tourism have begun to change ancient traditions, most Tibetans continue to lead a pastoral way of life. Their stoicism in the face of almost unimaginable isolation is legendary. Indeed, many spend their entire lives making pedestrian pilgrimages between the region's huge Buddhist temples. In contrast to other parts of "minority" China where cultural displays can seem staged, the religious rituals observed in Tibet are raw, passionate and quite unique. Tibetan temples come alive during the region's many festivals. If you have the opportunity to witness one, be sure to seize it.

Tibetan culture is not only confined within the provincial borders of the "Tibetan Autonomous Region". Nearly all of Qinghai, to the north, is ethnically Tibetan, as is the western half of Sichuan province. There are also smaller Tibetan outposts in Gansu and Yunnan.

Railway woman on the world's highest railway

★ Don't Miss

1 The Highest Railway in the World ➤ 142
2 Lhasa ➤ 144
3 Leshan and Emeishan ➤ 146
4 Jiuzhaigou ➤ 148

At Your Leisure

5 Lhasa's Outlying Monasteries ➤ 150
6 Shigatse ➤ 150
7 Chengdu ➤ 150
8 Wolong ➤ 151
9 Huanglong ➤ 151
10 Xiahe ➤ 152

Monks creating butter carvings at Jokhang Temple in Lhasa

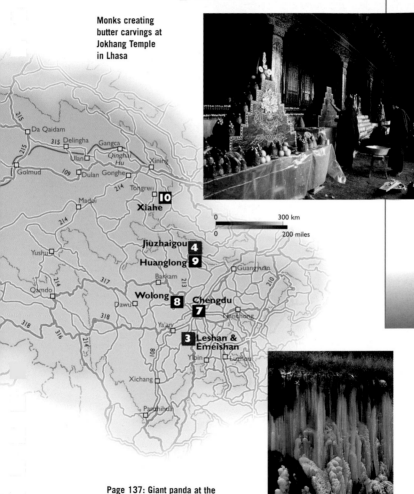

0 300 km
0 200 miles

Page 137: Giant panda at the Breeding Research Base, Chengdu

Right: Nuorilang Waterfall, Jiuzhaigou

Travelling in this remote part of China involves vast distances and breathless altitude. Even those taking the train to Lhasa will need to allow time to adjust to the Himalayan heights. Flying is essential.

Sichuan and Tibetan China in Two Weeks

Days One and Two

Direct trains to **2 Lhasa** (➤ 144–145) depart from Beijing, Shanghai, Guangzhou, Chengdu and Chongqing. Each train must first head to Lanzhou before diverting southwest. Travelling time for each is around 48 hours.

Day Three

Even the hike up to the Potala Palace may leave you breathless so stick to the flatter parts of Lhasa on your first day in town. Wander around the **Jokhang Temple** (➤ 145) and the nearby streets of **Barkhor** (➤ 145).

Day Four

Spend the morning between the **Potala Palace** (above) and **Norbulingka** (➤ 145). Apply for your ticket a day in advance and arrive early before the visitor limit is reached. Vist the cafés around Barkhor in the afternoon.

Day Five

Visit the two major temples in the Lhasa suburbs – the **5 Drepung Monastery**, northwest of Lhasa, and the **5 Sera Monastery** (➤ 150) in the northern suburbs.

Day Six

Rise early for the drive to **6** Shigatse (➤ 150). Take the riverside road, then explore the **Tashilhunpo Temple** in the afternoon (opposite, bottom).

Day Seven

Return journey to Lhasa. The alternative southern route has spectacular plateau vistas and passes **Yamdrok Yamtso Lake** and **Gynatse**.

Days Eight and Nine

Fly to **7** Chengdu (➤ 150). Stroll along **Qintai Lu** then spend the afternoon in a teahouse. Head to the **Bookworm Café** for an evening of good food and lively conversation. The next day visit Chengdu's **Giant Panda Breeding Base** (above; ➤ 151). Take a late afternoon flight to **4** Jiuzhaigou (➤ 148–149).

Days Ten and Eleven

Spend two days in **Jiuzhaigou National Park** (➤ 148–149). Take the bus to the far end of **Rize Valley** and walk back down to the **Nuorilang Waterfall**; take a bus back to the park gate. On the second day, walk along **Shuzheng Valley** to the Nuorilang bus terminus before riding up to **Long Lake**.

Day Twelve

Make a day trip to nearby **9** Huanglong (➤ 151)

DaysThirteen and Fourteen

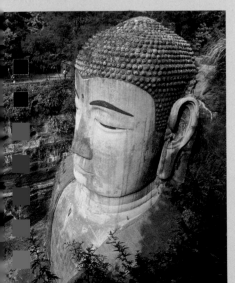

Fly back to Chengdu. Take a bus to **3** Leshan (➤ 146–147). Take a boat past the Leshan Buddha (left) before walking up to the Buddha Temple in the hills behind the giant carving. The following day hike up to **3** Emeishan (➤ 146–147), returning to Chengdu after dark.

❶ The Highest Railway in the World

The Tibetan railway is the greatest symbol of China's "can do" attitude. The line bores through rock and ice, and surmounts some of the bleakest, coldest and most oxygen-starved terrain in the world. Even the railway's critics agree it's an engineering marvel. The passage from wild, windswept Qinghai to Tibet's spiritual nerve-center has become one of the world's great train journeys.

The Qinghai-Tibet railway stretches 1,972km (1,225 miles) from Xining, in northeast Qinghai province, to Lhasa, and takes around 26 hours. Early on, it passes **Qinghai Lake**, China's largest salt-water lake. The rolling landscape turns more mountainous after **Golmud**. The stretch between here and Lhasa is truly breathtaking. The otherworldly **Kunlun Mountains** rise south of Golmud where the train begins its first major step up to the roof of the world. The track's highest point is at the 5,072m/16,641-foot) **Tanggula Pass**, which marks the border between Tibet and Qinghai. Here you are only a few hundred metres below the height of Mount Everest's base camp. The train heads downhill as it approaches Lhasa, weaving around mountains and over grassland.

Technical Challenge

In places the line has been built directly onto the vast sea of permafrost that forms the top layer of much of the Tibetan Plateau. Engineers have used rods of liquid nitrogen to ensure the ground remains frozen, though some 160km (100 miles) of earth was so delicate that the track had to be elevated on a series of viaducts. There are seven major tunnels, which bore straight through the middle of mountains. The longest tunnel – at **Yangbajing** – stretches 3.3km (2 miles), while the longest viaduct is 11.7km (7.2 miles).

Tinted windows offer protection from the fierce ultraviolet rays and concentrated oxygen is continually pumped through each carriage. Travellers have their own "diffuser" and can plug into any of the outlets – next to every seat and sleeper – and breathe from an air supply that's 40 per cent oxygen. The current altitude is recorded on a small digit display between each carriage.

The Train Experience

It's possible to take the train direct from five of China's biggest cities – Beijing in the north, Shanghai in the east, Guangzhou in the far south, and Chongqing and Chengdu in the southwest. Each route converges at the city of **Lanzhou**, just prior to Xining, and the total journey time is around two days.

At the time of writing, the train was still officially in a period of "testing". When the full "Tanggula Express" service opens, it will stop at six scenic spots, where passengers can disembark to enjoy the surroundings. New carriages will also feature deluxe sleeping compartments, complete with individual showers, glass-walled panoramic viewing cars and entertainment centres.

TAKING A BREAK

The **dining car** serves reasonable, although not gourmet, Chinese food.

Above: The Golmud to Lhasa
stretch of the Tanggula Express
is truly spectacular

Xining ✚ 198 C2
Lhasa ✚ 195 D1
Tanggula Pass ✚ 195 E2

THE HIGHEST RAILWAY IN THE WORLD: INSIDE INFO

Top tip There are four classes of ticket – hard and soft seats, hard and soft sleepers – and prices range from around 400RMB for a hard seat to around 1,200 RMB for a soft sleeper (prices vary according to departure point). Tickets can be booked at any of the major departure stations or with authorized agents in those cities. You'll need a **Tibetan Travel Permit**, available only to those who have booked a formal tour with an approved agency, and a signed **Passenger Health Registration Card**. The card is essentially a disclaimer for high-altitude travel and can be obtained when buying the ticket. The China Tibet Tourism Bureau has offices in Beijing, Shanghai, Chengdu and Hong Kong. The Sichuan China Youth Travel Service in Chengdu has a range of tour and permit services.

2 Lhasa

Though hardly a humming metropolis, Lhasa is a city changed. This once impenetrable stronghold of Tibetan Buddhism is now filled with Beijing-style boulevards, bland building developments and tourist throngs. On the plus side, it's never been easier to get there and, thanks to iconic attractions like the Potala Palace, Lhasa's ancient mystique remains.

Assuming you haven't been engaged in some serious mountaineering, Lhasa will be your first stop in Tibet. Its airport has direct links with several major Chinese cities (and Kathmandu in Nepal) and it is the terminus of the Qinghai–Tibet Railway (► 142–143). For Tibetans, Lhasa is often considered the *final* stop of a lifelong journey. The city is a place of pilgrimage, and every man, woman and child in Tibet will hope to make the ritual circumambulation around the Jokhang Temple at least once in their lifetime.

Residences of the Dalai Lamas

The **Potala Palace** is built upon a hillside overlooking the city and forms an imposing backdrop. This huge compound was the former winter residence of Tibet's religious and political leader, the Dalai Lama, and dates back to 1645. The palace is divided into White and Red sections. The **White Palace** is older and was the living area for former Dalai Lamas. The **Red Palace** is the religious citadel. The tombs of all but one of the former resident

The Potala Palace, seen from Chokpuri Hill through prayer flags

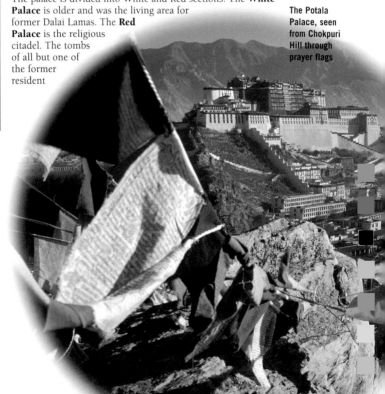

A Tibetan prayer wheel

Dalai Lamas are here. The highlight is the **Tomb of Lobsang Gyatso**, whose stupa contains 3,721kg (8,205 pounds) of gilded gold and thousands of encrusted jewels. Chapels and former living quarters are open for inspection, but much of the complex remains sealed. Tourist numbers have been capped at 2,300 daily, and in summer tickets must be applied for a day in advance. This can be done at the palace's west gate.

Three kilometres (2 miles) west of the Potala is **Norbulingka**, parkland where successive Dalai Lamas built their summer homes. The **New Summer Palace**, built in 1956, gives a fascinating glimpse into the life of the present Dalai Lama before his exile in 1959.

The Spiritual Heart of Tibet

The **Jokhang Temple** is unquestionably the holiest man-made structure in the Tibetan universe. Built in the 7th century, it houses the most precious Buddhist image in China – a golden statue of **Sakyamuni Buddha**. The temple's halls and shrines are always crowded with pilgrims, though access to the roof area seems to be a luxury reserved for fee-paying tourists. From the top you can gaze down onto the faithful, who will likely be either prostrating themselves before the main westerly gate, or tracing a clockwise path around the temple's circumference.

Around the temple are the streets of **Barkhor**, with many cafés. This web of narrow roads is the centre of traditional Tibetan life and a great place to wander among elaborately dressed locals.

TAKING A BREAK

There are many cafés around the Barkhor circuit and along Beijing Donglu and nearby Danjielin Lu. Most serve Western, Nepali amd Indian cuisine, as well as local favourites. The **New Mandala Restaurant** (► 155) on the west side of Barkhor Square has a rooftop garden with excellent views of the square and temple.

✚ 195 D1
Potala Palace
✉ Beijing Donglu ☎ 0891 682 4568 🕐 Daily 9–4 💷 Moderate

Norbulingka
✉ Luobulinka Lu (Norbulingka Road) ☎ 0891 682 6274 🕐 Oct–Apr daily 9:30–5:30; May–Sep 9–6:30 💷 Moderate 🚌 106, 109

Jokhang Temple
✉ Bakuo Jie (Barkhor Street) ☎ 0891 632 3129 🕐 Daily 9–5 💷 Moderate

LHASA: INSIDE INFO

Top tip There are still **restrictions** on foreigners travelling to Tibet. Visitors must have a Tibet Travel Permit before arriving in Lhasa (► 143), and a signed **Passenger Health Registration Card**.

3 Leshan and Emeishan

Temple fatigue is a common problem in China. If over-exposure to gilded statues and incense sticks has eroded your powers of appreciation, head immediately to Leshan and Emeishan. This eye-popping couplet of World Heritage sites will leave you fumbling for the camera. The former is home to the world's largest statue of Buddha, the second is the most spectacular of China's sacred mountains. You don't need to be a devotee to be impressed.

Although 30km (18.5 miles) apart, Leshan and Emeishan are two equally essential halves of the same experience. Leshan can be visited in half a day, while Emeishan demands between one and four full days, depending on whether you walk to the summit or hitch a ride.

Leshan

The 71m (233-foot) **Grand Buddha** of Leshan is the biggest of all Buddhas. He was carved into the cliff face over 90 painstaking years in the 8th and 9th centuries and gazes beatifically over the confluence of the Min, Dadu and Qingyi rivers. This once-dangerous passage of water has claimed many lives and the statue may have been created to protect passing boatmen.

It's difficult not to feel slightly humbled as you descend the narrow stair-case beside Buddha's body before passing in front of his feet at the base. Even Buddha's big toe dwarfs visitors. These close-up views are available by follow-ing what is essentially a one-way circuit of the hillside from the main gate. For a wider perspective, hop on a sightseeing boat from Leshan city.

Emeishan

At 3,099m (10,168 feet), Emeishan is the highest of China's sacred Buddhist mountains. Thousands flock here in pilgrimage or simply to scale the magnifi-cent heights. The route to the summit crosses a diverse landscape with pine and bamboo thickets, picturesque rock formations, waterfalls and gorges.

The first of Emeishan's temples were built during the Eastern Han dynasty (AD 25–220), but the area only really became a centre of Buddhism during the Ming and Qing dynasties, when more than 100 temples and monasteries dotted the mountain. The most famous temple these days is **Baoguo Temple**, the gateway to the hiking trails.

There are two main routes up the mountain. The northern route is shorter and more direct, the southerly route is longer, more strenuous but much more spectacular. Most choose to take the northerly path up and the southerly path down (don't feed the monkeys). A walk up and down the mountain requires at least two or three days and there are several guest houses on the mountain for overnight stays. Those more interested in the views than the climb can take a bus half way up the mountain before getting a cable car to the summit.

Leshan's Grand Buddha is carved into the rock

TAKING A BREAK
Restaurants can be found at the **Leidong Terrace**, just off the main mountain road.

Leshan Grand Buddha Scenic Area
✚ 198 C3 ✉ Sichuan province ☎ 0833 230 2416 ⏰ Apr–early Oct daily 7:30–7:30; early Oct–Mar 8–6 💰 Moderate 🚍 Frequent buses between Leshan and Chengdu. From Leshan city, take bus 3 or 13 to the park gate

Emeishan
✚ 198 C3 ✉ Sichuan province ☎ 0833 559 0111 ⏰ 24 hours 💰 Expensive 🚍 Emei town is 6km (4 miles) from Baoguo Temple; regular buses to Chengdu and Leshan 🚆 Emei town station

LESHAN AND EMEISHAN: INSIDE INFO

Top tip The Chinese like nothing better than a sunrise trip to a mountain peak. Your best bet to snatch some quiet time with the mountain is at **sunset**, an option only realistically available to those staying on the mountain.

④ Jiuzhaigou

Tucked away in the mountains of north Sichuan, Jiuzhaigou is perhaps China's most eulogized natural attraction. During a 1984 visit, former Communist Party boss Zhao Ziyang said the alpine scenery was "even better than Guilin" and, though 21st-century tourism has taken firm hold, the park's lakes, forests and waterfalls retain their captivating beauty.

Jiuzhaigou translates as "nine village valley", referring to the original Tibetan settlements that dotted the landscape. Though there are still a few prayer wheels and Tibetan stupa, the three remaining villages have lost much of their appeal and can hardly be described as attractions in their own right. The main motivation for modern visitors is the spectacular scenery – a fusion of snowy mountain peaks, tumbling waterfalls and hypnotically colourful lakes.

Jiuzhaigou National Park essentially comprises three valleys, joined in a Y-shape. It's more than 30km (18.5 miles) from the entrance, in the north, to the most southerly extremity of the park, which lies 3,060m (10,040 feet) above sea level. Shuttle buses whisk travellers to any of the scenic points in a matter of minutes. They set off roughly at 10-minute intervals, dropping and collecting passengers at stops along the route.

Hiking is not quite a lost art. A network of boardwalks allows visitors to meander through the forests, encircle the lakes and get close to the waterfalls. The pathways never stray too far from the main road though, and many are closed in winter. Wandering away from the marked paths is prohibited and camping among the swathes of pine is – sadly – a definite no-no.

Above and below: Spectacular foliage in Jiuzhaigou National Park

Three Valleys

Rize Valley is the right-hand branch of the Y-shape and the most colourful of Jiuzhaigou's three valleys. Many tourists take the bus to the **Ancient Forest**, at the end of the valley, and then bus hop, or walk back down the hill past the mesmerizing series of lakes, a kaleidoscope of jade, emerald and sapphire hues. The legendary colour of Jiuzhaigou's water has a scientific explanation, but talk of short-wave radiation, water dispersion and algae detracts from the hypnotic magic of staring into the water's depths.

Jiuzhaigou's left-hand branch, **Zechawa Valley**, offers a sharp contrast. The mountains here are dramatic and recall the North American Rockies. The lakes, however, are well spread out and, with boardwalks that hug the road, hiking in this area is fairly pointless. At the far end of the valley is **Long Lake**, the highest point in the park. The lake is spectacularly surrounded by glacial mountains. A few steps below is the colourful **Five Flower Lake**.

At the hub of the three valleys is the huge, horseshoe-shaped **Nuorilang Waterfall**. Even without the nearby bus station it would be difficult to miss this splendid sight. Below is the **Shuzheng Valley** – essentially an extended driveway into the park, flanked by more crystal-clear lakes and tumbling waterfalls, where cattle graze and birds fly low over the river reeds.

TAKING A BREAK

Shuzheng is the largest of the surviving villages and it's possible to get home-made fare here and feast in the gaudily decorated Tibetan dining rooms. If you're feeling thirsty, there's a natural spring close to the main road just south.

Jiuzhaigou National Park
🚩 198 C5 ✉ Sichuan province ☎ 0837 773 9753; www.jiuzhaigouvalley.com/english 🕒 Apr to mid-Nov daily 7am–7:30pm; mid-Nov to Mar daily 8–5:30 💰 Entrance expensive, bus ticket moderate (Apr to mid-Nov); entrance and bus ticket moderate (mid-Nov to Mar) 🚌 Up to 12 hours by public bus on the journey from Chengdu ✈ Daily flights from Chengdu

JIUZHAIGOU: INSIDE INFO

Top tip The authorities have outlawed the once-popular habit of staying at one of the Tibetan villages. Officially, guests should vacate the valley before closing time, though it's still possible to circumvent the rules. The main advantage of staying in one of the simple **guest houses** is being able to enjoy the park before and after the tour groups arrive and leave.

Hidden gem The valley was once famed for its amazing variety of **wildlife** – takins, monkeys and pandas, among others – though a sighting of these creatures is now a rarity.

At Your Leisure

5 Lhasa's Outlying Monasteries

Having spent a leisurely few days acclimatizing to the altitude in Lhasa, consider a visit to the two fantastic monasteries that lie just outside city limits. The **Drepung Monastery**, set against a bare hillside 10km (6 miles) northwest of Lhasa, was once the largest and wealthiest in Tibet. It was served by senior monks who were instrumental in training Dalai Lamas and specialized in "esoteric meditation".

On the northern outskirts of Lhasa is the 15th-century **Sera Monastery**, considered to be the most intellectually rigorous of the great centres of Tibetan Buddhism. If visiting in the afternoon, expect to see the daily "debating" rituals, a key part of any monk's training (except Sunday).

Drepung Monastery
➕ 195 D1 ☎ 0891 686 0727 ⏰ Daily 9–5 💰 Moderate 🚕 Taxi from Lhasa. At the foot of the monastery, transfer to a shuttle bus or make the steep hike up to the main gate

Sera Monastery
➕ 195 D1 ☎ 0891 638 3639 ⏰ Mon–Sat 9–5 💰 Moderate 🚕 Taxi from Lhasa

6 Shigatse

Set in the valley of the Yarlong Tsangpo (or Brahmaputra) River, Shigatse was once a spiritual and political rival to Lhasa. It's the historic base of the Panchen Lama, and his main temple, **Tashilhunpo**, remains one of the biggest and best preserved in Tibet. It's also one of the most beautiful, rising in stately terraces to a central gilded roof with decorated eaves. The

monastery is remarkable for its 26m-high (85-foot) gold and copper statue of Matreiya and its elaborate buildings which contain the gilded tombs of previous Panchen Lamas. The Kelsang Courtyard, enclosed by multistoreyed galleries, has a real Venetian grandeur.

The journey from Lhasa to Shigatse is very much part of the attraction. Buses take the direct route along the Yarlong Tsangpo, where the riverside road is cut dramatically from the cliffs, or you can go via an alternative southern route which passes the sacred Yamdrok Yamtso Lake and Tibet's third city, Gyantse, though you will need to hire a private vehicle for this.
➕ 195 D1 ✉ 270km (168 miles) west of Lhasa
Tashilhunpo
⏰ Daily 9–7 💰 Moderate 🚌 Irregular public bus, or tour booked in Lhasa

7 Chengdu

Chengdu is a key staging post for travellers visiting the wilds of Tibet or the scenic northern and western parts of Sichuan province. It's one of the few cities from where you can take a train or plane direct to Lhasa,

The teahouse at Wenshu Yuan, Chengdu's best-preserved Buddhist temple

and where picking up the necessary paperwork is relatively easy. The city itself is unremarkable and the weather not a great deal better. A local saying has it that clear skies are so rare that "dogs bark at the sun".

There are several redeeming features, notably the city's teahouses. Nowhere else in China are these institutions such a defining part of a city's character. They witness long, leisurely debates, never-ending games of mahjong and regular performances of **Sichuan Opera** – probably the most interesting of China's many genres. The **People's Teahouse** in People's Park has a pleasant lakeside location and is a great spot to enjoy the atmosphere. Look out for the ear-cleaners, shoe shiners and fortune tellers roaming among the crowd.

Like elsewhere in China, Chengdu's historic neighbourhoods have made way for new apartment blocks, but the re-created "traditional" street of Qintai Lu provides a reminder of the city's past.

➕ 198 C4 ✉ Sichuan province

🔟 Wolong

One of the last footholds of China's giant panda population, the **Wolong Nature Reserve** is the best place in China to see this most revered of animals in the flesh. There are pandas in other zoos around the country – notably those in Chengdu and Chongqing – but conditions are depressing. Here on this 200,000ha (494,200-acre) mountain reserve in western Sichuan, upwards of 100 pandas roam free. Many remain confined to the **Research and Conservation Centre** (Panda Park), where pandas live in enclosures liberally sprinkled with trees and climbing frames. Major work is currently ongoing to enlarge the centre and improve public access.

The **Giant Panda Breeding Base**, 10km (6 miles) north of Chengdu, is an alternative for anyone who can't make the three-hour trip to Wolong. The centre's recent breeding success means you may well be able to view newborn clubs with their mothers.

Wolong Nature Reserve
➕ 198 C4 ✉ 150km (93 miles) northwest of Chengdu, Sichuan province
☎ 0837 624 6773 🕐 Daily 8:30–5
🖐 Panda Park and museum both inexpensive 🚌 Buses depart from Chengdu daily and take around 3 hours

Giant Panda Breeding Base
✉ 26 Xiongmao Dadao, northern suburb of Chengdu ☎ 028 8351 6748; www.panda.org.cn 🕐 Daily 7–6
🖐 Inexpensive

🟧 Huanglong

Twinned with Yellowstone National Park in the USA, Huanglong is a stunning 3.6km-long (2.2-mile) alpine valley. It shares similar snow-capped mountain scenery with nearby Jiuzhaigou, but has a truly unique feature – a huge limestone terrace that cups a staircase of colourful ponds.

The official "Huanglong Scenic Area" also encompasses the Tibetan town of **Songpan**, 60km (37 miles) to the west, and the **Muni Valley**, a similar distance west again. In Songpan you can take guided horse treks into the mountains, while Muni is famed for its serene lakes (similar to but less busy than those at Jiuzhaigou) and the roaring Zhagu

Monks blowing the ceremonial horns at the Labrang Monastery, near Xiahe

Waterfall. There is a separate entry charge (70RMB). Because of the long distances and unreliable public transport, anyone on a tight itinerary should take an organized tour from Jiuzhaigou. The intrepid can take taxis or public buses from Songpan.

198 C4 ☒ Sichuan province ☎ 028 8773 8076; www.huanglong.com ⊙ Daily 8am–dusk ⓦ Expensive (Apr–19 Nov), inexpensive (20 Nov–Mar) ☐ Hire a taxi or minivan in Songpan or book a tour from Jiuzhaigou

⑩ Xiahe

For Tibetans living within a several hundred-kilometre radius of Xiahe, the **Labrang Monastery** is the greatest destination they hope to see in this lifetime. This 300-year-old lamasery domi-

nates the small mountain town in southwest Gansu province and is home to around 1,000 monks. They live in the charming warren of white-washed dwellings, and spend their days worshipping in the resplendent prayer halls or studying in the Buddhist colleges. Xiahe's resident population is supplemented by pilgrims who flock here to make the 3km (1.8-mile) trek around Labrang's circumference, pushing each of the 1,174 prayer wheels as they go.

Though Tibetan influences are strong, Xiahe also has a vibrant population of Hui Muslims. One of the most fascinating aspects of visiting this part of China is witnessing the co-existing religious communities. Look for the white skullcaps bobbing among the crowds of fuchsia-robed monks. In summer you can hike or take horse rides into the surrounding hills and nearby grasslands.

196 C2
Labrang Monastery
☎ 0941 712 1774 ⓦ Free to walk around the monastery complex; moderate for tour which includes entry to main prayer halls ⓦ Daily 8:30–6 ☐ Daily buses from nearby Xining and Lanzhou

Where to... Stay

Prices

Expect to pay per double room per night, including breakfast and taxes
$** under 400RMB **$$** 400–1,000RMB **$$$ over 1,000RMB

CHENGDU

Jinjiang Hotel $$

The Jinjiang is the grand old dame of Chengdu hospitality. Standards of service are excellent and the 480 rooms are elegantly appointed. The showpiece restaurant is the glass-roofed Louvre Garden. There's also a huge indoor swimming pool.

✚ 198 C4 ⊠ 80 Renmin Nanlu, Chengdu ☎ 028 8550 6666; www.jjhotel.com

Wen Jun Lou Hotel $

This pretty, YHA-affiliated hotel, with its signature classical architecture, is styled like a Qing mansion and has rooms set around two courtyards. It's on Chengdu's premier tourist street. There are two large dormitories, making it a popular choice with younger travellers. Private rooms have broadband access. The hotel can arrange tours and onward travel and pick you up from the airport and railway station if you have reserved in advance.

✚ 198 C4 ⊠ 12 Qintai Lu, Chengdu ☎ 028 8613 8884; www.dreams-travel.com/wenjun

EMEISHAN

Jinding Hotel $$

The Jinding Hotel, just below the 3,099m (10,168ft) summit, is the best option for those wanting to stay on Emeishan. It's an ideal place for a rest after climbing the sacred Buddhist mountain or before a sunrise visit to the peak. The rooms have air-conditioning and TVs. The restaurant is good for a decent meal, even if you aren't staying.

✚ 198 C3 ⊠ Golden Summit, Emeishan ☎ 0833 509 8088

JIUZHAIGOU

Jiuzhai Paradise Resort $$

This extraordinary resort has a faraway forest location, nestled up against the snow-capped mountains of north Sichuan. It's 30km (18 miles) from the entrance of Jiuzhaigou – the main attraction in the area. The spacious rooms have views over the forests and mountains and there's a huge spa centre with an indoor pool and excellent massage services. The highlight is the reception – a gigantic glass dome bubble with rock pools, rivers and bars within re-created traditional buildings.

✚ 198 C5 ⊠ Ganhaizi, Zhangzha Town, Jiuzhaigou County ☎ 0837 778 9999; www.jiuzhaiparadise.com

LHASA

House of Shambhala $$

This new 10-bed hotel, in a restored Tibetan courtyard home, has brought a touch of class to the roof of the world. It has a gourmet restaurant, and a second building next door includes a Tibetan spa.

✚ 195 D1 ⊠ 7 Jiri Erxiang (northeast of Jokhang Temple) ☎ 010 6402 7151; http://houseofshambhala.com

Kyichu Hotel $$

This friendly, family-run hotel is one of Lhasa's oldest privately run hotels and, until the recent opening of the Shambhala, was the classiest accommodation option in this touristy part of town. The hotel is located between the Jokhang Temple and the Potala Palace.

✚ 195 D1 ⊠ 149 Beijing Donglu, Lhasa ☎ 0891 633 1541

Where to...
Eat and Drink

Prices
Expect to pay for a meal for one, excluding drinks
$ under 50RMB $$ 50–100RMB $$$ over 100RMB

Baoguo Buyi $$

The home of what has become a popular national chain, Chengdu's Baoguo Buyi serves up fantastic, spicy Sichuanese cuisine in an elegant but informal dining hall. As with its sister restaurants, the decor is based around elaborate carved wood patterning. Ask for the "clothes hanger" dish, in which thin strips of cucumber and pork slices hang over a wooden railing.

✚ 198 C4 ⌖ 8 Guangfuqiao Beijie, Chengdu ☎ 028 8551 1999
⏱ Daily 10–2.30, 5.30–9

The Bookworm $$

This "literary restaurant" has a collection of 5,000 books in a variety of languages and a kitchen headed up by a French chef. Culinary highlights include "The Wordsworth", a plate of locally sourced grilled mixed vegetables, or "The Popeye", spinach with bacon strips, green onions and parmesan cheese. Unusually for this part of the country, the savvy bar staff have been well trained in coffee and cocktail making.

✚ 198 C4 ⌖ 28 Renmin Nanlu, Chengdu ☎ 028 8552 0177
⏱ Daily 9am–1.30am

Shunxing Old Teahouse $$

Some may find the "ancient" ambience slightly forced, but this expansive teahouse remains a great spot to enjoy the many facets of the Sichuan tea-drinking experience. The staff pour tea from an impossibly long spout (to better ferment the flavours) while ear-cleaners wander among the crowd with scary-looking metallic implements. Don't be alarmed. A Sichuanese ear clean may just be one of the nicest things you'll ever experience.

✚ 198 C4 ⌖ 3rd Floor, Chengdu International Exhibition and Convention Center, 258 Shawan Lu, Chengdu ☎ 028 8769 3202
⏱ Daily 11–10

Teddy Bear Café $

The Teddy Bear Cafe is in the Teddy Bear Hotel, a popular backpacker stop at the base of Emeishan. There's an English menu, which lists burgers and sandwiches with fries, as well as Chinese specials such as fried eggplant with garlic and ginger, and sweet and sour boneless chicken. You can also order a picnic to take up the mountain.

✚ 198 C3 ⌖ 43 Baoguo Lu, Baoguo, Emeishan ☎ 0833 559 0135;
www.teddybear.com.cn
⏱ Daily 7am–midnight

Pearl Court $$$

This is the plushest place to grab a bite to eat in what is a remote part of the country. The cuisine blends Tibetan and Sichuanese styles, though there are plenty of easy-to-digest Western options too. Wild local mushrooms and fish from the crystal-clean local lakes and rivers come particularly recommended.

✚ 198 C5 ⌖ Sheraton Jiuzhaigou Resort, Jiuzhaigou ☎ 0837 773 9988;
www.sheraton.com/jiuzhaigou
⏱ Daily 11:30–2, 6–10

Where to... Shop

New Mandala Restaurant $

This Nepalese-owned restaurant has a great second-floor location with an additional rooftop balcony with fabulous views of nearby Jokhang Temple. It's especially popular with foreign visitors and deservedly so: the Nepalese curries are creamy and the service is attentive. The menu also includes Western, Indian and Tibetan dishes.

➕ 195 D1 ✉ West side of Barkhor Square, Lhasa ☎ 0891 634 2235 🕐 Daily 8am–11pm

Norling Restaurant $$

The rock terrace and courtyard garden of the Kyichu Hotel make for a great al fresco option in Lhasa's warmer months. The chefs rustle up a wide variety of Tibetan, Nepali and Indian dishes, as well as the odd pasta meal.

➕ 195 D1 ✉ Kyichu Hotel, 18 Beijing Zhonglu, Lhasa ☎ 0891 633 1541 🕐 Daily 7am–10pm

One of Chengdu's more unusual crafts is bamboo weaving. The **Bamboo Weaving Arts and Crafts Factory** (12 Jiefang Lu) is one of many factories which have showrooms for customers.

Qingshiqiao Market (Xinkai Jie and Nanfu Jie) is one of Chengdu's largest markets, often referred to as the "Flower and Pets Market" because of its specialist stalls. The animals range from the exotic to the seriously cuddly.

Chengdu's **Tibetan nighbourhood** is around the intersection of Wuhouci Hengjie and Wuhouci Dongjie. You can find shops selling jewellery, prayer flags, lanterns, purses and incense, amongst other authentic Tibetan products.

The **Shu Brocade Institute** (268 Huanhua Nanlu) has weavers using traditional wooden looms to make silk, one of Sichuan's most celebrated products. Next door is an embroidery shop and a factory that offers tours to tourists.

Chunxi Lu is a pedestrian street where the trendy young things catch up with the latest fashions.

The vibrant **Barkhor Market** surrounds the Jokhang Temple in the old part of Lhasa and sells a mesmerizing variety of Tibetan wares, including rugs, knives, broadswords, traditional clothes and hats, gold and silver jewellery and various other handmade crafts. **Thangkas** are particularly popular. These scrolls are used in religious ceremonies and are notable for their bright colours and motifs of Tibetan Buddhism. Most are made either by painting or embroidery. Tibetan fashions are famously colourful.

Look for the gaudy and elaborately festooned aprons, fur hats and caps. Yak horns are just one of the many oddities. As always, bargaining is essential.

Many of Tibet's "traditional" products are actually now made in Nepal. The **Dropenling Handicraft Development Centre** (11 Chak Tsal Gang Lu) sells only locally made products like wall hangings, cushions and woven carpets.

The **Lhasa Department Store**, at the western end of Yutuo Lu (Yuthok Street), is the largest such store in the city. It sells handicrafts as well as practical items, such as cotton clothing, mugs, towels, toothpast and canned food.

There are three **Xinhua Book Stores** in Lhasa, one on Yutuo Lu, another on east Barkhor and the last on Beijing Zhonglu, west of the Tibet Hotel. They sell maps of Lhasa, dictionaries and Chinese and Tibetan books. A bookshop carrying dedicated Tibetan literature is on north Barkhor.

Where to...
Be Entertained

Nightlife

Chengdu is the region's hotspot for evening activities. **Sichuan opera** is a favourite. An integral part of each performance is *bianlian*, or "changing faces", where the actor changes between a series of traditionally patterned masks with lightning speed. The trick has always been a closely guarded secret within the operatic community. There are performances at many of Chengdu's teahouses, or a more formal show at the **Jinjiang Theatre** on Huaxing Zheng Jie on weekends.

Chengdu has a surprisingly large expatriate community and their presence has helped boost the drinking and dancing economy no end. The **Lotus Palace** bar (12 Jinli Jie; tel: 028 8553 7676) is nestled halfway down Jinli Old Street, off Wuhouci Dajie. Go early for a lounge experience or later for heavier club tracks. For a more full-on nightclub experience, try **MGM** (5th Floor, Yan Shi Kou Mansion, Li Hua Jie; tel: 028 8666 6618), the biggest, brashest and coolest club in the city. The second section of Renmin Nanlu (in the region of the US consulate) is clustered with bars and restaurants, including the ever popular Irish pub **Shamrock** (15 Renmin Nanlu; tel: 028 8523 6158; www.shamrockinchengdu.com) which has pool, live bands and sport on the big screen.

Wildlife

The **China Research and Conservation Centre for the Giant Panda** (Wolong Nature Reserve; tel: 0837 6246 773), several hours northwest of Chengdu, provides the best opportunity to see pandas in something approaching their natural habitat. For 200RMB it's possible to get temporary access to a giant panda enclosure and have your picture taken with an adult panda. Baby panda pictures cost 400RMB.

Out in the suburbs of Chengdu itself is the **Giant Panda Research Base** (26 Xiongmao Dadao; tel: 028 8351 6748; www.panda.org.cn). There are a number of enclosures which house the giant pandas and cubs which have been successfully reared here. The nursery area is open to the public so you can often see mothers with their newborns.

Scenic Reserves

Goddess Lake Scenic Area

(tel: 0837 778 8296; www.jiuzhaiparadise.com) is a "newly discovered" tourist area in northern Sichuan that claims to blend the best scenery of Jiuzhaigou and Huanglong into one neat package. Tours can be booked from the Jiuzhai Paradise Resort. Despite the hype, it can't really compare to its two UNESCO-listed neighbours, so make the trip a complement rather than a replacement for a visit to Jiuzhaigou proper.

Horse Trekking

Shun Jiang Horse Trek Company (tel: 0837 723 1201) offers guided treks up into the mountains that surround Songpan in northern Sichuan. A three-day trek costs as little as 350RMB. It's well worth stopping in this beautiful mountain town for a night or two on the way to Jiuzhaigou or Huanglong.

Skiing

Both **Emeishan** and **Xiling** (several hours to the west of Chengdu) have modest skiing facilities open during deepest winter. Neither is especially spectacular. Purists are better sticking to the far northeast of China or the man-made resorts around Beijing.

The Silk Road

Getting Your Bearings 158 – 159
In Two Weeks 160 – 161
Don't Miss 162 – 167
At Your Leisure 168 – 169
Where to… 170 – 172

Getting Your Bearings

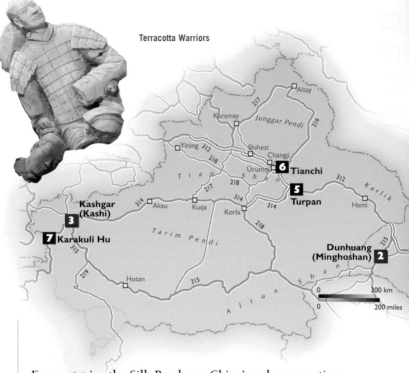

Terracotta Warriors

For centuries the Silk Road was China's only connection with the West. This lonely desert trail allowed the Middle Kingdom's most valuable inventions – paper and printing included – to spread west and opened up China to Islam and Buddhism. International trading has ceased, but the region remains coloured by an exotic mesh of races, religions and cultures.

Page 157: Snow-covered mountains loom behind Jiayuguan, at the western end of the Great Wall

Left: Typical yurt dwelling, Karakul Lake

★ Don't Miss
1 Xi'an ➤ 162
2 Dunhuang ➤ 165
3 Kashgar ➤ 167

At Your Leisure
4 Jiayuguan ➤ 168
5 Turpan ➤ 168
6 Tianchi ➤ 169
7 Karakuli Hu (Karakul
  Lake) ➤ 169

**Emin Mosque,
Turpan, at dusk**

The Silk Road was first pioneered after Qin Shihuang took charge of China in 221 BC. Business was particularly brisk during the glorious Han (3rd century BC–AD 3rd century) and Tang (AD 7th–10th century) dynasties when merchants arrived from across Persia, India and perhaps even Europe.

As China's ancient capital, Xi'an marked the point where East and West collided. Chang'an (as it was then known) was studded with palaces, mosques and market-places where strange foreign faces mingled with Chinese princes and scholars. In its day, the city rivalled Rome or Constantinople for imperial grandeur.

The camel-led caravans began their journey into the West along the Hexi Corridor, a narrow strip between the Mongolian steppe and the Tibetan Plateau. This is modern-day Gansu province, officially China's poorest region, but a land of haunting beauty. It also boasts China's most remarkable historical site – the Mogao Caves.

Further west the Silk Road forked either side of the Taklamakan Desert and converged again at Kashgar, close to the snow-capped mountains of China's western borders. In its culture and geography, this lively Islamic market town distills the best of Xinjiang province and represents China's final frontier.

The route once taken by camel convoys is now covered by railway tracks and a series of dry and dusty roads. Trains travel (slowly) from Xi'an to Kashgar, passing most of the major sights.

The Silk Road in Two Weeks

Day One

Walk atop the old City Walls of ❶ **Xi'an** (► 162–164) to survey what was once the biggest city on earth. Climb down from the South Gate to the **Beilin Museum**, then spend the afternoon visiting the legendary **Terracotta Warriors** (right).

Days Two and Three

Visit the **Great Mosque** and the **Bell and Drum Towers**, all within a walkable distance of one another. Head to the **Greater Wild Goose Pagoda** before lunch and spend a leisurely afternoon in the **Shanxi History Museum**. Board the 10:52pm sleeper train to ❹ **Jiayuguan** (► 168). The journey takes more than 18 hours, so lay back and watch the desert roll by.

Day Four

Visit **Jiayuguan Fort** (left) during the day and head up to the upper tower of the **Overhanging Great Wall** at sunset for a sweeping view of the desert and mountain peaks.

Day Five

From Jiayuguan, take a bus ride across the desert to ❷ **Dunhuang** (► 165–166). It's a 400km (248-mile) drive, but the roads here are straight and empty and the journey should take no more than five hours.

Day Six

Visit the **Mogao Caves** (below) in the morning. At sunset climb the giant sand dunes around the **Crescent Moon Lake** and hang around until nightfall to see the Gobi Desert stars come out.

Day Seven

Spend a relaxing day admiring the stunning scenery around Dunhunag before boarding the 8:16pm overnight sleeper train direct to **5 Turpan** (► 168).

Days Eight and Nine

Tour the outlying areas of Turpan. Organized trips take in the desert ruins of **Gaochang** and the **Flaming Mountains**, stopping for lunch in **Grape Valley**. The ruins of **Jiaohe** are the last stop. Kick back in Turpan on day nine.

Days Ten and Eleven

Take the bus to provincial capital **Urumqi**. If you have time, take a two-day hiking trip to nearby **6 Tianchi** (► 169). Fly to **3 Kashgar** (► 167).

Day Twelve

If possible, get to Kashgar for a Sunday. Once a week the town bursts into life as folk flock to the city from outlying areas for the **Livestock Market** (left).

Day Thirteen

Visit the **Id Kah Mosque** before heading out to the **Tomb of Abakh Khoja**.

Day Fourteen

Take a train or plane back to Urumqi, from where you can fly to any of China's major cities.

O Xi'an

Xi'an outshines even Beijing in terms of history and culture. As the final destination for the camel-led convoys of the Silk Road, Xi'an is the template for modern Hong Kong – a place where east and west collided with spectacular cultural and economic results. The city's ancient charm may have been eroded but, thanks to a chance discovery in 1974, it now boasts one of the world's greatest tourist attractions.

Xi'an was first made capital of China in the 11th century BC. The city rose and fell again and again until the Tang dynasty (7th–10th century AD) when it became firmly established as China's political and cultural centre. Under the stewardship of the Tang emperors, Xi'an saw a great flowering of the arts and science. Scholars and merchants flocked from all corners of the known world and the city became a huge, cosmopolitan melting pot. Xi'an may be one of the few cities in China that is smaller today than it was 1,000 years ago.

Walking the **City Walls** is the best way to conjure the atmosphere of that golden age. Even though the modern wall was built only in 1374, it was raised on the foundations of the former Imperial compound. The entire circumference is 13.7km (8.5 miles) and, for a fee, tourists can clamber up at each of the four compass points and hike the entire way around. Alternatively, there's a wall-top shuttle (5RMB per stop, 50RMB entire circuit).

Clay Army

Xi'an's greatest attraction actually lies 37km (23 miles) east of town. During a drought in 1974, peasant farmers digging a well made one of the world's greatest archaeological discoveries. And the mystery is still unravelling today.

The **Terracotta Warriors** (Bingmayong) form a vast underground army whose sole purpose was to guard the tomb of Qin Shihuang, the first man to unify China in 221 BC. The figurines are estimated to number around 8,000, although not all are on public display. Despite the astonishing work and sacrifice that went into creating it, the army was designed never to be seen and bears witness to Qin's power and megalomania.

Left: Riding along the top of the City Walls, near West Gate, Xi'an

Below: The Terracotta Warriors stand in rows under a giant roof

The figurines are displayed in three separate pits around which permanent buildings have taken shape. Pit One is bigger than a football field. So far more than 2,000 of an estimated 6,000 life-sized figurines have been unearthed. They are aligned in military formation and are extraordinarily expressive, each one boasting its own hairstyle and unique facial features. Pit Two contains chariot drivers, cavalry, archers and infantrymen, and broken arms and heads can still be seen scattered in the solidified mud. Pit Three is the smallest and is believed to represent the army headquarters.

Expect to spend around half a day exploring the pits and viewing the excellent exhibitions. You'll probably also need to factor in time at the huge market outside where you can buy Terracotta Army-inspired souvenirs.

Old Xi'an

Back in Xi'an proper, head towards the cluster of landmarks that lie in the middle of the city. The **Great Mosque** offers the best sense of Xi'an's cosmopolitan history. Originally built in 743 by Persian merchants, it was moved to its modern location in the 14th century, while the current building only dates from the 18th century. With a traditional Chinese pagoda serving as the minaret, the mosque melds a traditional Chinese temple layout with Arabic and Persian embellishments. The timber-built main prayer hall is a highlight. Just around the corner are the **Bell and Drum Towers**, facing each other across a newly built square. In Xi'an's glory days, the bell would have been rung as the city gates opened at dawn, and the drum struck as they were closed at dusk. Both are open daily.

The oldest building in town is the **Greater Wild Goose Pagoda**. The seven-storey structure was built in AD 652 at the request of legendary monk Xuanzang, who walked his way to India in the name of Buddhist learning and brought back invaluable translations of original texts. The 64.5m (212-foot) temple contains a few simple reproductions of these scriptures, but there's no English translation. It is one of the few places where you can witness original Tang-era masonry and is regarded by many as the symbol of the city.

TAKING A BREAK

Bars and cafés are clustered around **Defu Xi'ang**, an alley that runs parallel to Nan Dajie, just to the northwest of the South Gate. This is an atmospheric place to grab a beer or cup of coffee.

➕ 197 E1 ✉ Shanxi province

The Terracotta Warriors

☎ 029 8139 9001; www.bmy.com.cn ⏰ Mar–Nov daily 8:30–5:30; Dec–Feb 8:30–5 💵 Moderate, prices varies during the year 🚌 Book a tour in Xi'an, or take public bus 306 from the square beside the railway station

Shanxi History Museum
✉ 91 Xiaozhai Donglu ☎ 029 8521 9422; www.sxhm.com ⏰ Mid-Mar to mid-Nov daily 8:30–6:30; mid-Nov to mid-Mar daily 9–5:30 💵 Moderate, price varies during the year

Xi'an's South Gate (Yongning)

XI'AN: INSIDE INFO

Top tips The best spot to scale the city walls is at the **South Gate** (40RMB). The views of the city are excellent and the **Beilin Museum**, a few hundred metres to the east, has a fascinating collection of excavated stone tablets and carvings, many of which date back more than 2,000 years.

• The **Shanxi History Museum** is second only to the Shanghai Museum in showcasing the very best of Chinese history and culture. There are impressive displays from China's greatest two eras, the Han and Tang dynasties.

One to miss Qin Huangshi's Mausoleum is 1.5km (1 mile) east of the Terracotta Warriors. It's believed even more figurines are buried here, though full excavations have not taken place. Visitors are limited to climbing round the mound and walking around the exhibition halls.

2 Dunhuang

Dunhuang is long way from everywhere. Lying right at the far end of the Hexi Corridor in northwest Gansu province, this lush oasis town was the last stop for Chinese Buddhist pilgrims heading to India and a welcome return to civilization for those who made it through the Taklamakan Desert. Many of these adventurers were also artists and left their stunning legacy at the nearby Mogao Caves.

With the sand dunes of the Gobi Desert rearing up at the edge of the city, Dunhuang has an undeniable wow factor. The urban centre has benefited hugely from a recent makeover and is now leafy and pleasant, but the real attraction remains the **Mogao Caves**, which lie 25km (15.5 miles) southeast of the city.

Seated Tang Buddha (inset) in the Mogao Caves (bottom)

Mogao Caves

The so-called "caves" are actually a series of man-made shrines, each containing stone sculptures and rock paintings. They were excavated by hand across a 1.6km-long (1-mile) sandstone cliff face. There were once more than 1,000 caves, but only 428 remain today. Of these, only 30 are open to the public and you will be permitted to see a maximum of 10 on any given day. The number of accessible caves may dwindle even further as China gets serious about conservation.

The complex dates from AD 366, when a Chinese monk on his way to India had a vision of Buddha. Believing he was on holy ground, he convinced a wealthy Silk Road pilgrim to fund the creation of the first cave.

Pagoda at Crescent Moon Lake

Development continued through 10 dynasties, with pilgrims adding new caves and artistic interpretations of Buddha. Work reached its peak during the Sui and Tang dynasties (AD 581–907).

The caves show a mixture of influences. The earliest ones of the Northern Wei dynasty (AD 386– 534) display slim, ethereal figures that have a distinct Indian feel. More than half of the caves visible today date from the Tang dynasty (AD 618–907) and reflect the internationalism of the rulers of that era. The faces of these statues are often lively and expressive and there are discernible Greek and Western Asian influences.

As the Tang dynasty fell and China's economy slowed, the caves mysteriously became a dumping ground for a variety of documents and manuscripts before being sealed from the elements some time in the 11th century. The Western explorers who "discovered" the caves in 1900 were astonished to find texts more than 1,000 years old. Many were stolen and taken back home. The 8th-century AD "Diamond Sutra", the earliest printed book in existence, is now in residence at the British Library in London.

Other Attractions

Of the other attractions around Dunhuang, the best is the **Crescent Moon Lake**. This tiny pool lies at the point where the oasis meets the desert around 6km (3.5 miles) south of town. More impressive than the lake itself are the sand dunes that tower above visitors. From here you can enjoy camel rides, go dune surfing or take a scenic tour on the underside of a paraglider.

TAKING A BREAK

The area around the caves is undeveloped and **food options are limited**. Traditional "pulled noodles" – *la mian* – are popular in Dunhuang.

195 F4
Mogao Caves
☎ 0937 886 9060; www.dha.ac.cn 🏛 Expensive, including guide. It may be possible to pay extra to get access to non-public caves but expect a large asking price ⏰ Apr–Oct daily 8–6; Nov–Mar 9–5:30 🚌 30-minute bus or taxi ride from Dunhuang 🚉 Dunhuang railway station

Crescent Moon Lake
☎ 0937 888 3389 🏛 Moderate ⏰ Daily 7am–10pm 🚕 Take a taxi from the city

DUNHUANG: INSIDE INFO

Top tips The **best time to visit** is between April and October. High summer may be dry but the heat is tolerable, whereas winter is spine-numbingly cold.
• As the caves are an archaeological work in progress, the local authorities are very protective of them, and you must visit in the **company of a guide**. There are three English-language tours a day, at 9am, noon and 2pm.

❸ Kashgar

Lying between the Taklamakan Desert and the Tianshan mountains, Kashgar (Kashi) is China's most westerly city. This Silk Road oasis is home to the largest mosque in China, and has an overwhelmingly Muslim flavour.

Kashgar's Old Town is in the north of the city. Here you'll find the main tourist draw, the **Id Kah Mosque**. This yellow-trimmed building was originally built in the 15th century and is China's largest Muslim temple, capable of holding 20,000. The design – narrow minarets either side of an arched entrance – is similar to those in other parts of Central Asia.

The Id Kah Mosque

Kashgar is also home to several Muslim tombs, containing exquisite moaics. The most impressive is the **Tomb of Abakh Khoja**, a religious and political leader of the 17th century. His tiled mausoleum, 5km (3 miles) northeast of the city, is the holiest Muslim site in Xinjiang.

The legendary **Sunday Market** is now a daily occurance at Aizilaiti Lu (best on Sunday). The nearby weekly **Livestock Market** is worth a visit.

TAKING A BREAK

The stalls near the Id Kah Mosque, just off **Jiafang Beilu**, offer a variety of Muslim cuisine. The breads are delicious.

➕ 192 A2
Id Kah Mosque
☎ 0998 282 7113 ⏱ Daily 9–9. Avoid prayer times 💰 Inexpensive

Tomb of Abakh Khoja
☎ 0998 265 0630 ⏱ Daily 10am–dusk 💰 Inexpensive

At Your Leisure

4 Jiayuguan

Midway along the Hexi Corridor, Jiayuguan once marked the western tip of the Great Wall and the western boundary of the Chinese empire. The **Jiayuguan Fort**, guarding the pass that lies between snow-capped Qilianshan and Heishan mountains, has been so well restored that it has lost some of its ancient charm. Nevertheless, the surrounds are scenic and an epic sense of history remains. Even though China controlled territory far beyond this point, the fort was the last major military stronghold of Chinese civilization.

The **Overhanging Great Wall**, linking the town with Heishan, is believed to have been constructed in 1539, but then crumbled to dust and was only rebuilt by students in 1987. From the upper tower, high on a ridge, there are sweeping views of the desert and snow-capped mountain peaks.

➕ 196 B3 ✉ Gansu province
🚉 Jiayuguan railway station

5 Turpan (Tulufan)

Xinjiang's bountiful summer fruit harvest is sold at stalls across China. Things always taste better at source, and so it is in Turpan, where the bustling markets are piled with a colourful mixture of melons, pears, apricots, peaches, pomegranates and grapes. That anything grows here at all is a miracle. Lying in a deep depression 154m (505 feet) below sea level, Turpan is one of the hottest, driest places on earth. This is a classic desert oasis city, with water channelled from distant glaciers through an ingenious series of irrigation channels.

The 40m-tall (130-foot) **Emin Ta**, an Iranian-style brick minaret dating from 1778, is the pick of the city-centre cultural trips, but ensure you also make time to tour the outlying areas. The ancient desert ruins of **Jiaohe** and **Gaochang** are a short drive out of town and the nearby **Flaming Mountains**, so named because of their deep red hue, are simply breathtaking.

➕ 193 E2 ✉ Xinjiang province
🚌 Buses regularly make the 180km (112-mile) trip from Urumqi. Journey time is 4 hours. Minibus tours of the city ruins and the Flaming Mountains can be booked in Turpan

Turpan's Flaming Mountains catch the early morning sun

6 Tianchi

Tianchi is a deep-blue lake nestled amid the magnificent scenery of the snowy Tianshan mountain range, 110km (68 miles) north of Xinjiang's provincial capital, Urumqi. The mountains rise spectacularly from the desert plains and it's possible to take a horseback ride up through the fir trees all the way to the snow line. During the summer months local Kazakhs set up tents for tourists and it's worth making the two-day hike around the lake. Lying at an elevation of 1,980m (6,500 feet), the lake freezes over in winter and the roads are often closed, so check on conditions before setting out.

➕ 193 E3 ✉ Xinjiang province
🖐 Moderate 🚌 Bus from Urumqi. The return trip can be made in a day though it's possible to stay in one of the semipermanent camps on the lakeside

7 Karakuli Hu

Several hours southwest of Kashgar lies Karakuli Hu (Karakul Lake), a dreamy vista of teardrop blue water and snow-tipped mountain peaks. Lying at 3,600m (11,800 feet) above sea level, the lake is famed for its hypnotizing azure hues. Assuming the highway is in good

Yurts (portable dwellings) and camels at Karakul Lake

order (and you're travelling in a private car), the 200km (124-mile) journey can be done in a very long daytrip, but to properly enjoy the area, stay in simple accommodation around the lake. There is a Chinese-run hotel with rooms for around 50RMB and a scattering of Tajik settlements of yurts and stone houses which travellers can rent.

The three mountains to the east of the lake soar to impressive heights. Muztagata is 7,546m (24,758 feet) high, Kongur Tagh 7,649m (25,096 feet) and Kongur Tube 7,530m (34,705 feet). Travellers continuing on the road past Karakul Lake will reach the Pakistan border at the Karakoram Pass.

➕ 192 A2 ✉ Xinjiang province
✉ Daily public buses run Mar–Nov from Kashgar and return buses from the nearby town Taskkurgan. Due to the condition of both road and bus, the journey takes up to 6 hours. Tours can also be arranged in Kashgar

Where to... Stay

Prices

Expect to pay per double room, including breakfast and taxes, per night
$** under 400RMB **$$** 400–1,000RMB **$$$ over 1,000RMB

Chini Bagh Hotel $$

This hotel has been built in the gardens of the old British Consulate and, in spite of the depressing outer appearance, has comfortable rooms, particularly in the Friendship Wing, at the front of the complex. There are also dormitory rooms. Facilities include a snooker room and sauna.

➕ 192 A2 ✉ 144 Seman Lu, Kashgar
📞 0998 298 0671

Silk Road Dunhuang Hotel $$

The Silk Road Hotel has been built in the style of a Ming-dynasty palace amid the sand dunes south of town. The rooms are decorated in warm desert hues and vary in style from ancient courtyard villa to modern western. The hotel can organize camel riding and sand sledging, and there are nightly cultural performances.

➕ 195 F4 ✉ Dunyuet Lu, Dunhuang
📞 0937 888 2088;
www.the-silk-road.com

Sofitel on Renmin Square $$$

This top-notch hotel slots into China's new "Five-Star Platinum" rating category standard. It has two huge wings and 432 rooms, cosily decorated in soft furnishings. There are four restaurants, including one specializing in Muslim cuisine, and two bars.

➕ 197 E1 ✉ 319 Dongxin Jie, Xi'an
📞 029 8792 8888; www.sofitel.com

Where to... Eat and Drink

Prices

Expect to pay for a meal for one, excluding drinks
$** under 50RMB **$$** 50–100RMB **$$$ over 100RMB

Charley Johng's Café $

This is one of a number of Western-style cafés that have grown up around the backpacker trail throughout this remote part of China. Charley Johng's serves classic Chinese favourites, such as sweet and sour pork (*gulu rou*) and spicy tofu (*mala doufu*), as well as such Western standards as banana pancakes, muesli with local fruit and some very decent coffee. Bike rental and internet access are also available.

➕ 195 F4 ✉ Mingshan Lu, Dunhuang 📞 0937 883 3039
🕐 Daily 7:30am–11pm

Defachang Dumpling Restaurant $$$

This is one of China's most famous and popular restaurants, thanks in part to its prime location between the Drum and Bell towers in Xi'an, and also because of its fantastically juicy *jiaozi* (dumplings). Try the famous Dumpling Feast to sample a spread of the dizzying varieties on offer. Their shapes vary according to the type of fillings used, which include duck, shrimp and walnut marzipan.

➕ 197 E1 ✉ 1 Xi Dajie, Zhongulou Guangchang, Xi'an 📞 029 8721 8260
🕐 Daily 10–9:30

Feng Yi Ting $$

The Feng Yi Ting serves excellent Sichuan and Cantonese dishes, as well as Dunhuang's regional cuisine. This courtyard restaurant is decorated in classical Chinese style, with red lanterns hanging from the ceiling.

⊞ 195 F4 ⊠ Silk Road Dunhuang Hotel, Dunyue Lu, Dunhuang ☎ 0937 888 2088 ☻ Daily 6:30am–10pm

John's Information Café $$

A friendly and relaxed place, popular with backpackers, John's is located within the grounds of the Seman Hotel. The food and drink is very simple but satisfying, with a range of Western choices – such as burgers and a cooked breakfast – alongside Xinjiang delicacies. John Hu, the owner, speaks good English, and is a great source of information, both about what to do around Kashgar and how to do it.

⊞ 192 A2 ⊠ 337 Seman Lu, Kashgar ☎ 0998 258 1186; www.johncafe.net ☻ Daily 8:30am–1am

Lao Chayuan Jiudian $$

This hotel restaurant serves up traditional Uyghur dishes in comfortable surroundings. Unusually for this part of the country, food is attractively presented and, street stalls excepted, it's the most popular place to sample local cuisine. Try the beef noodle soup or the lamb shish kabobs.

⊞ 192 A2 ⊠ 251 Renmin Xilu, Kashgar ☎ 0998 282 4467 ☻ Daily 8am–11pm

Muslim Street $

Muslim Street has market stalls during the day but really comes alive at night time when the eating begins. It's lined with small restaurants serving traditional Muslim food, offering a taste for what's in store ahead on the Silk Road. Be sure to try the Yangrou Pao Mo, a famous soup in which flat bread is broken into a broth and served up with slices of lamb.

⊞ 197 E1 ⊠ Huimin Jie, Xi'an (north of the Drum Tower)

Where to... Shop

DUNHUANG

Dunhaung was called "Gua (melon) Zhou (region)" in ancient times and the city markets still abound with fragrant fruits. For local crafts and products, head to **Fanggu Shangye Yitao Jie** (Ancient Shopping Street), a long pedestrian strip that runs from Yangguan Donglu to Kinjian Lu (open 5pm–midnight daily). Among the cultural odds and ends are jade, carpets and Dunhuang's famous "Yangguan" luminous cups. These drinking vessels glow in the dark, thanks to the mineral content of the jade quarried from nearby Mount Qilian. You can also buy the local wine, made with Dunhuang's famously sweet grapes. It may be too sweet for some, but makes for an unusual gift.

KASHGAR

More than anywhere else en route, Kashgar captures the commercial spirit of the Silk Road. The most celebrated of its many trading gatherings is the legendary **Sunday Market** (the Yekshenba Bazaar), off Aizilaiti Lu. The din of rumbling carts, camels and traders rushing to set up their stalls begins before dawn. Everything you can think of is on sale, from Central Asian clothes and carpets, to buckets of lard, to DVD players. The market is a seething labyrinth of stalls. The only area where there's space to get your bearings is the horse-trading area, due to the necessity of a having a test-drive track for prospective clients. Though the market is now a daily occurrence, things still only get really busy on Sunday.

In the eastern suburb of Kashgar is the **East Gate Bazaar** (Dongmen Dabazha), which is particularly good for hats and knives. The **Old Town Bazaar** along Jiefang Beilu and surrounding streets makes for another great shopping (and eating) experience.

XI'AN

Huajue Xiang is a narrow, under-cover alley that leads from the Drum Tower up to and beyond the entrance to the Great Mosque. It is lined with many great souvenir shops selling everything from jade and jewellery to cheap trinkets. The **Arts Street** (Shuyuanmen) runs between the south gate of the City Walls and the Beilin Museum, and has stores selling craft and souvenirs. It's a good spot for calligraphy and ink paintings, as well as Terracotta Warrior reproductions in miniature. Also try the stalls and shops in between the many restaurants along **Muslim Street** (Huimin Jie). Up-market shopping can be found in abundance off **Nan Dajie** and in the **Century Ginwa mall**, beneath the square that divides the Drum and Bell towers.

Where to...
Be Entertained

Nightlife

As one of China's most important cities, Xi'an has all the usual nightlife options, from dance clubs to smoky snooker halls. The towns farther west are more remote and nightlife often revolves around the hotel, or the backpacker bars.

XI'AN

Tang Dynasty Theater Restaurant (75 Chang'an Lu, Xi'an; tel: 029 8782 2222; www.xi'antangdynasty. com) offers a spectacular dining experience. The set menu dishes are served in an opulent auditorium when nightly traditional song and dance shows are put on for patrons. It's a super-slick, made-for-tourist experience, but the performance is well-honed and hard not to enjoy.

It's possible to buy separate tickets for the food or the theater, or combine them. In keeping with the imperial décor, the prices are high. Visit the website for more details.

Defu Xiang, an alley just west of Nan Dajie near the Bell Tower, has a cluster of bars and cafes. This is an atmospheric place to grab a beer or cup of coffee.

The **Entertainers Pub and Pizzeria** in the Hyatt Regency Hotel (158 Dong Dajie; tel: 029 8769 1234; www.hyatt.com) has nightly live music, a disco area and a snooker room, making it a pleasant place to wind down after seeing the many sights of Xi'an.

Anyone wanting to take things one stage further should head for the **One Plus One** (Yi Jia Yi) night-club (285 Dong Dajie; tel: 029 872

0008; 8pm–3am), which plays extremely loud house and Chinese rock and disco to a mixed local and international crowd.

DUNHUANG

The **Sand Dunes and Crescent Moon Lake** (5km/3 miles south of Dunhuang; tel: 0937 888 3389) is open 24 hours and is a great place to play on the sand dunes, either early in the morning or even under the stars at night. It's possible to take short camel rides into the dunes here, go sand sledding, or indulge in a bit of dune paragliding.

KASHGAR

Kashgar is bazaar city and the selling doesn't stop with the sun going down. The **Night Bazaar** is held immediately in front of the Id Kah Mosque and is something of a social event for locals. The stalls include tea and coffee outlets and the occasional street entertainer.

Walks

1 Beijing's Hutong
  174 – 176
2 Shanghai's French
  Concession 177 – 179
3 Sheung Wan to Central, Hong
  Kong 180 – 182

1 Beijing's Hutong

Walk

DISTANCE 5.5km (3.5 miles) TIME 5 hours
START POINT Yonghegong Metro ✚ 210 C5 (off map) END POINT Beihai Park North Gate,
Di'anmenxi Dajie ✚ 210 B4

Once upon a time, the whole of Beijing was composed of *hutong* alleys. These charming residential neighbourhoods were defined by proximity to the Forbidden City – the higher class the *hutong*, the closer it was to the emperor's palace. Thus the maze of alleys around the Drum and Bell towers were once home to some important folk. These days they make for a picturesque and relaxing stroll in the heart of China's bustling capital.

Note: This route involves a long walk between the Imperial Academy and the Houyuan'ensi Hutong (approx 1.5km/1 mile). For a shorter stroll, begin at the entrance to Houyuan'ensi Hutong on Jiaodaokounan Dajie. Alternatively, cover the route on bicycle.

1–2

Walk south from Yonghegong metro station, away from the flyover of the Second Ring Road and towards the incense-shrouded **Lama Temple** (➤ 58). The entrance is on Yonghegong Dajie at the far south of the temple complex. Expect to spend at least an hour exploring the colourful prayer halls and marvelling at the Buddhist rituals unfolding within. A long row of shops selling Buddhist talismans and trinkets is outside the temple on Yonghegong Dajie. Having picked up a lucky charm or two, wander beneath the ornamental archway (*paitou*) that marks the entrance to Guozijian Jie. A few metres along the street is the **Temple of Confucius**, a haven of spacious courtyards and ancient cypress trees, and much quieter than its Buddhist neighbour. Inside the temple proper are stone slabs which record the names of students

who successfully sat their imperial examinations in this spot. Continue west on Guozijian Jie to reach the **Imperial Academy**, where emperors of old would expound the Confucian classics to an audience of kneeling officials, scholars and students.

Page 173: The Bell Tower, Beijing
Right: The Lama Temple's Hall of the Wheel of the Law

lathered onto the rippling snack. Add some bean sprouts and shredded lettuce, fold up in a square and you have a classic Beijing meal-to-go. From the crossroads, head south on Jiaodaokounan Dajie and take the third right into **Houyuan'ensi Hutong**. This marks the beginnings of a large *hutong* quadrant. At No. 13 is the **Former Residence of Mao Dun**, a celebrated communist-era writer. The museum is fairly low key but it's worth exploring Mao's classic courtyard *hutong* home. Continue along the street to reach **Nanluogu Xiang**, one of Beijing's most famous alleyways lined with fantastically snug courtyard coffee shops and street-side kebab sell-

Taking a Break

Xiaoxin Café (tel: 010 6403 6956; open: 9am–2am) is one of the most light and airy of the cluster of cafés on Nanluogu Xiang (it's at No 103). It does some fantastic homemade cheese and chocolate cakes.

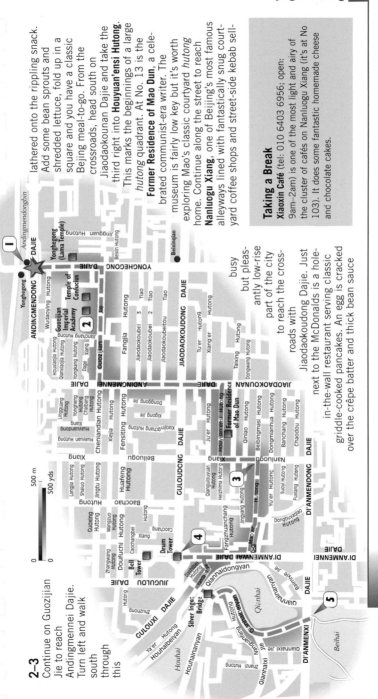

2–3

Continue on Guozijian Jie to reach Andingmennei Dajie. Turn left and walk south through this

busy but pleasantly low-rise part of the city to reach the crossroads with

Jiaodaokoudong Dajie. Just next to the McDonalds is a hole-in-the-wall restaurant serving classic griddle-cooked pancakes. An egg is cracked over the crêpe batter and thick bean sauce

ers. Turn left and walk south towards the entrance to the Mao'er Hutong, around which some of the best cafés are clustered.

3–4

Having refuelled, turn west into the **Mao'er Hutong,** home to the rich and famous of Beijing past. Among them was Wan Rong, wife to "Last Emperor" Puyi. She lived at Nos 35 and 37. These courtyards, like most of the historic buildings along this stretch, are not open to the public, but if you spot a door

One of the red drums in the Drum Tower

Beijing's "Lake District"

The manmade lakes of Xihai, Houhai and Qianhai were excavated under Mongol leadership during the Yuan dynasty (AD 1206–1368) and used to connect China's newly anointed capital with the Grand Canal. For years the 1,600km-long (995-mile) waterway had been used to transport grain and silk from the fertile south to the dry plains of the north. Thanks to the lakes, barges could unload their precious cargo close to the market street of Yandai Xiejie. In Yuan times the nearby Drum Tower marked the centre of the city and, with it, the huge Mongol empire.

ajar, feel free to poke your head in and flash a smile at whoever is inside – you may be allowed to look around. Continue until you hit Di'anmenwai Dajie. This road lies on a north-south trajectory that passes through all the main ceremonial halls of the Forbidden City.

The palace is obscured by Jingshan, which rises to the south, while to the north are the **Drum and Bell towers.** The large trapezoid tower visible now is the Drum Tower, while the Bell Tower is obscured from view immediately behind it. These two buildings were used to mark the beginning and end of the

day in imperial times. They can both be climbed (for a fee) and boast tremendous views of this attractive part of the city.

4–5

From the Drum Tower, retrace your steps south and take a right (west) into **Yandaixi Jie,** a popular market area during the Ming dynasty (AD 1368–1644) and now a trendy café and shopping street with the buildings refurbished in a traditional style. Bear left and head towards Qianhai, one of the three major bodies of water that comprise Beijing's so-called "Lake District". Cross Houhai Beiyan to reach the elegant **Silver Ingot Bridge,** from where – on a rare clear day – it's possible to see all the way to the Fragrant Hills, northwest of the city. Having crossed the bridge, bear left and wander beneath the willows that line the lakes. The waterfront bars and cafés here are especially popular in summer, while in winter the lake ices over and becomes a giant rink where locals play hockey or skate. At the south end of the lake is a Starbucks café, housed in a Ming-era building. Cross Dianmen Xidajie to reach the walled entrance of Beihai Park.

2 Shanghai's French Concession

Walk

DISTANCE 4km (2.5 miles) **TIME** 4 hours
START POINT Fuxing Park ✚ 208 B2 **END POINT** Nanjing Xilu Metro ✚ 208 B3

Following the First Opium War in 1842, the Treaty of Nanjing made Shanghai a British-controlled trading port. A few years later, France joined the colonial gold rush and took a slice of the city for itself. Instead of filling its patch with banks and trading houses, the French built stylish villas, theatres and clubs, connected by a series of leafy boulevards. The area soon became the beating heart of swinging Shanghai – and remains so to this day.

1–2

Once known as "French Park", **Fuxing Park** (Fuxing Gongyuan) offers fascinating cultural contrasts. By day, locals gather under the century-old plane trees to practise tai chi and play chess. By night, they canoodle in the shadows, *à la Français*. Exit at the more southerly of the two western gates onto Xiangshan Lu. To the left lies the pebble-covered **Former Residence of Sun Yat-sen**,

revolutionary father of modern China. Sun is adored within China and his home remains a place of pilgrimage. Turn right onto Sinan Lu, heading past the grand mansions that were once home to diplomats and celebrities. After the communist revolution these beautiful villas were divvied up between multiple families. Note the rusty bikes parked in once-stately lobbies. Nevertheless, in the elaborate gables and terraces there is still the distinct whiff of past decadence. Take a short detour down Gaolan Lu to view the Russian-built **St Nicholas Church**.

2–3

Emerge onto **Huaihai Zhonglu** to find yourself back in the 21st-century comfort zone,

Starbucks and all. Turn left and join the throng shuffling slowly past the string of international boutiques. Up ahead is the **Cathay Theatre**, easily identified by its distinctive spire. Built in 1932, this was one of Shanghai's earliest cinemas and showed the new breed of Hollywood "talkies" to an exclusively foreign audience. Turn right down Maoming Nanlu to view the **Okura Garden Hotel** ahead on your left. Built in 1926 as the "Cercle Sportif Français", this was once Shanghai's most lively club. Upper-crust members would come to swim in the Olympic-sized pool and sip cocktails on the roof terrace. It later became Mao Zedong's headquarters, and an eight-

Outside the colonial-style Lyceum Theatre

The Hengshan Moller Villa, now a hotel

room air-raid shelter was built beneath the garden. Try to ignore the uninspired hotel tower – a relatively modern extension – and concentrate your attentions on the lobby and the first two floors. Be sure to sneak a peek at the stained-glass roof and the sprung dance floor of the Grand Ballroom. Across the road is the distinctive black and white brick **Jinjiang Hotel**. Built in 1928, this building was the very first high-rise apartment block in a city that is now dominated by such structures. It was here that US president Richard Nixon and Zhou Enlai signed the historic Sino-US communiqué in 1972. Further north, on the corner of Maoming Nanlu and Changle Lu, is the **Lyceum Theatre**, where a young Peggy Hookham danced while her father worked as an engineer in Shanghai. Peggy later returned as prima ballerina Dame Margot Fonteyn and her portrait still hangs in the lobby.

Taking a Break

The cosy **Boonna Café** (tel: 021 5404 6676; 9am–1am) has some interesting brews from Yunnan province and is just across the road from the Russian Mission Church on Xinle Lu. If you are feeling hungry at the end of the walk, head for **Wujiang Lu**. It's packed with noodle and dumpling joints and is a great place to refuel after a hard day's walk.

3–4

Turn left onto Changle Lu to enjoy some window shopping at the tailor-made Cheongsam stores. At Shaanxi Nanlu, take another left to enter shoe heaven. Prices are great, but you'll need petite feet to take full advantage. Consider making a short detour down Lane 180, on your right, to visit **Torana House**. This superb gallery has a fabulous collection of Tibetan rugs. Continue down Shaanxi Nanlu and take a right onto Xinle Lu. This stretch of tiny boutiques is where Shanghai's fashionistas come to stockpile local designer gear. History buffs might want to check out the nearby green-domed **Russian Mission Church**. From

The White Russians of Shanghai

Many of the "White Russians" fleeing the Bolshevik Revolution in their homeland headed for the safety of the colonial settlements of Shanghai. By 1932 they formed the second largest foreign community in the city (after the Japanese) and were so numerous that work began on several impressive Russian Orthodox churches, two of which can be seen on the walk. Portraits of the last tsar, Nicholas II, used to hang inside St Nicholas Church. After 1949, these were replaced by photos of Mao Zedong.

the church, head north on Xiangyang Beilu until you reach Julu Lu, another tree-lined avenue well endowed with boutique shops. Turn right and head east to rejoin Shaanxi Nanlu. Turn left here and walk towards the **Hengshan Moller Villa**. This bizarre Gothic vision is now a hotel (▶ 84) but the Bonomi Café gives non-residents the excuse to head inside.

4–5

Cross Yanan Zhonglu, passing under the elevated highway of the same name that bisects the western half of Shanghai. Keep

walking north until you meet Weihai Lu. Turn right and walk for a few hundred metres until you pass the south entrance to a

sprawling residential compound on your left. This is the south part of Taixing Lu, one of Shanghai's best-preserved and most atmospheric **longtang neighbourhoods**. The street vendors and cheerful washing lines prove the area is still very much lived in. The atmospheric side streets offer a non-reconstructed glimpse into "old Shanghai". Emerging onto Nanjing Xilu, turn right to reach the recently renamed Nanjing Xilu metro station (previously "Shimen Yi Lu").

The art deco ballroom in the Okura Garden Hotel

3 Sheung Wan to Central

Walk

Hong Kong Island is far more than the sum of its flash cars, glitzy malls and newfangled glass skyscrapers, as this walk proves. Let the hustle and bustle of the metropolis melt away as you head into the fragrant backstreets of Sheung Wan and Central. Peel back the layers of history to reveal traditional markets and delightful colonial buildings rubbing shoulders with Hong Kong's modern constructions.

DISTANCE 3.5km (2 miles) **TIME** 4 hours
START POINT Sheung Wan MTR station **END POINT** Central MTR station

1–2

Turn right out of Exit B of the Sheung Wan MTR station and walk for a few minutes to reach the **Western Market**. Built in 1906, this distinctive Edwardian building fell into disuse before being declared a historical monument in 1990 and restored to its former glory. Next to it is the **Sheung Wan Fong** piazza – a good base from which to explore the many traditional shopping streets around Sheung Wan. Head off towards Morrison Street before

taking a right into **Wing Lok Street**. This thoroughfare is lined with speciality shops selling ginseng and bird's nest, two of the vital ingredients in Hong Kongers' complex recipe for longevity. At the end of the street, turn left into **Des Voeux Road West**, where there are yet more bags stacked with fragrant preserva-

Land Reclamation in Hong Kong

It may not look like it, but Possession Street was once located on a cape that commanded a magnificent ocean view. This steep central street marks the point where Queen Victoria's foreign legion first landed in Hong Kong in 1841. Noting the scarcity of developable land, the new colonial masters began experimenting with land reclamation and never really looked back. Victoria Harbour is now barely half its original 2km (1-mile) width and the poor proprietors on Possession Street haven't so much as a letterbox view of the sea.

tives. This street is particularly famous for exotic dried seafood. Walk along Des Voeux Road West and turn left into **Ko Shing Street**. This is the wholesale centre of Hong Kong's thriving medicine trade. It is renowned for its wide selection of herbal medicine and expert

Food shop in Des Voeux Road West

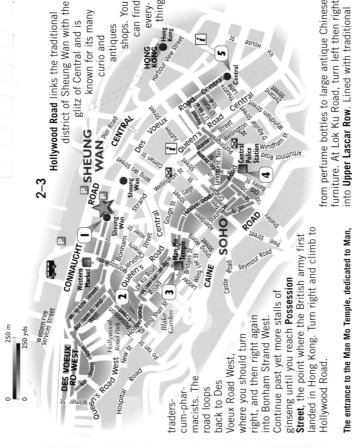

2-3

Hollywood Road links the traditional district of Sheung Wan with the glitz of Central and is known for its many curio and antiques shops. You can find everything

traders-cum-pharmacists. The road loops back to Des Voeux Road West, where you should turn right, and then right again into Bonham Strand West. Continue past yet more stalls of ginseng until you reach **Possession Street,** the point where the British army first landed in Hong Kong. Turn right and climb to Hollywood Road.

The entrance to the Man Mo Temple, dedicated to Man, God of Literature and Mo, God of War

from perfume bottles to large antique Chinese furniture. At Lok Ku Road, turn left then right into **Upper Lascar Row.** Lined with traditional stalls, this street is a great place to pick up a wide variety of collectables. Take a right at Ladder Street and head back up the hill to Hollywood Road. Just opposite is the **Man Mo Temple**, one of the first traditional temples built during the colonial era. The magnificent façade reflects its historical roots, while inside the air is thick with aromatic incense smoke, said to carry prayers to the spirit world. Gold altars and red shrines pay homage to the Taoist gods of literature ("Man") and war ("Mo"), Man with his calligraphy brush and Mo with his sword. The temple's historical artefacts include a bronze bell dating to 1847 and imperial sedan chairs made in 1862.

3–4

Continue east along Hollywood Road until you join the **Mid-Levels Escalator**. Built primarily as a transit link for residents of the Mid-Levels district, this 800m-long (2,625-foot) escalator runs one-way downhill from 6am to 10am, and uphill from 10:20am to midnight. Take a right and ride the escalator up to Staunton Street, the gateway to **Soho**. This buzzing dining district takes its name from its location, SOuth of HOllywood Road, and consists of Staunton Street, Shelley Street, Elgin Street, Peel Street and Old Bailey

Antiques shop on Cat Street, Sheung Wan

Street, each of which are lined with great restaurants, coffee shops and funky bars. Walk a loop by heading west along Staunton Street before turning left into Peel Street, left again onto Elgin Street and making a final left onto Shelley Street. Walk back down the steps beside the escalator to Hollywood Road. Turn right to view the former **Central Police Station**, a four-storey colonial classic that dates to 1864.

4–5

Head across the road into Cochrane Street (beneath the escalator) and walk downhill. Turn right when you reach Stanley Street.

Taking a Break

As you walk downhill on Cochrane Street, look for **Gage Street** on your left. This lively lane will be recognizable for the billows of steam that spew from its traditional Cantonese restaurants. For something more up-market, try **Elgin Street** in Soho. **Craftsteak**, at No 29 (tel: 852 2526 0999), is the pick of the international bistros

This is a popular spot for photographers and there are hundreds of new and used cameras and accessories available at reasonable prices. Turn left onto the stone-slab **Pottinger Street steps**. Traditional stalls line this charming pedestrian thoroughfare and, set against the nearby modern buildings, it's one of the best spots to appreciate Hong Kong Island's singular mix of old and new. Continue along Pottinger Street to Des Voeux Road Central, turn right and right again into **Li Yuen Street West**. Between here and parallel **Li Yuen Street East** there is a warren of alleys selling knick-knacks and cheap clothing. When you're done browsing, rejoin Des Vouex Road Central and turn right to reach the Central MTR station, a few steps away.

Practicalities

Websites

- China National Tourism Adminsitration http://old.cnta.gov.cn/lyen/index.asp
- China National Tourist Office (CNTO, overseas office of the CNTA): www.cnto.org
- Beijing Tourism Administration: http://english.bjta.gov.cn
- Hong Kong Tourism Board: www.discoverhongkong.com
- Beijing 2008 Olympic Games: http://en.beijing2008.org

BEFORE YOU GO

WHAT YOU NEED

		UK	Germany	USA	Canada	Australia	Ireland	Netherlands	Spain
●	Required								
○	Suggested								
▲	Not required								
△	Not applicable								
Passport/National Identity Card		●	●	●	●	●	●	●	●
Visa (regulations can change – check before booking your trip)		●	●	●	●	●	●	●	●
Onward or Return Ticket		○	○	○	○	○	○	○	○
Health Inoculations (tetanus and polio)		○	○	○	○	○	○	○	○
Health Documentation		▲	▲	▲	▲	▲	▲	▲	▲
Travel Insurance		○	○	○	○	○	○	○	○
Driver's Licence (national)		△	△	△	△	△	△	△	△
Car Insurance Certificate		△	△	△	△	△	△	△	△
Car Registration Document		△	△	△	△	△	△	△	△

Some countries require a passport to remain valid for a minimum period (usually at least six months) beyond the date of entry – contact their consulate or embassy or your travel agent for details.

WHEN TO GO

Beijing

High season   Low season

JAN	FEB	MAR	APR	MAY	JUN	JUL	AUG	SEP	OCT	NOV	DEC
1°C	4°C	11°C	21°C	27°C	31°C	31°C	30°C	26°C	20°C	9°C	3°C
34°F	39°F	52°F	70°F	81°F	88°F	88°F	86°F	79°F	68°F	48°C	37°C

☀ Sun   ☁ Cloud   🌧 Wet   ⛅ Sun/Showers

Temperatures listed are the **average daily maximum**. China's climate varies greatly from region to region, but only Yunnan province has a truly pleasant year-round climate. Northern and western China have the clearest skies, but can be very dry and extremey cold in winter. Shanghai's climate is similar to the UK's, except for the extremely hot and humid summer. Hong Kong is warm and sticky, but cools off considerably during the winter. Chongqing is China's hottest city, but still suffers from lack of sun for most of the year. Summer is probably the least pleasant time to travel in China, but it's still regarded as high season for tourism. If you can bear occasionally chilly temperatures, there's much to recommend late autumn or early winter. Avoid the Chinese New Year holidays (Jan/Feb), Labour Day holidays (first week of May) and National Day holidays (first week of October).

GETTING THERE

By Air Hong Kong, Shanghai and Beijing are the main international airports, though Guangzhou does host some arrivals direct from mainland Europe and the USA. The major domestic carriers, Air China, China Southern Airlines and China Eastern Airlines, all operate internationally. Cathay Pacific is Hong Kong's well-connected flagship airline.

From the UK Virgin Atlantic flies to Shanghai and Hong Kong. British Airways flies to Beijing, Shanghai and Hong Kong. Oasis Hong Kong Airlines, a budget carrier, operates between Hong Kong and London Gatwick. Return tickets start from as little as £250. Flight time to the three major Chinese hubs is 10–12 hours.

From the rest of Europe Lufthansa, KLM and Air France are among the many airlines that fly between Europe and China (Beijing, Shanghai and Hong Kong). Air France and Lufthansa also fly direct to Guangzhou.

From the US and Canada American Airlines, United Airlines, Delta Airlines and Continental Airlines have direct flights to mainland China but often code share with Chinese airlines. United's flight between Washington DC and Beijing is the only direct flight between east coast USA and China. Flight time from Los Angeles is 12–15 hours.

From Australia Qantas operates direct flights to Beijing, Shanghai and Hong Kong. Flight time is 9–12 hours from Sydney.

TIME

 Beijing Standard Time is eight hours ahead of Greenwich Mean Time (GMT). There is no daylight saving. Despite spanning five time zones, the entire country adopts Beijing time. Locals in Xinjiang province sometimes adopt an unofficial local time, two hours behind Beijing.

CURRENCY AND FOREIGN EXCHANGE

Currency The *renminbi* (RMB) is the main unit of currency in China. It is divided into 10 *jiao*. Notes are in denominations of 0.1, 0.2, 0.5, 1, 2, 5, 10, 20, 50 and 100RMB. The renminbi is alternatively known as the *yuan*, but is normally called *kuai* in colloquial speech. The Hong Kong dollar (HK$) is the currency of Hong Kong, and notes are in denominations of 10, 20, 50, 100, 500 and 1,000. The *pataca* (MOP) is the currency of Macau. Notes are in denominations of 5, 10, 20, 50, 100 and 500. All three currencies are roughly equal in value, though the *renminbi* is marginally the strongest and the *pataca* the weakest.

Exchange Most foreign currencies can be exchanged through the Bank of China, though hotels and exchange booths provide similar services. It is normally more economical to exchange currency in China, where rates are reasonable. In contrast, Western banks rarely have a surplus of *renminbi* and normally offer terrible value.

Credit and debit cards It's easy to withdraw local currency direct from ATMs across China using your debit or credit card. No local charge is applied, though your own bank will likely levy a service fee. It is becoming easier to pay direct with plastic, but China has its own credit card system and many places do not accept foreign cards.

TIME DIFFERENCES

GMT
12 noon

Beijing
→ 8 pm

USA New York
← 7 am

USA LA
→ 4 pm

Germany
→ 1 pm

Australia
→ Sydney 10 pm

WHEN YOU ARE THERE

CLOTHING SIZES

UK	Rest of Europe	USA	
36	46	36	Suits
38	48	38	
40	50	40	
42	52	42	
44	54	44	
46	56	46	
7	41	8	Shoes
7.5	42	8.5	
8.5	43	9.5	
9.5	44	10.5	
10.5	45	11.5	
11	46	12	
14.5	37	14.5	Shirts
15	38	15	
15.5	39/40	15.5	
16	41	16	
16.5	42	16.5	
17	43	17	
8	34	6	Dresses
10	36	8	
12	38	10	
14	40	12	
16	42	14	
18	44	16	
4.5	38	6	Shoes
5	38	6.5	
5.5	39	7	
6	39	7.5	
6.5	40	8	
7	41	8.5	

NATIONAL HOLIDAYS

1 Jan	New Year Holiday
Jan/Feb	Chinese New Year (7 days)
1–7 May	Labour Day Holiday
1–7 Oct	National Day Holiday

CLOTHING SIZES

Many of the clothes and shoes produced for China end up in domestic shops and use international sizing methods. Most Chinese clothes use a simple "S, M, L, XL" system, but values may differ from the West. Shoes follow the mainland European model (39, 40, 41 etc).

OPENING HOURS

○ Shops   ● Post Offices
● Offices ● Museums/Monuments
● Banks   ○ Pharmacies

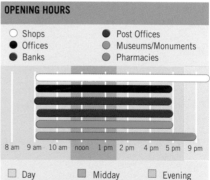

8 am 9 am 10 am noon 1 pm 2 pm 4 pm 5 pm 9 pm

☐ Day   ☐ Midday   ☐ Evening

Shops Shops in mainland China open early and close late (10pm). Few shut for lunch. Hong Kong shops may not open till 11, but stay open very late.
Banks Some services (including foreign exchange services) may not be available during lunch (11:30–2:30) and on weekends, especially in smaller cities. Mainland Chinese banks normally open on the weekend, but hours may be limited.
Post offices Times vary, but post offices often stay open much later than 5pm. Many open on weekends, but close for public holidays.
Pharmacies Opening hours vary but long working hours are the norm.

PERSONAL SAFETY

- Violent crime is extremely rare, though petty theft has become common in the bigger cities. Keep an eye on valuables in busy areas.
- It's safe to walk around Chinese cities at any time of day or night.
- Police officers usually speak a little English and are normally friendly and helpful. They may be reluctant to get involved with foreigners because of language difficulties.
- Train and air travel is very safe, road transport less so. Seat belts are rare on buses and in taxis, and driving standards are poor.

Police assistance:

 110 from any phone

TELEPHONES

buys around 37 minutes call time to the US and 27 minutes to Europe. There are also many phone "shops", which use IP technology and have metered public booths. Telephone boxes are not always easy to find. The easiest way to use them is to buy a prepaid IC card, also available from street vendors and stores.

IP cards can be used to make cheap international calls from any phone and are available from street vendors. A 100RMB card

International Dialling Codes
Dial 00 followed by

UK:	44
USA / Canada:	1
Irish Republic:	353
Australia:	61
Germany:	49

POST

Post offices are recognizable by their dark-green signs. The service is reliable and reasonably cheap. International postcards cost 4RMB to send and take 5–10 days to reach their destination. The post office also offers EMS express delivery internationally.

ELECTRICITY

Mainland China uses a 220-volt power supply. Plugs come in a variety of shapes,

 and most sockets cater to at least two varieties.

Most modern plugs are two-pin, similar to those used in the US. Hong Kong uses British-style three-pin plugs.

TIPS/GRATUITIES

Tipping is not customary in China, although tour guides and hotel porters may expect a small gratuity. Some restaurants might include a 10–15 per cent service charge in the bill.

Drivers	5RMB per person per day
Tour guides	10RMB per person per day
Porters	8RMB per person for groups; 5–10RMB per bag for individuals
Taxis	No tip necessary

UK	**USA**	**Ireland**	**Australia**	**Canada**
☎ 010 8529 6600	☎ 010 6532 3831	☎ 010 6532 2691	☎ 010 5140 4111	☎ 010 6532 3536

HEALTH

 Insurance Full travel insurance is essential when visiting China. Ensure your policy includes emergency evacuation to your own country. There is some excellent private health care available in the major cities but it is expensive. China has no national healthcare service as such, and local hospitals can be unpleasant and unreliable.

 Dental Services Have a dental check-up before coming to China. There are good dental services in the big cities but fees are high.

 Weather China is extremely humid in summer and dehydration may become a problem. Northern and western parts of China can be fiercely cold in winter. The reduced level of atmospheric oxygen in Tibet often causes altitude sickness. Wear sunscreen when visiting elevated regions, regardless of the temperature.

 Drugs It's best to bring whatever medication you may need from home. Chinese pharmacies are well stocked with Chinese and Western medicines but, due to the language problem, it can be difficult picking out the right product.

Safe Water Tap water is only safe to drink after being boiled. Purified water is available from most shops.

TIBET TRAVEL PERMIT

Foreign visitors must obtain a "Tibet Travel Permit" before visiting. Officially, you must be booked on a government-sanctioned tour to be granted a permit, but some companies may be able to supply just the paperwork. See also page 143.

CONCESSIONS

Young People/Senior Citizens Children and students get sizeable discounts at most major attractions, although ticket offices will often only accept Chinese student ID cards. Similarly, senior citizen discounts are common, but often only applicable to Chinese elders.

TRAVELLING WITH A DISABILITY

Major airports and large hotels generally have adequate facilities for visitors with a disability, but elsewhere services and amenities are poor. Thanks to the Olympic preparations, Beijing has begun introducing tactile paths and wheelchair ramps. Hong Kong is better. www.discoverhongkong.com/eng/travelneeds/disabled is good for information.

CHILDREN

The Chinese adore children. There are many attractions for children, including amusement areas in most parks. On the downside, few restaurants have children's menus and China's crowds can make keeping an eye on them a challenge. Ensure your kids carry a note in English and Chinese with a contact telephone number and address.

TOILETS

Sinks and urinals are often blocked with cigarette butts or worse, privacy is non-existent and running water is a bonus rather than the norm. Most public facilities have squat toilets and paper is rarely supplied. Carry tissues with you at all times. If in doubt, visit the nearest KFC, McDonalds or shopping mall.

MANDARIN AND PINYIN

China's official language is Mandarin. There may be thousands of different written characters, but the language uses surprisingly few spoken syllables. Consequently, Mandarin relies on tones to help users communicate clearly. There are four main tones (plus a neutral tone) and every syllable must be pronounced (roughly) in the correct tone for any sentence to be quickly understood.

Pinyin ("pin" means "spell" and "yin" means "sound") is a system of Romanization, which uses the Roman alphabet to guide pronunciation of Mandarin. Each syllable (relating to one character of written text) is composed of an initial, a final and the tone. Pinyin is primarily used by children and foreign students of Chinese. Consequently, native speakers of Mandarin may not be able to understand written pinyin, especially if the appropriate tones are not indicated.

Tones
– = The first (1) tone is high and flat
/ = The second (2) tone rises from a mid- to high-pitch
v = The third (3) tone falls to a low pitch before rising slightly
\ = The fourth (4) tone falls from a high- to low-pitch
     The neutral tone (5) is spoken softly with no particular emphasis

Note: If you have two "tone three" (v) words together, the first word becomes "tone two" (/).

INITIALS

b	as **p** in speak
p	as **p** in park
m	as **m** in mother
f	as **f** in father
d	as **t** in stay
t	as **t** in tag
n	as **n** in nurse
l	as **l** in lay
g	as **g** in girl
k	as **k** in kangaroo
h	as **h** in he
j	similar to **j** in jeep but sharper
q	similar to **ch** in cheap, but preceded by a sharp "t" sound
x	similar to **sh** in sheep, but not as full
zh	as **j** in jerk
ch	as **ch** in church
sh	as **sh** in ship
z	as **ds** in beads
c	as **ts** in coats
s	as **s** in see
r	a cross between the "y" in "you" and "r" in "roo"
y	as **y** in hymn
w	as **w** in water

FINALS

a	as **ar** in car
o	as **ar** in war
e	as **e** in her
i	as **e** in English
u	as **oo** in book
er	as **are** in are, with a vocalized final "r"
ai	as **y** in sky
ei	as **ay** in play
ao	as **ow** in cow
ou	as **o** in so
an	as **an** in can
en	as **un** in under
ang	as **ang** in clang
ong	as **ong** in long
in	as **in** in in
ing	as **ing** in sing
ie	as **ye** in yes
ia	as **ya** in yard
ian	as **yen** in yen
un	as **on** in won

USEFUL WORDS AND PHRASES

hello/goodbye **nǐ hǎo/zài jiàn**
thank you **xiè xiè**
you're welcome **bú kè qi**
sorry/excuse me **duì bu qǐ**
good morning (6–9am) **zǎo shàng hǎo**
good morning (9am–noon) **shàng wǔhǎo**
good afternoon **xià wǔhǎo**
good evening **wǎn shàng hǎo**
good night **wǎn ān**
yes/no **shì/bù**
please **qǐng**
where **zài nǎ lǐ**
here **zhèr**
there **nàr**
when **shén me shí hou**
why **wèi shén me**
who **shéi**
how are you? **nǐ hǎo ma?**
fine, thank you **wǒ hěn hǎo, xiè xiè**
my name is... **wǒ jiào...**
I am... **wǒ shì...**
what's your name? **nǐ jiào shén me míng zi?**
do you speak English? **nǐ huì shuō yīng wén ma?**
I don't speak Chinese **wǒ bú huì shuō zhōng wén**
I don't understand **wǒ bù dǒng**
help! **jiù mìng!**
police **jǐng chá**
on/to the right **zài/dào yòu biān**
on/to the left **zài/dào zuǒ biān**
opposite **duì miàn**
near **jìn**
far **yuàn**
north **běi**
south **nán**
east **dōng**
west **xī**
free **miǎn fèi**
open **kāi**
closed **guān bì**
church **jiào táng**
museum **bó wù guǎn**
palace **gōng diàn**
town **chéng zhèn**
road **lu**
street **jiē dào**
bridge **qiáo**

DAYS/MONTHS/HOLIDAYS

day **rì**
month **yuè**
year **nián**
today **jīn tiān**
tomorrow **míng tiān**

yesterday **zuó tiān**
Monday **xīng qī yī**
Tuesday **xīng qī yī**
Wednesday **xīng qī èr**
Thursday **xīng qī sì**
Friday **xīng qī wǔ**
Saturday **xīng qī liù**
Sunday **xīng qī tiān(rì)**
January **yī yuè**
February **èr yuè**
March **sān yuè**
April **sì yuè**
May **wǔ yuè**
June **liù yuè**
July **qī yuè**
August **bā yuè**
September **jiǔ yuè**
October **shí yuè**
November **shí yī yuè**
December **shí èr yuè**
national holiday **guó dìng jià rì**
Easter **fù huó jié**
Christmas **shèng dàn jié**
New Year's Eve **chú xī**
New Year's Day **yuán dàn**

NUMBERS

zero **líng**
one **yī**
two **èr**
three **sān**
four **sì**
five **wǔ**
six **liù**
seven **qī**
eight **bā**
nine **jiǔ**
ten **shí**
eleven **shí yī**
twelve **shí èr**
thirteen **shí sān**
fourteen **shí sì**
fifteen **shí wǔ**
sixteen **shí liù**
seventeen **shí qī**
eighteen **shí bā**
nineteen **shí jiǔ**
twenty **èr shí**
twenty-one **èr shí yī**
thirty **sān shí**
forty **sì shí**
fifty **wǔ shí**
sixty **liù shí**
seventy **qī shí**
eighty **bā shí**
ninety **jiǔ shí**
one hundred **yì bǎi**
one thousand **yì qiān**

Atlas

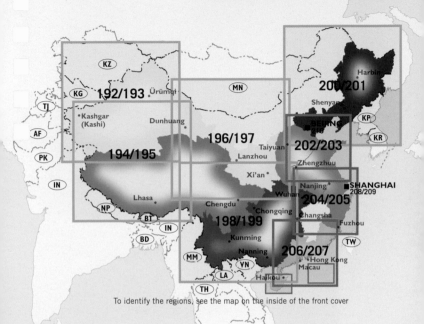

KZ

KG 192/193 Ürümqi MN

TJ

AF •Kashgar Dunhuang 200/201 Harbin

PK (Kashi) 196/197 Shenyang

IN 194/195 Taiyuan 202/203 KP

Lanzhou KR

Zhengzhou

Xi'an SHANGHAI

Lhasa Nanjing 208/209

NP Chengdu Wuhan 204/205

BT 198/199 •Chongqing Changsha Fuzhou

IN Kunming

BD Nanning 206/207 TW

MM VN Hong Kong

LA Macau

TH Haikou•

To identify the regions, see the map on the inside of the front cover

Regional Maps

▬▬▬ Major route	▫ City
▬▬ Motorway	▫ Town/village
─── National road	✈ Airport
── Regional road	🏛 Featured place of interest
─ Other road	🌳 Natural place of interest
─·─·─ International boundary	⁶⁴⁶⁰ Height in metres
------- Undefined international boundary	⚓ Port/Ferry route
─··─ Province/Administrative region boundary	⌂⌂⌂ Great Wall of China
	National park

192–201   0 ___ 200 km
           0 ___ 100 miles

202–207   0 ___ 100 km
           0 ___ 50 miles

City Plans

═══ Main road/minor road	▮ Important building
─── Railway	▮ Park
▪ Featured place of interest	● Metro

208–210   0 ___ 500 metres
           0 ___ 500 yards

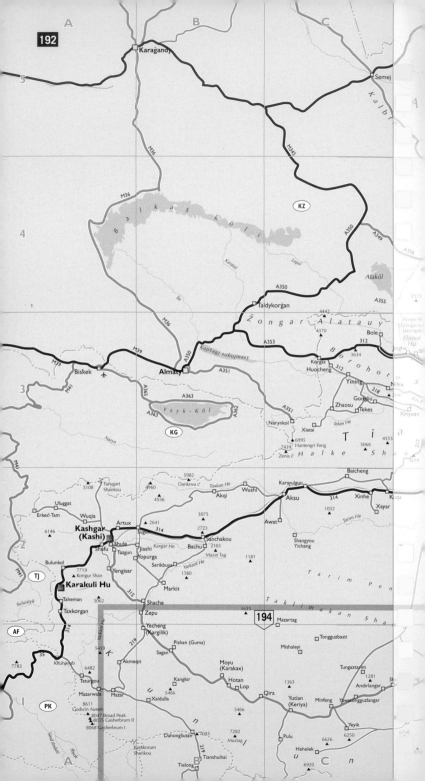

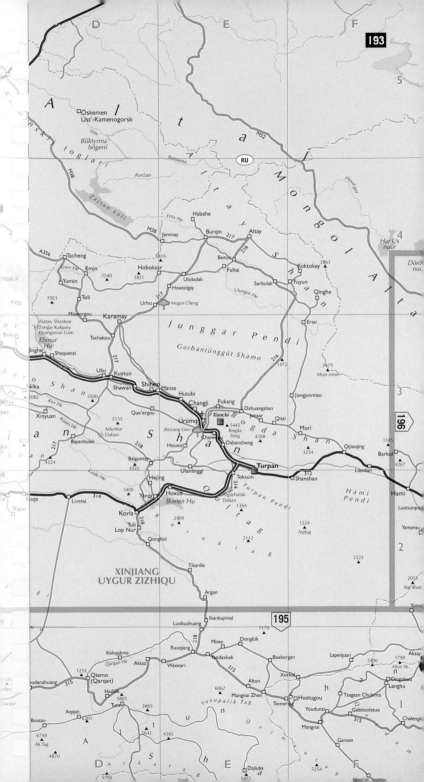

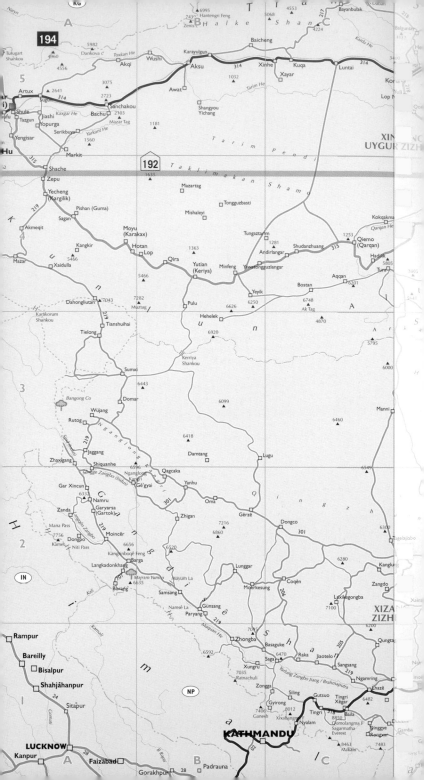

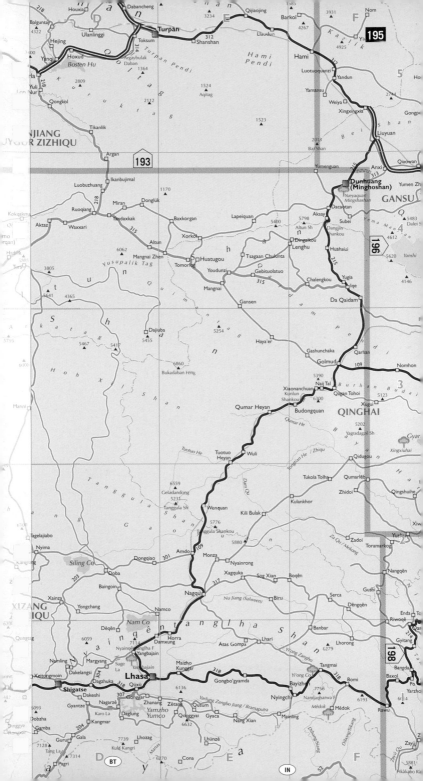

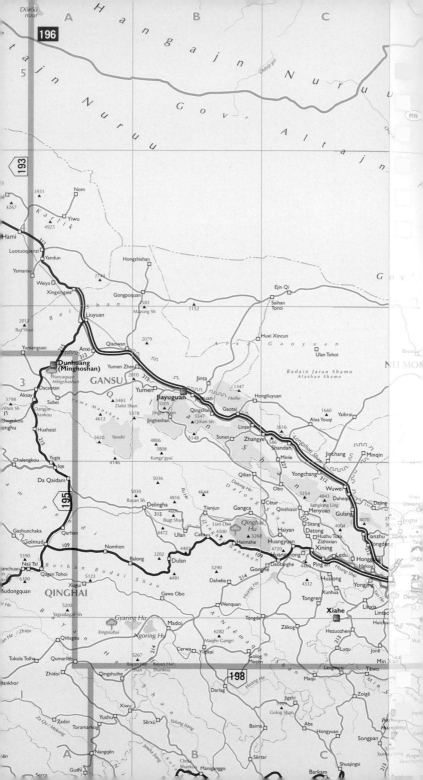

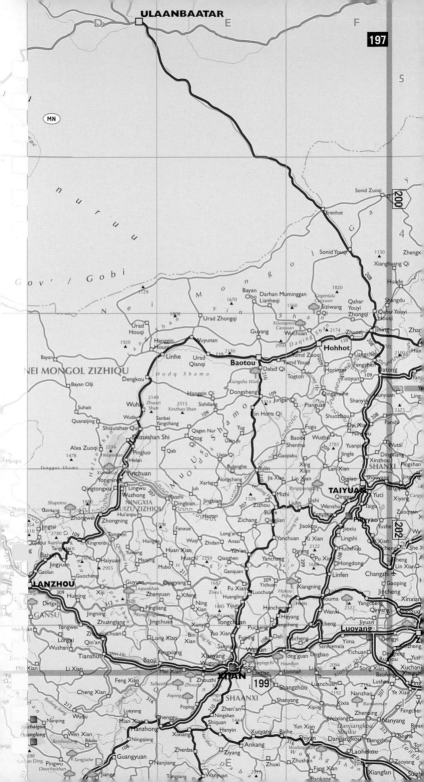

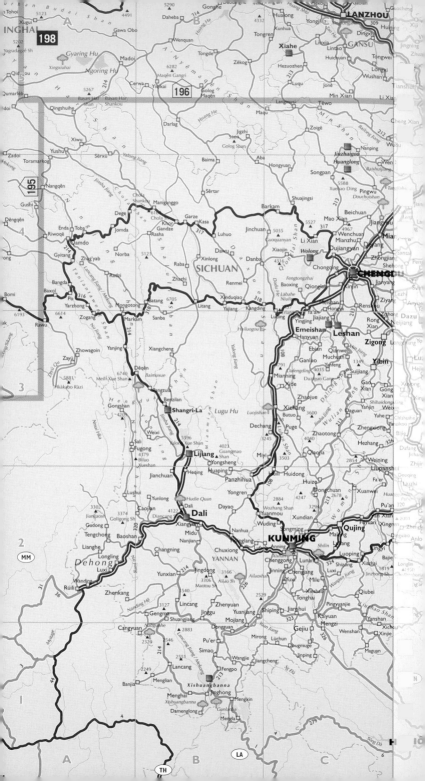

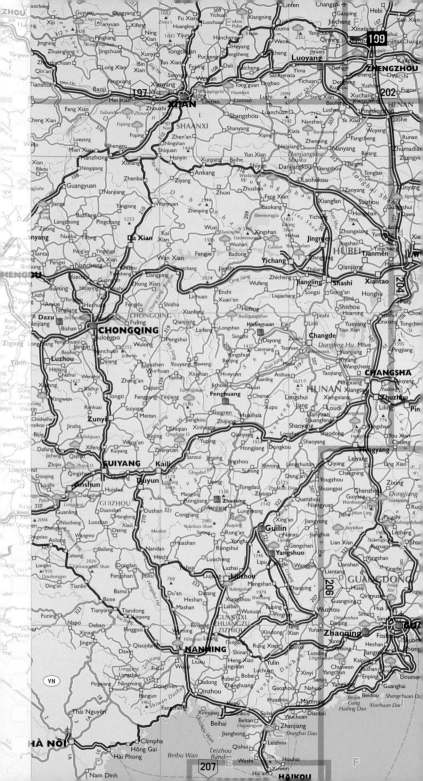

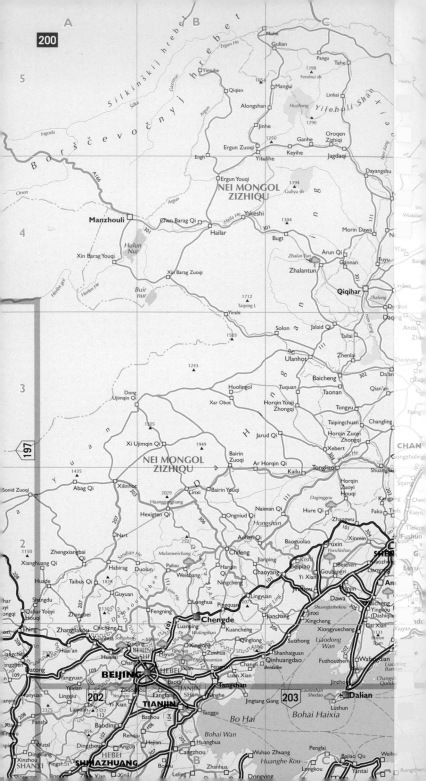

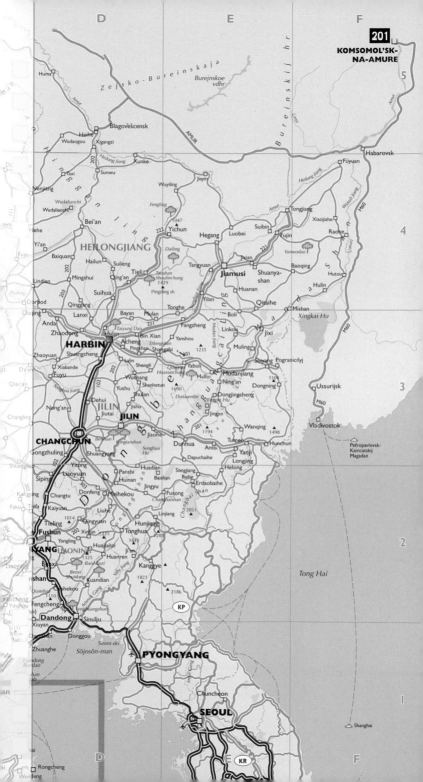

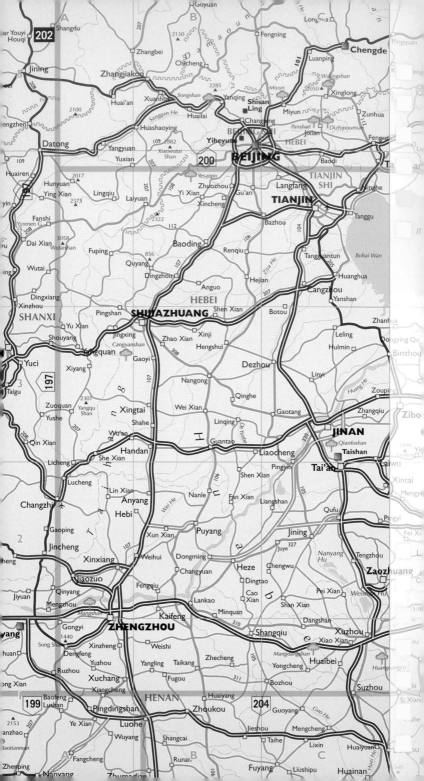

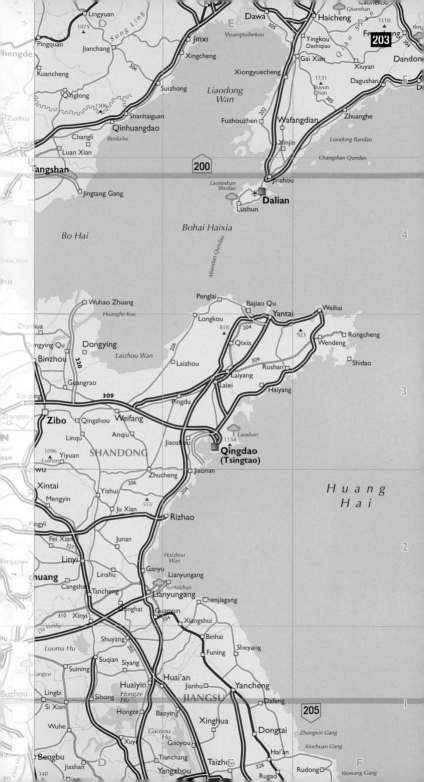

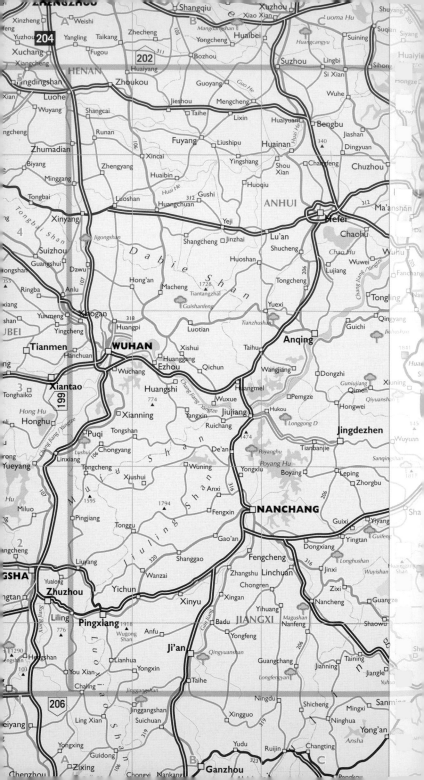

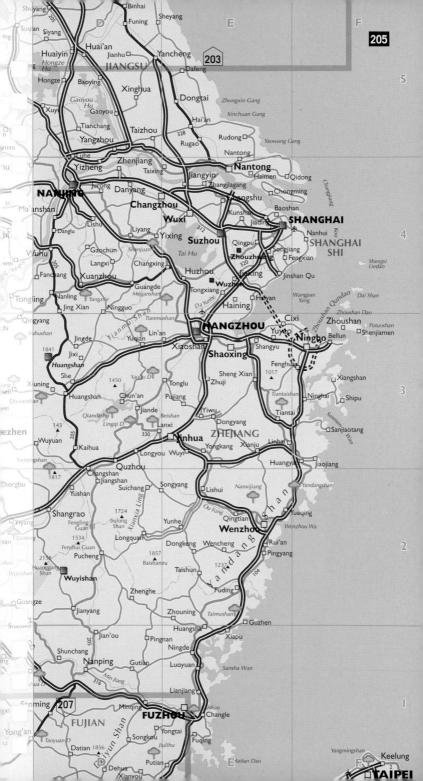

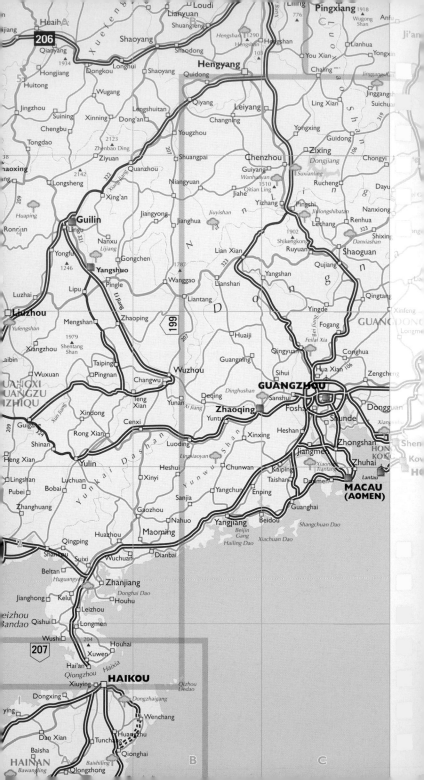

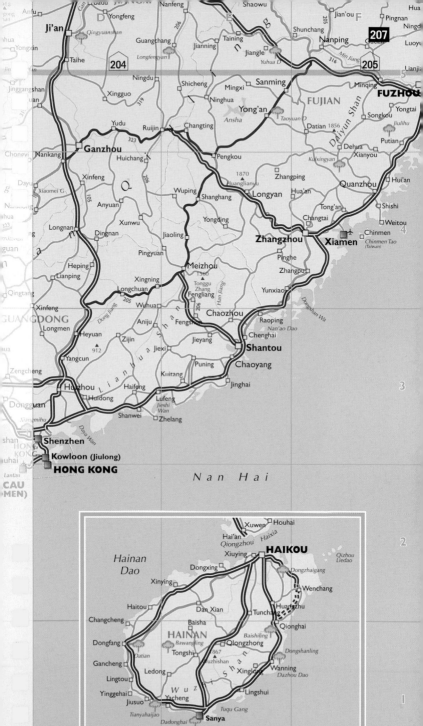

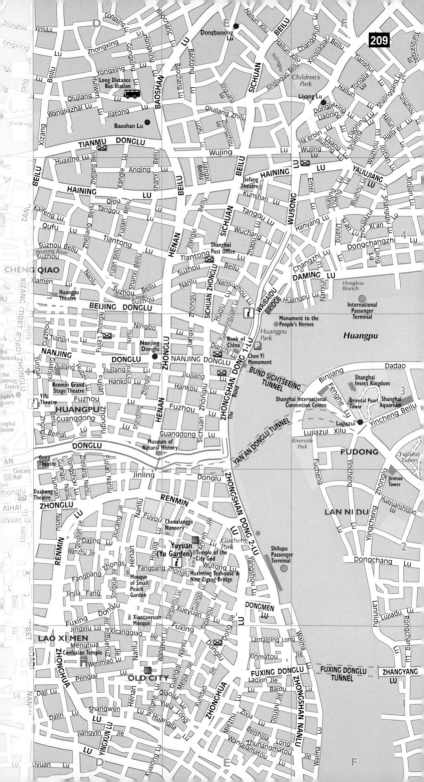

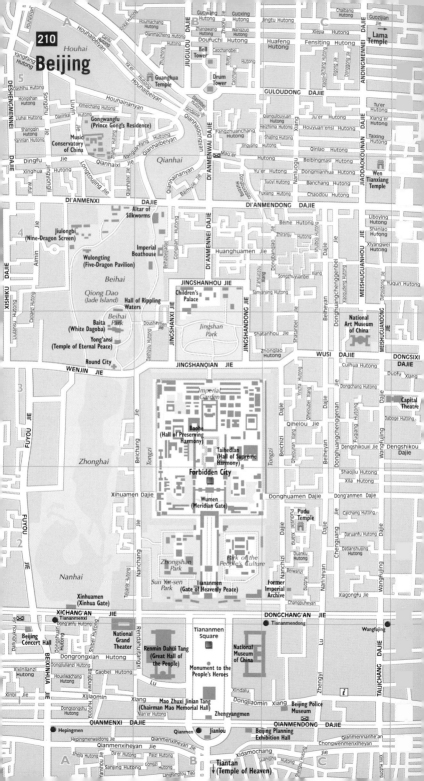

A   B   C

5

4

3

2

1

Houhai

Yangfang Hutong

Houhaibeiyan

Houhainanyan

Guowang Hutong   Guoxing Hutong

Jingtu Hutong

Chaibang Hutong

Guozijian Jie

Houmachang Hutong

Zhangwang Hutong

Qiancheng Hutong

Doufuchi Hutong

Huafeng Hutong

Xiejia Hutong

Fensiting Hutong

Lama Temple

Guanghua Temple

Bell Tower

Caochangbei

Drum Tower

GULOUDONG DAJIE

Tu-r Hutong

Xiang-r Hutong

Taixing Hutong

Gongwangfu (Prince Gong's Residence)

Qianglouyuan Hutong

Ju-r Hutong

Houyuan'ensi Hutong

Helzhima Hutong

Shailing Hutong

Jingyang Hutong

Qinlao Hutong

Music Conservatory of China

Qianhai

Mao-r Hutong

Yu-er Hutong

Belbingmasi Hutong

Dianmianhua Hutong

Namulogu

Banchang Hutong

Suoyi Hutong

Fuxiang Hutong

Chaodou Hutong

Wen Tianxiang Temple

DI'ANMENXI DAJIE   DI'ANMENDONG DAJIE

Altar of Silkworms

Beihe Hutong

Uboying Hutong

Shanliao Hutong

Zhiranlu Hutong

Xiyangwei Hutong

Jiulongbi (Nine-Dragon Screen)

Huanghuamen Jie

Dongchangdao Xiang

Shoubei Hutong

Yuqun Hutong

Imperial Boathouse

Wulongting (Five-Dragon Pavilion)

Beihai

JINGSHANHOU JIE

Xizhizou Xiang

Songzhuyuanbei Xiang

Songzhuyuanbei Hutong

Dongchangchengnanbei

Dacheng Hutong

Qiong Dao (Jade Island)

Children's Palace

Hall of Rippling Waters

Jingshan Park

Sanyanjing Hutong

Baita (White Dagoba)

Yong'ansi (Temple of Eternal Peace)

Doushanmen

Shatanhou Jie

Shatanbei

National Art Museum of China

Round City

WENJIN JIE

JINGSHANQIAN JIE

Zhonglao Hutong

WUSI DAJIE

Cuihua Hutong

DONGSIXI DAJIE

Duofu Xiang

Imperial Garden

Dongchang Hutong

Capital Theatre

Baohe (Hall of Preserving Harmony)

Qihelou Jie

Daboge Hutong

Dengshikouxi Jie

Zhonghai

Taihedian (Hall of Supreme Harmony)

Forbidden City

Dengshikou Dajie

Xihuamen Dajie

Wumen (Meridian Gate)

Donghuamen Dajie

Dong'anmen Dajie

Shaojiu Hutong

Xila Hutong

Pudu Temple

Nanhai

Zhongshan Park

Park of the People's Culture

Calchang Hutong

Daruanfu Hutong

Datianshuijing Hutong

Sun Yat-sen Park

Tiananmen (Gate of Heavenly Peace)

Former Imperial Archive

Changpuheyan

Xiagongfu Jie

Xinhuamen (Xinhua Gate)

XICHANG'AN JIE

DONGCHANG'AN JIE

Tiananmen

Dong'anfu Hutong

Tiananmendong

Wangfujing

Beijing Concert Hall

National Grand Theater

Tiananmen Square

National Museum of China

Dongrongxian Hutong

Renmin Dahui Tang (Great Hall of the People)

Monument to the People's Heroes

Houxiwachang Hutong

Gaobei Hutong

Xijiaomin Xiang

Mao Zhuxi Jinian Tang (Chairman Mao Memorial Hall)

Nian-r Hutong

Dongjiaomin Xiang

Beijing Police Museum

Dongsongshu Hutong

Zhengyangmen

Beijing Planning Exhibition Hall

QIANMENXI DAJIE

QIANMENDONG DAJIE

Hepingmen

Hepingmenwaidong Jie

Qianmen

Jianlou

Qianmennanhe'an

Qianmenxiheyan Jie

Chongwenmenxiheyan

Sheila Hutong

Da'er Hutong

Paizi Hutong

Xidamochang

Sanjing Hutong

Langfangtou Tiao

Tiantan ↓ (Temple of Heaven)

(street/hutong labels transcribed as legible)

Aberdeen 99
accommodation
36–37
Beijing and the
Northeast 60
camping 37
guest houses 37
Hong Kong and the
South 109–110
hotels 12–13,
36–37
reservations 37
Shanghai and the
East 84–85
Sichuan and
Tibetan China 153
Silk Road 170
Southwest China
133
youth hostels 37
acrobatic shows 42,
90
admission charges 35
air travel 32–33, 185
airports 32–33
domestic 35
alcohol 39
Ancient Forest 148
antiques 41, 63
ATMs 185

Badaling 57
Bailong Lift 122
banks 185, 186
Baodingshan 130
Baoguo Temple,
Emeishan 147
basketball 42
batik 129
Beijing and the
Northeast 43–64
accommodation 60
airport 32
Chengde 58–59
Dalian 59
eating out 61–62
entertainment 64
five-day itinerary
46–47
Forbidden City
48–49
Great Wall 30, 57
Harbin 59
hutong 27, 52–53,
174–176
Lama Temple 58,
174
map 44–45
Ming Tombs 58
798 Art District 58
shopping 40, 63
Summer Palace
55–56
Temple of Heaven
54
Tiananmen Square
50–51
tourist information
33

Beishan 130
Black Dragon Pool
Park 128
Buddhist grottoes 130
budget travellers
37
The Bund 74–75
Bund Sightseeing
Tunnel 74–75
buses 34
intercity buses 35

Caicun 131
calligraphy 21
camping 37
chauffered car rental
34
Chengde 58–59
Chengdu 150–151
Cheung Chau 106
Chi Lin Nunnery,
Hong Kong 101
children 188
China Research and
Conservation
Centre for the
Giant Panda 156
Chinese medicine
16–17, 98,
180–181
Chongqing 129–130
chopsticks 17, 38
cinema 42, 64, 90
climate 184
clothing sizes 186
coffee shops 39
Coloane 105
concessions 188
Confucius 11
consulates and
embassies 188
cooking courses
136
credit and debit cards
185
Crescent Moon Lake
166
crime 187
currency 185

Dabao Temple 131
Dai people 132
Dalai Lama 144, 145
Dali 131
Dalian 59
Dapeng Ancient City
106
Dazu Rock Carvings
130
dental services 188
Dinghu Mountain
107
disabilities, travellers
with 188
Dong people 129
Drepung Monastery
150
dress codes 38
driving 34–35, 184

drugs and medicines
188
Dunhuang 165–166
DVDs 41

eating out 14–17, 38
beers and wines 39
Beijing and the
Northeast 61–62
Chinese restaurants
38
coffee shops 39
dress code 38
etiquette 17
Hong Kong and the
South 110–111
meal times 38
menus 38–39
Shanghai and the
East 86–87
Sichuan and
Tibetan China
154–155
Silk Road 170–171
smoking 38
Southwest China
134–135
teahouses 39
tipping 38
vegetarian food 39
Western food 39
economic growth 7
electricity 187
Elephant Trunk Hill
120
Emeishan 146–147
emergency telephone
numbers 187
Emin Ta, Turpan 168
entertainment 42
Beijing and the
Northeast 64
Hong Kong and the
South 114
Shanghai and the
East 89–90
Sichuan and
Tibetan China 156
Silk Road 172
Southwest China
136
Everest 7

Fengdu 126
Fenghuang 129
festivals and events
42, 59, 82, 83, 132
Flaming Mountains
168
Folded Brocade Hill
120
food and drink 38–39
alcohol 39
cooking schools
15–16
drinking water 188
tea and coffee 39,
41
see also eating out

football 42
Forbidden City
48–49
foreign exchange 185
Forest of Stone Lions
Garden, Suzhou 80
Former Residence of
Mao Dun, Beijing
175
Former Residence of
Song Qing Ling,
Shanghai 71
Former Residence of
Sun Yat-sen,
Shanghai 71, 177
French Concession,
Shanghai 70–71,
177–179
Fuxing Park,
Shanghai 71, 177

Ganlanba 132
Gaochang 168
Giant Panda Breeding
Base 151, 156
Goddess Lake Scenic
Area 156
Goddess Peak 125
golf 42, 64
Grand Buddha of
Leshan 147
Grand Canal 78, 79
Great Hall of the
People, Beijing
50–51
Great Mosque, Xi'an
163
Great Wall 30, 57
Great Wall of South
China 129
Greater Wild Goose
Pagoda, Xi'an 164
Green Lake Park 132
greyhound racing 114
Guangzhou 30,
40–41, 107
guest houses 37
Guilin 116, 120–121
Gulangyu 108
Gyantse 150

Hainan 108
Hangzhou 79
Happy Valley
Racecourse, Hong
Kong 98, 114
Harbin 59
health 184, 188
Highest Natural
Bridge in the
World 123
Highest Railway in
the World
142–143
Hong Kong Cultural
Centre 100
Hong Kong
Disneyland 103,
114

Hong Kong Island 96–99, 180–182
Hong Kong Museum of Art 100, 101
Hong Kong and the South 91–114
accommodation 109–110
airport 32
Cheung Chau 106
eating out 110–111
entertainment 114
Guangzhou 40–41, 107
Hong Kong Island 96–99, 180–182
Kowloon 100–101
Lantau Island 102–103
Macau 104–105
map 92–93
Sanya 108
seven-day itinerary 94–95
Shenzhen 106
shopping 40, 112–113
tourist information 33
Xiamen 108
Zhaoqing 107
Hong Kong Space Museum and Theatre 100, 101
horse-racing 30, 98, 114
horse trekking 156
hot spring resorts 108
hot-air ballooning 121, 136
hotels 12–13, 36–37
budget travellers 37
Chinese 36
international 36–37
see also accommodation
Huanghua 57
Huanglong 151–152
Huangpu River 74–75
Huangshan 81
Humble Administrator's Garden, Suzhou 80
hutong, Beijing 27, 52–53
Huxingting Teahouse, Shanghai 76, 77

Ice Lantern Festival, Harbin 59
Id Kah Mosque, Kashgar 167
Imperial Academy, Beijing 174
insurance 184, 188
intercity transport 34–35

International Beer Festival 82
International Photography Festival 83
inventions 8–11

jade 41, 113, 171
Jade Dragon Snow Mountain 127, 128
Jiangnan 78
Jiaohe 168
Jiayuguan 168
Jinghong 132
Jingshan Park 49
Jinmao Tower, Shanghai 75
Jiuzhaigou 148–149
Jiuzhaigou National Park 148, 149
Jokhang Temple, Lhasa 145

Karakuli Hu (Karakul Lake) 169
karaoke 18, 30, 42, 64, 114
karst towers 120
Kashgar 167
Kowloon 100–101
Kunlun Mountains 142
Kunming 131–132
Kunming Lake 55–56

Labrang Monastery 152
Lama Temple, Beijing 58, 174
language 20–21, 25, 189–190
Lantau Island 102–103
Lanzhou 143
Leshan 146–147
Lesser Three Gorges 126
Lhasa 144–145
Li River cruise 120–121
Lijiang 127–128
live music 64, 90
Longmen Caves 82–83
Longsheng 121
longtang neighbourhoods, Shanghai 77, 179
Luoyang 82–83

Macau 104–105
Maglev 30, 32
malls 40
Man Mo Temple, Hong Kong 182
Manchuria 44
Mao Zedong 14, 51

markets 40, 63, 101, 113, 135, 155, 167, 171
Mausoleum of Mao Zedong, Beijing 51
medical treatment 188
Mekong River 132
metro 34
Ming Tombs 58
minority groups 108, 121, 127–128, 129, 132
Mogao Caves 165–166
Mohe 7
money 185
Monument to the People's Heroes, Beijing 51
motor racing 42
motorcycle taxis 34
Muni Valley 151
Museum of Chinese Sex Culture, Shanghai 75
museum and monument opening hours 186

Nanjing 81
national holidays 186
Naxi people 127–128
New Wushan 126
newspapers and magazines, foreign 63
Ngong Ping Skyrail, Lantau 102, 103
nightlife 42
see also entertainment
Nine Bends River 80
noise and crowds 18–19
Norbulingka 145
Northern Lights 7
Nuorilang Waterfall 149

Ocean Park, Hong Kong 99, 114
Old City, Shanghai 76–77
Olympic Games 2008 28–29
one-child policy 27
opening hours 186
opera, Chinese 42
opera, Sichuan 156
Opium Wars 22–23
Oriental Pearl TV Tower, Shanghai 75
Overhanging Great Wall 168

paintings 41
Panchen Lama, Shigatse 150

pandas 151, 156
passports and visas 184
Peace Hotel, Shanghai 75
Peak Tram, Hong Kong 98
pearls 41
pedicabs 34
People's Square, Shanghai 72–73
personal safety 187
pharmacies 186, 188
Pingyao 83
Po Lin Monastery 102
police 187
population 7
porcelain 41
post offices 186, 187
Potala Palace, Lhasa 144–145
Prince Gong's Residence, Beijing 53
public transport 33–34

Qin Huangshi's Mausoleum 164
Qingdao 82
Qinghai Lake 53, 142
Qinghai-Tibet railway 142–143
Qu Gorge 126

rafting 80
Repulse Bay 99
restaurants see eating out
rice wine 39
Riyuegu 108
Rize Valley 148
road safety 34, 35
Rowswell, Mark 24–25

sacred mountains 30, 82, 146–147
St Ignatius Cathedral, Shanghai 71
Sakyamuni Buddha, Lhasa 145
sampans 125
Sand Dunes and Crescent Moon Lake 166, 172
Sanya 108
seals 41
senior citizens 188
Sera Monastery 150
798 Art District, Beijing 58
Seven Star Cave 120
Seven Star Park 120
17 Arch Bridge, Kunming Lake 56
Shamian Island 107

Shanghai Art
  Museum 73
Shanghai and the East
  65–90
  accommodation
  84–85
  airport 32
  eating out 86–87
  entertainment
  89–90
  five-day itinerary
  68–69
  French Concession
  70–71, 177–179
  Hangzhou 79
  Huangpu River
  74–75
  Huangshan 81
  Luoyang 82–83
  map 67
  Nanjing 81
  People's Square
  72–73
  Pingyao 83
  Qingdao 82
  shopping 40, 88
  Suzhou 80
  Taishan 82
  tourist information
  33
  water towns of
  Jiangnan 78
  Wuyishan 80
  Yuyuan and the Old
  City 76–77
Shanghai Grand
  Theatre 73
Shanghai Museum
  72–73
Shanghai Urban
  Planning
  Exhibition Center
  73
Shangri-La 130–131
Shanxi History
  Museum, Xi'an
  164
Shenzhen 106
Shihaozhai Temple
  126
Shigatse 150
shopping 12, 13,
  40–41
  Beijing and the
  Northeast 40, 63
  Hong Kong and the
  South 40, 112–113
  malls 40
  markets 40
  opening hours 186
  Shanghai and the
  East 40, 88
  shopping trips 19
  Sichuan and
  Tibetan China 155
  Silk Road 171–172
  Southwest China
  135
Shuzeng Valley 149

Sichuan and Tibetan
  China 137–156
  accommodation
  153
  Chengdu 150–151
  Drepung
  Monastery 150
  eating out 154–155
  Emeishan 146–147
  entertainment 156
  Huanglong
  151–152
  Jiuzhaigou
  148–149
  Leshan 146–147
  Lhasa 144–145
  map 138–139
  Qinghai-Tibet rail-
  way 142–143
  Sera Monastery 150
  Shigatse 150
  shopping 155
  two-week itinerary
  140–141
  Wolong Nature
  Reserve 151, 156
  Xiahe 152
Silk Road 157–172
  accommodation
  170
  Dunhuang
  165–166
  eating out 170–171
  entertainment 172
  Jiayuguan 168
  Karakul Lake 169
  Kashgar 167
  map 158–159
  shopping 171–172
  Terracotta Warriors
  30, 162–163, 164
  Tianchi 169
  Turpan (Tulufan)
  168
  two-week itinerary
  160–161
  Xi'an 159, 162–164
Simatai 57
Site of the 1st
  National Congress
  of the Chinese
  Communist Party,
  Shanghai 71
skiing 59, 64, 156
smoking etiquette 38
snow sculptures 59
software piracy 41
Solitary Beauty Peak
  120
Songpan 151
Songzanlin Lamasery
  130
Southwest China
  115–136
  accommodation
  133
  Chongqing
  129–130
  Dali 131

Dazu Rock
  Carvings 130
  eating out 134–135
  entertainment 136
  Fenghuang 129
  Guilin 116,
  120–121
  Kunming 131–132
  Lijiang 127–128
  map 116–117
  Shangri-La
  130–131
  shopping 135
  Three Gorges 26,
  124–126
  two-week itinerary
  118–119
  Wulingyuan
  122–123
  Xishuangbanna
  132
  Yangshuo 120–121
  Zhaoxing 129
souvenirs 41
sports 42, 64
Stanley, Hong Kong
  99
Star Ferry, Hong
  Kong 96, 101
statistics 7
Stillwell Museum,
  Chongqing 130
stilt houses 129, 132
student travellers
  188
Summer Palace
  55–56
sun safety 188
Sun Yat-sen 177
Suoxi Valley 122
Suzhou 80
Suzhou Silk Museum
  80
Symphony of Lights,
  Kowloon 100

Tai Chi 26, 27
Taipa 105
Taishan 82
Tanggula Pass 142
Tanziling Ridge 124
Tashilhunpo, Shigatse
  150
taxis 33–34
tea 41
teahouses 39
telephones 187
Temple of Confucius,
  Beijing 174
Temple of Heaven,
  Beijing 54
Temple Street Night
  Market, Hong
  Kong 101, 113
Terracotta Warriors
  30, 162–163, 164
theatre 64, 90
Three Gorges 26,
  124–126

Three Gorges Dam
  26, 124
Three Pagoda
  Temple, Dali 131
Tian Tan Buddha 102,
  103
Tiananmen Square,
  Beijing 50–51
Tianchi 169
Tianzi Mountain
  123
Tibet Travel Permit
  143, 188
Tiger Leaping Gorge
  128
time differences 185,
  186
tipping 38, 187
toilets 36, 188
Tomb of Abakh
  Khoja, Kashgar
  167
Tomb of Lobsang
  Gyatso, Lhasa 145
Tongli 78
tourist information
  33, 184, 185
train services 35,
  142–143
travel arrangements
  32–33, 185
Tsing Ma suspension
  bridge, Lantau 103
Turpan (Tulufan) 7,
  168

Victoria Peak,
  Hong Kong 98

walks
  Beijing's hutong
  174–176
  Shanghai's French
  Concession
  177–179
  Sheung Wan to
  Central 180–182
Water Splashing
  Festival, Jinghong
  132
water towns of
  Jiangnan 78
West Lake, Hangzhou
  79
White Horse Temple,
  Luoyang 83
White Russians of
  Shanghai 179
Wolong Nature
  Reserve 151, 156
Wu Gorge 125
Wulingyuan 122–123
Wuyishan 80
Wuzhen 78

Xiahe 152
Xiamen 108
Xi'an 159, 162–164
Xiling Gorge 125

Xingping 121
Xinhaoshan Ying
  Binguan, Qingdao
  82
Xintan 125
Xishuangbanna 132
Xizhou 131

Yabuli 59
Yak Meadow 128

Yalong Bay 108
Yamdrok Yamtso
  Lake 150
Yangbajing 142
Yangshuo 120–121
Yangtze River
  124–126
Yarlong Tsangpo
  (Brahmaputra)
  river 150

Yellow Dragon Cave
  123
Yellow Mountain 81
youth hostels 37
Yuanjiajie 123
Yunnan 117
Yuyuan 76–77

Zechawa Valley 149
Zhangjiajie Forest

Park 122
Zhaoqing 107
Zhaoxing 129
Zheng He 11
Zhouzhuang 78
Zhumulangma
  Feng 7

Picture Credits

The Automobile Association would like to thank the following photographers, companies and picture libraries for their assistance in the preparation of this book.
Abbreviations for the picture credits are as follows – (t) top; (b) bottom; (c) centre; (l) left; (r) right; (AA) AA World Travel Library.

Front and back covers (t) AA/N Hicks; (ct) AA/B Bachman; (cb) AA/G Clements;
(b) AA/G Clements; spine AA/A Kouprianoff; 2(i) AA/B Madison; 2(ii) AA/D Henley; 2(iii) AA/G Clements; 2(iv) AA/A Mockford & N Bonetti; 2(v) AA/N Hicks; 2(vi) AA/D Henley;
3(i) AA/D Henley; 3(ii) AA/I Morejohn; 3(iii) AA/A Mockford & N Bonetti; 3(iv) AA/G Clements; 5 AA/B Madison; 6/7 AA/D Henley; 7 inset AA/B Bachman; 8 AA/G Clements;
9t AA/A Mockford & N Bonetti; 9b AA/M Lynch; 10 AA/A Mockford & N Bonetti;
11 AA/A Mockford & N Bonetti; 12tl AA/J Holmes; 12cr AA/A Mockford & N Bonetti;
13t AA/A Mockford & N Bonetti; 13b AA/A Mockford & N Bonetti;14tl Stockbyte Royalty Free; 14cl AA/A Kouprianoff; 14br AA/B Madison; 15 AA/D Henley; 16t AA/B Madison;
16b AA/A Mockford & N Bonetti; 17 AA/D Henley; 18 AA/B Bachman; 19 AA/A Mockford & N Bonetti; 20 AA/A Mockford & N Bonetti; 21 AA/I Morejohn; 22 AA/R Strange;
23r AA/R Strange; 23b AA/A Mockford & N Bonetti; 24t AA/A Mockford & N Bonetti;
24c AA/A Mockford & N Bonetti; 25 AA/N Hicks; 26 AA/A Mockford & N Bonetti;
27c AA/B Madison; 27b AA/A Mockford & N Bonetti; 28tl © View Stock/Alamy;
28tr AA/A Mockford & N Bonetti; 28/29 © Lou Linwei/Alamy; 29b © View Stock/Alamy;
30t AA/A Mockford & N Bonetti; 30c AA/B Madison; 30b AA/A Mockford & N Bonetti;
31 AA/D Henley; 43 AA/G Clements; 45 AA/B Madison; 46c AA/A Mockford & N Bonetti;
46b AA/A Mockford & N Bonetti; 47t AA/A Mockford & N Bonetti; 47b AA/A Mockford & N Bonetti; 48 AA/A Mockford & N Bonetti; 49 AA/A Mockford & N Bonetti;
50/51 AA/A Mockford & N Bonetti; 50b AA/G Clements; 52 AA/A Mockford & N Bonetti;
53 AA/A Mockford & N Bonetti; 54 AA/A Mockford & N Bonetti; 55 AA/G Clements;
56 AA/A Mockford & N Bonetti; 57 AA/A Mockford & N Bonetti; 59tl AA/D Henley;
59br AA/B Madison; 65 AA/A Mockford & N Bonetti; 66 AA/A Mockford & N Bonetti;
68 AA/A Mockford & N Bonetti; 69t AA/A Mockford & N Bonetti; 69b AA/A Mockford & N Bonetti; 70 AA/A Mockford & N Bonetti; 71 AA/A Mockford & N Bonetti;
72/73 AA/A Mockford & N Bonetti; 72b AA/G Clements; 74 AA/A Mockford & N Bonetti;
75 AA/G Clements; 76 AA/A Mockford & N Bonetti; 77 AA/A Mockford & N Bonetti;
78 © Mike Stone/Alamy; 79 AA/I Morejohn; 80 AA/A Mockford & N Bonetti;
81 AA/I Morejohn; 82 AA/I Morejohn; 83 AA/I Morejohn; 91 AA/N Hicks; 93t AA/I Morejohn;
93b AA/N Hicks; 94 AA/B Bachman; 95 AA/B Bachman; 97 AA/B Bachman; 98 AA/B Bachman;
99 AA/B Bachman; 100t AA/N Hicks; 100b AA/B Bachman; 101 AA/A Kouprianoff;
102 AA/B Bachman; 103 AA/B Bachman; 104t AA/D Henley; 104/105 AA/D Henley;
105t AA/D Henley; 106 AA/B Bachman; 107 AA/I Morejohn; 108 AA/I Morejohn;
115 AA/D Henley; 117tl AA/D Henley; 117tr AA/D Henley; 117br AA/D Henley;
118c © Robert Harding Picture Library Ltd/Alamy; 118b AA/D Henley; 119c AA/D Henley;
119b AA/D Henley; 120/121 AA/D Henley; 121c AA/D Henley; 122/123 © Keren Su/China Span/Alamy; 123t © AM Corporation/Alamy; 124/125 AA/D Henley; 126 AA/D Henley;
127 AA/D Henley; 128 AA/D Henley; 130 AA/A Kouprianoff; 131 AA/D Henley;
132 AA/I Morejohn; 137 AA/D Henley; 138 © Suzy Bennett/Alamy; 139c AA/L K Stow;
139b © Panorama Media (Beijing) Ltd/Alamy; 140c AA/L K Stow; 140b AA/I Morejohn;
141t AA/D Henley; 141b AA/D Henley; 142/143 © Suzy Bennett/Alamy; 143c © Suzy Bennett/Alamy; 144 AA/I Morejohn; 145 AA/I Morejohn; 146 AA/D Henley; 148b © Keren Su/China Span/Alamy; 148/149 © Panorama Media (Beijing) Ltd/Alamy; 150 AA/D Henley;
152 AA/I Morejohn; 157 AA/I Morejohn; 158tl AA/B Madison; 158bl AA/D Henley;
159 AA/D Henley; 160c AA/B Madison; 160b AA/I Morejohn; 161t AA/D Henley;
161b AA/D Henley; 162t AA/B Madison; 162/163 AA/B Madison; 164 AA/B Madison;
165c AA/W Guanmin; 165b AA/D Henley; 166 AA/D Henley; 167 AA/D Henley;
168 AA/D Henley; 169 AA/D Henley; 173 AA/A Mockford & N Bonetti; 174 AA/A Mockford & N Bonetti; 176 AA/A Mockford & N Bonetti; 177 AA/A Mockford & N Bonetti;
178 AA/A Mockford & N Bonetti; 179 AA/A Mockford & N Bonetti; 180 AA/B Bachman;
181 AA/D Henley; 182 AA/N Hicks; 183 AA/G Clements; 187t AA/B Madison; 187cl AA/A Mockford & N Bonetti; 187cr AA/B Bachman

Every effort has been made to trace the copyright holders, and we apologise in advance for any accidental errors. We would be happy to apply the corrections in the following edition of this publication.

SPIRAL GUIDES

Questionnaire

Dear Traveler

Your comments, opinions and recommendations are very important to us. So please help us to improve our travel guides by taking a few minutes to complete this simple questionnaire.

Send to: Spiral Guides, MailStop 66, 1000 AAA Drive, Heathrow, FL 32746–5063

Your recommendations...
We always encourage readers' recommendations for restaurants, nightlife or shopping – if your recommendation is added to the next edition of the guide, we will send you a FREE AAA Spiral Guide of your choice. Please state below the establishment name, location and your reasons for recommending it.

_____

_____

_____

_____

_____

Please send me AAA Spiral _____
(see list of titles inside the back cover)

About this guide...
Which title did you buy?

_____ AAA Spiral

Where did you buy it? _____

When? mm/ y y

Why did you choose a AAA Spiral Guide? _____

_____

_____

_____

_____

Did this guide meet your expectations?

Exceeded ☐   Met all ☐   Met most ☐   Fell below ☐

Please give your reasons _____

_____

_____

_____

_____

continued on next page...

Were there any aspects of this guide that you particularly liked?

_____

_____

_____

_____

_____

Is there anything we could have done better?

_____

_____

_____

_____

_____

About you...

Name (Mr/Mrs/Ms) _____

Address _____

_____

_____ Zip _____

Daytime tel nos. _____

Which age group are you in?

Under 25 ☐ 25–34 ☐ 35–44 ☐ 45–54 ☐ 55–64 ☐ 65+ ☐

How many trips do you make a year?

Less than one ☐   One ☐   Two ☐   Three or more ☐

Are you a AAA member? Yes ☐   No ☐

Name of AAA club _____

About your trip...

When did you book? m m / y y   When did you travel? m m / y y

How long did you stay? _____

Was it for business or leisure? _____

Did you buy any other travel guides for your trip? ☐ Yes   ☐ No

If yes, which ones? _____

_____

Thank you for taking the time to complete this questionnaire.